Detective Fi

'The Death of Sherlock Holmes'. Reproduced from 'The Final Problem',
printed in *The Strand Magazine*, November 1893. Illustrator: Sidney Paget.

Detective Fiction

Charles J. Rzepka

polity

The right of Charles Rzepka to be identified as Author of this Work has been asserted in accordance with the UK Copyright, Designs and Patents Act 1988.

First published in 2005 by Polity Press

Polity Press
65 Bridge Street
Cambridge CB2 1UR, UK

Polity Press
350 Main Street
Malden, MA 02148, USA

ISBN: 0-7456-2941-5
ISBN: 0-7456-2942-3 (pb)

A catalogue record for this book is available from the British Library.

Typeset in 10.5 on 12 pt Sabon
by SNP Best-set Typesetter Ltd., Hong Kong
Printed and bound in Great Britain by TJ International Ltd, Padstow, Cornwall

For further information on Polity, visit our website: *www.polity.co.uk*

Contents

For my mother, Lillian,
who taught me how to read,
and for my wife, Jane,
who is still teaching me how to write.

Acknowledgements

Casebook Entry No. 4 is based on material originally published as ' "I'm in the Business Too": Gothic Chivalry, Private Eyes, and Proxy Sex and Violence in Chandler's *The Big Sleep*', *Modern Fiction Studies* 46:3 (2000): 695–724.

The author and Polity Press also express their gratitude to the Howard Gottlieb Archival Research Center at Boston University for providing the cover art for this volume, which is taken from the original book jacket for Mignon G. Eberhart's *The Glass Slipper* (1941).

Introduction

This book is intended primarily for college undergraduates, preferably English concentrators, although anyone with some training in the interpretation of imaginative writing and some knowledge of the history of English and American literature should find it useful. Students for whom a course in detective fiction constitutes their first introduction to the study of literature will benefit from the guidance of their instructors as they make their way through this book.

Graduate students, teachers, and scholars of detective fiction, who will have no need of such assistance, may also find the book of some interest. At least, that is my hope. For in addition to providing a basic introduction to terminology and approaches, and following the development of the detective genre in relation to cultural change, I have tried to offer a new explanation of that development in the context of one cultural change in particular: the rise of the modern historical sciences. In a book intended primarily as an introduction, this explanation can hardly appear as more than an extended correlation, but I hope readers will find it suggestive enough to warrant at least a suspension of disbelief pending further research and investigation.

Detective fiction may seem like a tidy and well-defined topic, but it offers difficult problems of generic designation and narrative analysis. Solving these problems requires the use of concepts that may be unfamiliar to many readers, and I will do my best to explain them in terms that will not try the patience of more knowledgeable fans and critics. Let me assure newcomers that while many of these concepts may be difficult to grasp initially, they will prove well worth the effort. As for the old hands, I ask them to bear with me.

Simplification can reveal relationships too large-scale for finer instruments of analysis. The difficult thing is to keep the focus sharp and deep while widening the field of view.

In order to preserve sharpness and depth of focus, I have included extended essays, called 'Casebook Entries', on seminal works by four of the most important writers of detective fiction over the last two centuries: Edgar Allan Poe, Arthur Conan Doyle, Dorothy Sayers, and Raymond Chandler. In addition, readers will find substantial, if shorter, essays embedded in the text on Émile Gaboriau, Wilkie Collins, G. K. Chesterton, Agatha Christie, Dashiell Hammett, and Ross Macdonald. In these essays, I trace the cultural and generic assumptions common among writers of detective fiction, examine the individual perspective on these assumptions afforded by each writer, provide some sense of the expanding critical landscape within which these perspectives have been situated in recent decades, and try to add some fresh insights. The cultural history of detection offered by this book is meant to provide an interpretive context for reading this series of essays. The essays are, in turn, meant to be provocative, in the literal sense of 'provoking' discussion between teachers and students, and among students themselves.

As of this moment, there are several good histories of detective fiction available in libraries and bookstores. Nearly all of these address social, political, and institutional influences, and the more recent ones base their arguments on considerations of class, gender, or race, focusing on the 'cultural work' that popular writing performs in each of these areas. Many of these studies have proved helpful to me, as will soon become clear.

However, this book offers neither an armchair guide to reading detective fiction nor an ideological critique of the genre.

This is not to say that ideological criticism hasn't an important role to play in explaining the development of detective fiction. Clearly, the first move of ideological scoundrels is to try to pass off the constraints of culture as the dictates of nature, and ever since the Enlightenment, which was supposed to put a stop to such things, there have been deplorable acts of oppression and discrimination in the West directed against women, labourers, and people of colour, all in the name of 'what nature intended'. Just as clearly, detective fiction has often contributed to this process of rationalization. Since the durability of such ideological hocus-pocus largely depended on its popularity, we should not be surprised to learn that many writers became popular by confirming their readers' self-serving ideas of where culture stopped and nature began. As for expressions of indignation at the phenomenon

I think John Stuart Mill may have said it best: 'To find fault with our ancestors for not having annual parliaments, universal suffrage, and vote by ballot, would be like quarrelling with the Greeks and Romans for not using steam navigation, when we know it is so safe and expeditious' (21–2).

Many recent critics have found detective fiction unrelievedly conservative, 'a literature of reassurance and conformism', in the words of Dennis Porter (220). But in fact, the tendency of the genre over the long run has been toward ever greater self-criticism, inclusiveness, and breadth of appeal. Values inherent in the very form of literary detection have encouraged this trend. Deriving from the eighteenth-century Enlightenment faith in the universality of reason, these values gradually became a potent weapon against claims to authority based solely on inherited 'customary' or 'prescriptive' rights attached to class position (as in monarchies sharing power with wealthy landowners) and, eventually, against claims based on the presumably inherited, 'natural' traits of gender and race.

Culture is propagated in and by individual responses to the prevailing customs, modes of communication, material artefacts, and bodily displays (gesture, dress, ornament) by which its codes are expressed. According to one popular account, Louis Althusser's, no one can avoid socialization or 'interpellation' by these codes. As a result, it is alleged, free individuals become administered and monitored 'subjects' of the modern state, which perpetuates the power of the ruling classes while deluding both the empowered and disempowered into believing that this very process makes them free and self-determining citizens of a liberal democracy.

What the most significant works of detective fiction demonstrate is that such processes can never be total and are often far from it, for 'interpellation' (socialization, enculturation, indoctrination) cannot fully control the idiosyncratic process at work in any particular individual's response to what Mill and others of his generation termed 'the spirit of the age'. The most interesting and lasting works of detective fiction, like those in other types of popular literature, do not simply reproduce the values of their cultures or the inherited formulas, clichés, and truisms of the best-sellers that preceded them, but pursue the individual writer's unique, often critical, vision of what the Gothic crime writer William Godwin called 'Things as They Are'.

This may sound like an easy thing to do, until the writer realizes that no one will pay much attention to, let alone money for, his or her critical vision of 'Things as They Are' unless that vision is informed by the literary tradition that has attracted readers and shaped their expectations over the course of many years, perhaps centuries. Each of the writers I have chosen for extended discussion will be found, I trust, to have satisfied both of these requirements: visionary originality and knowledge of that tradition.

Since it is a *cultural* history, this book focuses on trends and writers that most clearly reflect major cultural changes. Because the most important of these cultural changes for our purposes occurred, first of all, in concepts and practices of history that shaped the very form of the detective story, and, secondly, ideas of class, gender, and race that shaped the genre's central protagonist and audience expectations, knowledgeable readers and fans may sometimes feel that their favourite writers or works are not getting the attention they deserve. For any shortcomings of that sort, I apologize. Size constraints, and the requirements of my overall argument, simply would not allow a more inclusive narrative.

At the same time, because it is meant to be an introduction to the *history* of the genre and its critical and theoretical approaches, this book may often be felt to include facts, events, and critical readings that are not necessarily 'cultural' in their significance, or germane to its larger argument. (One reading omitted on grounds of both cultural and historical irrelevance is Jacques Lacan's famous 'Seminar' on Edgar Allan Poe's 'The Purloined Letter'.) If, in shifting my weight repeatedly between the two stools of culture and history, I sometimes fall between them, I ask my generous readers to remain patient while I try to pick myself up off the floor and resume my awkward dance.

The book is divided into three main parts. In the first, following a theoretical introduction to the genre, the main cultural trends shaping the origins of detective fiction in modern times are examined. Primary among these was the rise of modern sciences devoted to the study of material history, such as geology, palaeontology, and evolutionary biology, and of the human mind, especially psychoanalysis, which focused on reconstructing an individual's past experiences from the evidence of present behaviour.

In the second part, the development of the genre is traced from its beginnings in the broadsheet criminal 'confessions' and *The Newgate Calendar* of the early eighteenth century to the so-called 'Golden Age' of detective fiction spanning the years between the First and Second World Wars. Aside from a few important innovations that took place in America and France, the major setting for developments during this period was Great Britain.

In the third part of the book, I will focus on the evolution of detective fiction in the United States from the end of World War I ('The

Great War') to the present day. During this period the classic 'who-dunit' that had emerged by the end of the nineteenth century in Britain, with its perpetually foregrounded challenge to the reader's reasoning skills, gave way to the so-called American 'hard-boiled' detective story, which emphasized physical action while adapting to new ends many of the devices of its classical, puzzle-posing counterpart.

The periods covered in parts II and III overlap in the two decades following World War I, a cataclysm that not only changed the course of world events, but profoundly affected Britain's and America's attitudes toward history, toward their respective national destinies on the world stage, and toward relations between the classes, races, and genders making up the readership and subject matter of detective fiction in each country. In the midst of these changes, America became the primary influence on the later development of the genres of detection and crime throughout the world.

A final warning: although I have tried not to give away the endings of stories discussed in this book, the attempt has almost invariably failed. *Caveat lector* – let the reader beware! In addition, the Casebook entries presume familiarity with the stories being discussed.

Part I

Narratives of Detection and the Sciences of History

1

What is Detective Fiction?

Types and Elements

Before we can relate the history of something, we must define what we are talking about. There are several ways to go about defining detective fiction. One is taxonomic. This means placing it in relation to other types of popular literature, such as love stories, Westerns, science fiction, spy tales, and so on. John G. Cawelti (*Adventure*) has grouped these types into larger categories called 'archetypes', which are convenient for making an initial distinction between two major kinds of detective fiction, 'Mystery' and 'Adventure'.

Because it often begins with an unsolved crime of some sort, the detective story seems to fit snugly within Cawelti's 'Mystery' archetype, rather than either of his other two groups, 'Adventure' or 'Romance'. Crimes, however, can appear in all three, while some detective mysteries do not, technically, involve crimes at all. In addition, many crime stories including a detective or similar character offer no mystery to be solved, but rather a difficulty to be overcome: making an arrest or eluding one, stealing something or retrieving it, taking or freeing a hostage. Such 'caper' or crime-suspense tales have a long pedigree reaching back to 'The Purloined Letter' (1845) of Edgar Allan Poe (1809–49). While gripping, they are not particularly mysterious, for the culprits and their schemes are known almost from the beginning. 'Caper' tales clearly belong to Cawelti's Adventure archetype, where the virtues to be displayed are ingenuity, daring, and resolve, not the decipherment of clues or weighing of evidence.

In what follows, we will focus on detective fiction of the Mystery type, whether the detectives in question are official, private professional, or amateur. Nonetheless, the Adventure crime story, both with and without detectives, will be seen to play an important early role in the development of its Mystery counterpart.

Within the Mystery type of detective story some elements are fairly consistent. A Mystery detective story usually contains a detective of some kind, an unsolved mystery (not always technically a crime), and an investigation by which the mystery is eventually solved. There is another component, however, that may be present in varying degrees, or may not be present at all. This is the so-called 'puzzle element': the presentation of the mystery as an ongoing problem for the reader to solve, and its power to engage the reader's own reasoning abilities. The first three elements of detective fiction – detective, mystery, investigation – make a conjoint appearance quite early in the history of the genre. However, the fourth, the 'puzzle element', is conspicuous by its absence during most of this period.

Bleak House (1853), for instance, by Charles Dickens (1812–70), features one of the earliest official police detectives to appear in mainstream English fiction, Inspector Bucket. It also includes the murder of a prominent attorney, Mr Tulkinghorn, and a train of detection that involves testing alibis, sifting motives, and collecting material evidence, all leading to the arrest of the culprit, Lady Dedlock's French maid, Mademoiselle Hortense. Along the way we encounter at least two innocent suspects (one of them Lady Dedlock herself) and several techniques of detection (such as close surveillance) dear to the heart of early crime writers. Tulkinghorn's murder is only one among many mysteries in Dickens's huge tapestry of London high and low life, at the centre of which lurks the tragedy of Lady Dedlock's deadly, locked-up secret: her former love affair with Captain Hawdon and her abandonment in infancy of the child they conceived, Esther Summerson. In fact, Bucket's most important investigation is directed not at apprehending a murderer, but at preventing a suicide. Over the course of twenty-four hours, the detective helps Esther track Lady Dedlock to Hawdon's anonymous grave, whither she has fled from the mansion of her husband, Sir Leicester, in disgrace.

As for amateur detectives, consider Emily St Aubert, heroine of *The Mysteries of Udolpho* (1794), a popular Gothic novel by Ann Radcliffe (1764–1823). Many critics have cited Radcliffe's book as a detective story prototype. Here we have a young Englishwoman trapped in a decrepit castle owned by a predatory Italian Count named Montoni. She is surrounded by mysteries defying rational explanation: cadavers in hidden rooms, strange night sounds, secret passages behind fluttering curtains, and the like. Emily makes several discoveries for herself as she tries to escape from the castle, and is later told that smugglers hiding contraband have contrived some of the other 'supernatural' occurrences to scare away casual interlopers.

Dickens's and Radcliffe's novels illustrate the three constant factors we have identified as essential to detective fiction. In each, we find a detective (one professional, one amateur), mysteries to be solved, and an investigation which eventuates in the solution to these mysteries. But neither author enables the reader to participate very actively in the investigation. Radcliffe offers few if any resources in the course of Emily's adventures by which we might arrive at a solution before the author provides it. Tulkinghorn's murder in *Bleak House* fails the same test. We know early on that Mademoiselle Hortense has reason to despise Lady Dedlock, and thus sufficient motive to frame her employer for the crime. But we are denied the most vital information pointing in the maid's direction until after her arrest. This includes the source of the paper fragment used to wrap the gunpowder in the pistol that killed Tulkinghorn. The remainder of the page from which that fragment was torn is recovered from Mademoiselle Hortense's wastebasket by Inspector Bucket's wife.

Granting the reader access to information essential to solving the mystery is thought by many readers and critics, at least nowadays, to be crucial to stories of detection. Just as crucial, for those holding this view, is withholding from the reader for as long as possible the complete solution to the mystery. For this reason, one might argue that Inspector Bucket's discovery of Lady Dedlock's sordid past does not qualify as a plot of detection any more than his solution of Tulkinghorn's murder, even though the reader is provided with enough hints to 'connect the dots', as it were. Indeed, the problem here is not too few dots, but too many, all neatly lined up. Long before Lady Dedlock's flight, her connection to Captain Hawdon and to Esther has been surmised by a number of unsavoury characters, whose suspicions are conveyed to us though they have not yet become public.

Given these reservations, some critics consider *Bleak House* less a novel of detection than of 'Sensation', a term coined by Margaret Oliphant (1828–97) in a *Blackwood's Edinburgh Magazine* essay of May 1862. Oliphant was describing books much like Dickens's, where a long train of carefully prepared hints, suggestions, and implications is laid down not so much to astonish the reader with something altogether unexpected as to reveal some dreadful secret that most readers have suspected all along.

Clearly, stories that feature a detective, a mystery, and an investigation may or may not engage the reader's own powers of detection. That is, they may or may not have a 'puzzle element'. Those that do, as we shall see, also have a special relationship to the act of reading, and to cultural attitudes toward history and its narrative recovery in the modern world. Because this distinction is crucial to our understanding of the development of the genre in relation to these attitudes, I shall use the term 'detec*tive* fiction' in what follows to refer to any story that contains a major character undertaking the investigation of a mysterious crime or similar transgression, and reserve the term 'detec*tion*', as in 'literary detection', 'stories of detection', and the like, for that category of detective writing in which the puzzle element directly engages the reader's attention and powers of inference.

Formulas, Rules, and 'Fair Play': The Basis of the Puzzle Element

The puzzle element is often linked in discussions of detective fiction with the word 'formula', a term also applied to popular genres such as Westerns and love stories. A 'formula' is like a recipe: it describes the specific kinds of characters, settings, and plots that readers have come to expect in their favourite popular genre. For instance, in the 'hard-boiled' American detective formula the hero is typically a 'tough guy' and good at making wise-cracks. Because it is a constant, the formula can create a sense of ritualization, an integral part of what makes some popular genres attractive to their fans. Thus, according to W. H. Auden, the 'classical' English detective story typically re-enacts rites of scapegoating and expulsion that affirm the innocence of a community of good people supposedly ignorant of evil. Formally expelled from an Edenic 'Great Good Place' (19) by imprisonment, transportation, or execution, the evil snake-in-the-grass who has been lurking unsuspected among its inhabitants takes away the stain of sin along with him or her upon expulsion: Paradise is Regained.

Writing to a formula will probably ensure sales, but it can become boring. In detection, however, formulaic rules also present opportunities for the display of authorial ingenuity through 'rule subversion' (Owen, 78), which is intended to enhance the challenge of the puzzle element: having reached the point of cliché, for instance, the formulaic rule that 'the butler did it' is ripe for violation. Literary detection seems to generate, in writers and readers alike, a distinct disciplinary impulse that paradoxically encourages 'rule subversion' by perpetuating the expectation of formulaic adherence, a self-contradictory impulse largely foreign to other popular literary genres.

The glory days of rule-bound literary detection arrived during the 1920s and 1930s, the so-called 'Golden Age', when 'classic' or 'analytic' stories of detection challenging the reader to answer the question of 'Whodunit?' dominated the best-seller lists. These decades also saw the first appearance of serious critical reflection on the form itself and on its historical development, including Régis Messac's magisterial dissertation on the detective novel and scientific thought (1929) and critical 'prologues' to popular anthologies edited by Willard Huntington Wright (a.k.a. S. S. van Dine, 1887–1939), Dorothy Sayers (1893–1957), and others.

In general, Golden Age commentators saw a progressive pattern in the evolution of literary detection from its 'invention' by Edgar Allan Poe in 1841, when 'The Murders in the Rue Morgue' was published, through the consolidating masterpieces of Arthur Conan Doyle (1859–1930) in the 1890s, to popular examples of classical detection by contemporaries such as Sayers, Agatha Christie (1891–1976), Ngaio Marsh (1895–1982), and John Dickson Carr (1906–77). It is impossible to ignore the line of influence embodied by these writers. But as Martin Kayman warns us (3), temporal succession can easily be mistaken for inevitable advance.

There is nothing inevitable about detection's advance along the path that the Golden Age critics laid out, and much, in fact, that remains inexplicable if we adhere too closely to their itinerary. Why, for instance, did it take some twenty years for Poe's example, inspired as it was, to make any impact on detective fiction? What was it about the decades after World War I that enhanced the allure of 'classical' detection in England, while inciting the 'hard-boiled' reaction against it in the United States? As I hope to show, the answers to such questions lie to some degree in changes that were taking place in the reading public's general concepts of history and historical reconstruction.

While we may question the assumption of inevitability among Golden Age theorists of detective fiction, their cooperative attempt to regulate the genre by formulating rules is not without interest. The source of that regulatory impulse appears in Wright's opening statement to 'Twenty Rules for Writing Detective Stories': 'The detective story is a kind of intellectual game. It is more – it is a sporting event' (189). As in any game or sporting event, rules are needed to ensure fair play between opposing sides – in Wright's view, between the author and the reader. Put succinctly, the author proposes a mystery and provides clues adequate to solve it, while the reader, using the clues, tries to solve the mystery within a predetermined time-limit, i.e., the length of the story itself. This limit is usually restricted to the length of time it takes the fictional detective to arrive at and state the solution. Tsvetan Todorov has distilled this adversarial relationship into a succinct analogy almost universally recognized by theorists of the genre: the author is to the reader as the criminal is to the detective (49).

Looked at from another point of view, however, the reader and the detective can be seen as rivals, and the author as their referee. Holmes's famous wake-up call to Watson, 'The game is afoot!' (Doyle, 'Abbey Grange', 881), referring to prey rather than poker, suggests that detective fiction is less like a card or board game, or a team sport, than like a hunt, probably the oldest human activity requiring detective skills. In hunting, one's quarry is rarely considered one's opponent, rival, or adversary, terms more aptly directed at one's fellow hunters. In this analogy reader and detective compete in pursuit of the criminal like two hunters in pursuit of the same pheasant, with the author presiding as a kind of 'master of the hunt', ensuring fair play between the competitors. This is certainly what Wright had in mind in formulating his first rule, which states, 'The reader must have equal opportunity with the detective for solving the mystery. All clues must be plainly stated and described' (189).

As we shall see, reassigning the assumed rivalry between reader and author to the relationship between reader and detective will help clarify the specific appeal of the narrative of detection as a reading experience. For in the actual reading of detection the only 'person' with whom one feels truly competitive, moment to moment, is the detective, not the author who has devised the competition, nor the criminal who is (imaginatively) the object of pursuit. Both author and criminal, after all, can be presumed to know the solution to the mystery from the outset.

Analogies to the sports of tracking and predation can help clarify another common feature of literary detection, in which the detectives' designated 'prey' is limited, so to speak, to the members of one species ('suspects') and confined within the boundaries of a single 'game preserve'. Wright's rule number ten, 'the culprit must turn out to be a person who has played a more or less prominent part in the story'

(191), indicates the importance of maintaining a closed circle of suspects from the beginning. This explains the high rate of crime to be found at boarding schools, colleges, country houses, and on moving trains in the land of classical detection.

The importance of sustaining our appetite for play (Caillois) or 'ludic interest' (Champigny, 4–5) in the narrative of detection is reflected in several other rules. 'The culprit must be determined by logical deductions,' says Wright, 'not by accident or coincidence or unmotivated confession' (190–1). This implies not only that the criminal cannot surrender in mid-hunt, but also that the hunt must conform to the requirements of causal logic, from which chance and the supernatural are excluded. Similarly, 'the problem of the crime must be solved by strictly naturalistic means', making 'the method of murder, and the means of detecting it [. . .] rational and scientific' (191). Thus Wright indicates that the imaginary world of detection must conform to the universe described by modern science, the world familiar to most educated readers living in the industrially developed nations.

Rules that do not conform to those of the known modern universe, of course, often govern events in science fiction, fantasy, and supernatural horror stories. That is to say, the rules governing the world of detection also govern the succession of events unfolding in any realistic piece of fiction written in the last two centuries. What makes them particularly important to literary detection is that they ensure not only that the story will appear nominally realistic, but also that the writer is setting up the intellectual game of detection 'fairly'.

This concept of fairness is alien to nearly every other form of literary realism, where we rarely assume the author to be ethically delinquent when he or she withholds certain facts, feeds us misinformation, or is mistaken him- or herself. When Mr Krook, the rag and paper shop owner in *Bleak House*, mysteriously dies of 'spontaneous combustion', readers may object on the grounds of physical impossibility, despite Dickens's citations of evidence he considers scientific. It would make no sense, however, to call Dickens unfair. Nothing is jeopardized by the mode of Krook's death beyond the willing suspension of disbelief necessary to the enjoyment of any made-up story trying to mimic reality. As for Dickens's general skill as a writer, questions of fairness are simply irrelevant: debates over the author's use of coincidence or accidental discovery or intuition may result in negative aesthetic judgements, but not accusations of being 'unfair' to the reader.

Prototypes, Rhetorical Devices, and Narratology

Detective fiction prototypes predate by many centuries the idea that a story of detection must 'play fair'. Some critics have traced the genre as far back as the Jewish Apocrypha's stories of Daniel defeating the Elders in the trial of Susanna, or exposing the priests' theft of grain from the temple of Bel (Wrong, 42; Sayers, 'Omnibus', 72). Others have held up Sophocles' *Oedipus Rex* as an early example, featuring as it does a detective and a criminal combined in one character, a device more common in detective fiction than one might expect. Still others have sought to limit the genre to the rise of eighteenth-century empiricism, as exemplified in *Zadig, ou le Destinée* (*Zadig, or Destiny*, 1748), by Voltaire (François-Marie Arouet, 1694–1778). Here the title character infers the size, colour, and trappings of a horse that has escaped from the emperor's stable, relying solely upon physical signs of the animal's passage along the road. Finally, some have argued that detective fiction began with modern policing methods in the early nineteenth century. Like Wright, they insist that 'the detective novel must have a detective in it' (190).

Régis Messac first traced in detail the ancient and medieval history of the logical method that is central to all detective fiction, as well as to modern science: induction. Inductive logic relies on the inferring of conclusions from empirical evidence, as opposed to the deriving – or 'deducing' – of conclusions from indisputable premises or axioms, which is the method of deductive logic. In detective fiction, the two forms of logic are rarely distinguished. However, the distinction is crucial to understanding the function and origins of the genre, and can be demonstrated with some simple examples.

Geology, for example, uses induction: we can infer that present-day mountaintops once lay below sea-level from the discovery of fossilized sea-life embedded in them. Geometry, however, uses deduction: if a straight line is the shortest distance between two points (which we assume, axiomatically, to be the case in plane geometry), and the line connecting two points, A and B, is straight, then this line is also the shortest distance between them. Both types of logic depend on syllogistic reasoning of the form: (1) all B are A; (2) C is B; (3) therefore, C is also A. Inductive logic, however, does not always begin from self-evident, axiomatic premises.

For instance, our geology example begins with the unspoken premise, 'All fossils that look like seashells originated in the sea'; moves on to the observation, 'There are seashell-looking fossils on the tops of these mountains'; and arrives at the logical conclusion that these mountains were once below sea-level. And yet, it is only recently in human history that our premise about fossilized seashells would have been taken for granted. Well into the eighteenth century many 'natural philosophers', as scientists then called themselves, thought that such fossils were crystals mimicking living forms, or miraculous creations implanted directly in the earth by God for his own mysterious purposes. Even admitting them to be the remains of aqueous creatures, some argued that they might have been deposited atop the Alps by birds or pilgrims from the Holy Land. In short, inductive logic usually depends on many previous acts of empirical inference, as well as the testing of such inferences through experiment, comparison, and repeated observation. By such means we arrive at estimates of the probability (often beyond a reasonable doubt, but never deductively certain) of past events and their relationships to one another.

Of course, other important historical factors contributed to the emergence of modern detective fiction besides the popularization of a scientific interest in inductive logic. Among the most important were the eighteenth-century shift in law-enforcement methods from public exhibitions of punishment to private surveillance and arrest, the explosive growth of Western cities, the spread of literacy, and innovations in the publication and distribution of printed matter.

But whether the story in question is less than two centuries old or more than two millennia, what matters to the reader seeking to 'play the game' of literary detection is what seems to have mattered most to the formal theorists of the Golden Age: first, that the solution to the mystery employ the inductive methods characteristic of the modern sciences while conforming to the laws of physical cause and effect presumed by those methods; and, second, that the solution be withheld until the reader has been given access to all the evidence by which the mystery is finally, and plausibly, solved by the fictional investigator. Attempting to 'subvert' either of these two rules almost invariably tends to nudge an author's work out of the category of detection, since it diminishes the puzzle element that defines 'detection' as such.

With the rise to prominence of detec*tion* as a sub-genre of detec*tive* fiction toward the end of the nineteenth century, the purpose of writing detective stories began to shift from the reporting and display of induction to the incitement and prolonging of inductive activity in the reader. Before turning to the cultural history of this transformation, we must try to better understand the process itself. We may begin by observing that induction can only be incited in the reader by a particular kind of narrative, using a particular kind of rhetorical figure: metonymy.

Metonymy is a figure of speech in which effect stands for cause or part for whole. (The latter is also called synecdoche.) Metonymy is based on connection, whereas other rhetorical figures of substitution like metaphor and simile (a metaphor using 'like' or 'as') are based on shared qualities or appearances. A crown that stands for a monarch is a metonym, as is a fingerprint for the suspect who left one at the scene of a crime. An animal that stands for a warrior, however, is a metaphor. The warrior may be described as a 'lion' in battle, but only conceptually, in his fierceness or rage or power: he has no mane or tail, for instance.

Like the 'rules' stipulating that in detective fiction the ordinary laws of the physical universe (as conceived by modern science) are assumed to apply, metonymy is crucial to the development of the realistic and naturalistic traditions of the European and American novel. In literary detection, however, it is the basic figure governing the creation and interpretation of *clues*. Metonymic clues, unlike special powers of intuition, chance associations, angelic voices, or other private forms of experience, are taken to be interpretable by all observers sharing a common point of view, knowledge base, and powers of thought. This is why, in fictional detection, giving the reader full access to clues is considered essential to ensuring fair play.

Clues can be made accessible to the reader either directly within the master narrative of the story as a whole or indirectly through statements from various characters in it, that is, through *testimony*. Testimonies usually offer particular points of view – reliable, unreliable, or yet to be tried – on the relevance and meaning of the clues appearing in them. When testimony takes the form of a first-person master narrative, either spoken by one of the characters in the story or written down after the fact by an eye-witness, it may coincide with the story itself.

The narrative structure of testimonies within which clues appear in fictional detection has become a prominent part of contemporary narratology, which is the study of the principles, forms, and functions of narrative. The primary and constant feature of the narrative of detection is that its structure is always two-fold. As Todorov puts it, the reader of a story of detection encounters 'not one but two stories: the story of the crime and the story of the investigation'. 'In their purest form, these two stories have no point in common. [. . .] The first story, that of the crime, ends before the second begins. But what happens in the second? Not much. The characters of this second story, the story of the investigation, do not act, they learn' (44). The first story, Todorov goes on to say – 'the story of the crime – tells "what really happened", whereas the second – the story of the investigation – explains "how the reader (or the narrator) has come to know about it"' (45). Drawing on the terminology of Russian Formalist critics of the early twentieth century, Todorov calls the first story 'story' and the second 'plot': 'The story is what has happened in life, the plot is the way the author presents it to us. The first notion corresponds to the reality evoked, to events similar to those which take place in our lives; the second [. . .] to the narrative, to the literary devices the author employs' (45).

The French narratologist Gérard Genette uses the terms *récit* and *histoire* to describe these two notions (25), but the cognate associations of such terms with English words like 'story', 'history', and 'recitation', and the ambiguous use of terms like 'story' itself by Todorov and others, make a clearer, simpler terminology desirable.

In what follows, then, I will use the term *array* to refer to the events appearing in a text as they are conceived by the reader in the order of their original occurrence, whether that occurrence takes place before or after the story begins. The master array of a story is imaginatively constructed and reconstructed by the reader as a single, coherent sequence in the projected time-frame of the world the story represents. I will use the term *narrative* to refer to these same events as they appear in the sequence of their actual telling, that is, in the time-frame of the reader's immediate, serial experience of the text – word by word, sentence by sentence. I shall reserve the word *plot* to refer to the interplay between array and narrative, and *story* to refer to the complete textual entity that comprises array, narrative, and plot.

The plot relationship between the array and the narrative of any story is often characterized by what Genette calls *analepsis* (40), that is, the narrative construction of arrays that may precede the inception of the narrative itself. It is easy to see the vital role that analepsis plays at the end of the classical detective story, when the detective (or sometimes the criminal himself) provides a summary narrative that connects and puts in proper order both the array of events leading up to the crime and the array of events by which the detective himself arrived at the correct sequence of the first array.

Also important to the narratology of detective fiction, according to Genette, is *prolepsis*, a narrative device which causes the reader to anticipate a discovery or realization in the future that has analeptic consequences, or that merely sets up, without causing the reader to anticipate them, the conditions for such an analeptic recovery later on. The first-person narrators in many of the suspense novels of Mary Roberts Rinehart (1876–1958) often resorted to the explicitly anticipatory version of this device, which Genette calls the 'advance notice'. This technique came to be known to Rinehart's fans and parodists alike by the acronym 'HIBK', for 'Had I But Known' – as in 'Had I but known then what I know now, I would never have set foot on Baron von Rotshnitzel's private yacht.' The more subtle form of prolepsis, 'well-known to connoisseurs of detective stories' (77), says Genette, is the 'advance mention', a 'simple marker without anticipation' intended to acquire significance later in the narrative, through analeptic recovery (75). Clearly, Genette is thinking of clues here.

Narratives also include non-temporal devices. The most important of these for the literature of detection is 'modality' or 'mood', which controls the reader's access to information. This is achieved by the narrative's 'adopting or seeming to adopt what we ordinarily call the [. . .] "vision" or "point of view"' of 'one or another participant in the story' (Genette, 162). The standard detective sidekick, such as Holmes's Watson or Hercule Poirot's Captain Hastings, usually performs this modal function in a seemingly natural way calibrated to match his or her presumably ordinary intelligence.

As with nearly all the other features of detective fiction, its doubled, analeptic narrative structure has earned extensive commentary. Some critics, like Todorov, Franco Moretti, Peter Huhn, and William Stowe, believe that such plots epitomize the practice of encoding and decoding that shapes our everyday encounters with social and cultural reality. Thomas Sebeok, Umberto Eco ('Horns'), and Gian Paolo Caprettini have connected the techniques of induction that knit together array and narrative with those of 'abduction', a form of induction characterizing scientific hypothesis rather than scientific proof.

Few of these writers have paid close attention to what Peter Brooks calls 'the temporal dynamics that shape narratives in our reading of them, the play of desire in time that makes us turn pages and strive toward narrative ends' (xii). In the literature of detection this 'play of desire in time' takes the specific form of the reader's engagement with the puzzle element. Before examining this engagement specifically in Brooks's terms, however, we need to understand how the reader's interest in detective fiction has ordinarily been conceived.

Reading for Identification

Most analysts of detective fiction see the genre as a form of wish-fulfilment. The wishes to be fulfilled may be psychological and common to all readers, or socially determined, or both, but their fulfilment is nearly always conceived as vicarious, that is, achieved through a process of identification with the activities of one or several characters. We have already mentioned W. H. Auden's view that detective stories enable readers to experience the cathartic ritual of scapegoating. More generally, Michael Cohen speaks of humanity's innate desire to throw off the restraints of civilization and release its suppressed impulses toward violence by identifying with the criminal or with those who vengefully hunt him down (14–15).

Among hidden cultural motives, the public legitimation of privileges specific to the class, race, and gender of dominant social groups ranks high with many critics. Most of these, like Dennis Porter, Stephen Knight (*Form*), Martin Kayman, and D. A. Miller, draw heavily on the work of social and political theorists such as Louis Althusser and Antonio Gramsci.

Althusser viewed modern culture as a device for the perpetuation of norms of behaviour that enforce the power of ruling groups extra-legally, primarily through civil institutions. These include schools, churches, families, business and civic organizations, the medical profession, and the arts, especially mass forms of popular entertainment and communication where detective stories thrive. The socializing process by which this enforcement is achieved is called 'interpellation'. Gramsci believed that the cultural values authorizing any group's dominance necessarily took a form that seemed so natural and right in the eyes of all classes as to foreclose the possibility of direct challenge by oppressed groups. This naturalized form of dominance he called 'hegemony'.

According to followers of Gramsci and Althusser, hegemonic control of the populace is maintained through interpellation. As a part of modern mass entertainment, detective fiction helps interpellate its readers into conformity with the hegemony of white, male, middle-class values in Western capitalist-industrial societies. In the words of Dennis Porter, detective writers are 'distillers of familiar national essences', 'effectively suppress[ing] the historical reality that they seem to represent' (218–19).

The writings of Roland Barthes and Fredric Jameson (*Political*) are also cited in connection with this view of popular culture as the perpetuation of power relations in society by other than official means, that is, through the symbolic mirror, or 'mythologies', as Barthes calls them, of culture. The single most influential ideological critic of detective and crime fiction, however, was Michel Foucault. Foucault's ground-breaking study of the shift in eighteenth- and nineteenth-century law-enforcement methods, from public execution as a form of deterrence to targeted investigation and surveillance, provided a specific historical rationale for applying concepts like hegemony and interpellation, with their implications of surreptitious cultural control over individual thought and behaviour, to the materials of detective and crime fiction. According to Miller, the very point of view commonly adopted by nineteenth-century novelists – third person, objective, and all-knowing – embodies Foucault's notion that middle-class society is obsessed with exercising social control through modes of surveillance.

All of these critics advance, to one degree or another, a mimetic or vicarious explanation for the kinds of satisfaction that detective fiction gives its fans. In their approaches to the genre, detection is nearly always conceived as an imagined spectacle of crime, investigation, and solution into which the reader projects himself or herself (or is 'interpellated') imaginatively. Even among ritualists like Auden, or David Grossvogel, who sees solving the puzzle as analogous to ancient Gnostic initiation ceremonies (4), there is the unspoken assumption that we read detective fiction for the sake of identifying with a character in the story, usually the detective, but sometimes the criminal and sometimes both.

The assumption that the reader's primary identification is with the detective, the defender of hegemonic norms and self-perpetuating cultural value-systems, is based on the fact that the reader and the detective perform the same mental activity of inductive reasoning. By contrast, any vicarious release of anti-social impulses must take the shape of a relatively passive, imaginative identification with the criminal transgressor.

However, there is no reason why the reader cannot identify with the detective in the same manner as with the criminal, or, for that matter, in the same manner as with any other character in any other work of fiction. The proof of this statement is to be found in the hundreds of crime-suspense stories and novels of mystery featuring both a detective figure and a criminal, but lacking the puzzle element. Clearly, the reader need not imitate the *practice* of detection when identifying with the detective, defender of order and upholder of hegemonic values, any more than he or she need imitate the *practice* of crime when identifying with the criminal, the rebellious, free-thinking challenger of that order.

In short, theories of identification with or 'interpellation' by the detective figure, whether psychological, psycho-social, or ideological, do not require the foregrounding of the puzzle element as something with which the reader must actively engage, although that engagement may help to intensify the reader's ordinary process of identification. What, then, can the puzzle element do that no other narrative or rhetorical device can do? What unique purpose does it serve that cannot also be served through the reader's merely vicarious participation in the events, characters, and activities that appear in the story itself?

These are the kinds of questions raised by Peter Brooks with respect to narrative in general. Watching him try to answer them can bring us closer to answering the larger question posed by this book: what cultural and historical developments during the nineteenth and early twentieth centuries helped make literary detection, originally a small sub-genre of detective fiction in general, its dominant form?

'Reading for the Plot' of Detection: The Desire to Invent

Unlike theorists of narrative like Todorov and Genette, who examine popular narrative as a static structure, Brooks professes interest in 'the motor forces that drive the text forward' (xiii–iv) and that are to be found, not in the text, but in the mind of the person who actively brings the text to life by reading it. Only by studying the actual process of reading induced by different types of narrative can we understand the 'structuring operation' performed by each of them on the reader's ability to make sense of what he or she reads (9). 'Plot' is the engine of that 'structuring operation', according to Brooks, a 'logic of narrative' that unfolds its meanings in time, sequentially and cumulatively, whenever we are 'reading for the plot'.

According to Brooks, 'plot' is a function of the continual interplay between what I have called 'narrative' and 'array' in the unfolding of the story. Readers may be motivated to read stories for any number of reasons besides plot, including escapism, sexual titillation, or curiosity about life in an unfamiliar milieu. Or they may read for artistic gratification or insight into 'the human condition' or intellectual stimulation. These are the usual motives that have been attributed to readers of 'high-brow' literature as opposed to 'low-brow' mass entertainment since the early twentieth century, when 'reading for the plot', the central narrative dynamic of the nineteenth century novel, fell into disrepute.

The lowly detective story, says Brooks, has retained the narrative allure of the traditional novel, stimulating 'the active quest of the reader for those shaping ends that, terminating the dynamic process of reading, promise to bestow meaning and significance on the beginning and the middle' (19). Brooks's *tour de force* interpretation of Arthur Conan Doyle's Sherlock Holmes story 'The Musgrave Ritual' (1893) illustrates this point.

Here, Holmes deciphers a document whose recitation has been part of a coming-of-age ritual in the wealthy Musgrave family for two centuries. No one in the family understands its meaning after all this time, but Holmes figures out that it provides coded directions for finding the hidden location of the crown of Charles I, whose execution ended the English Civil War in the seventeenth century. The ancestors of Reginald Musgrave, Holmes's client, provided aid and comfort to Charles's adherents and buried the crown on their estate after the king's son, Charles II, fled to France. The Musgrave Ritual sets out the literal steps to be taken on the grounds of the estate, relative to landmarks and compass points, that will lead to the underground chamber where the treasure is hidden. There Holmes also discovers the body of Reginald's head butler, Brunton, who was entombed in the chamber when he tried to steal the treasure after deciphering the Ritual himself.

Referring to the doubled plot of detection proposed by Todorov and others, Brooks points out (23–9) that in 'The Musgrave Ritual' Holmes physically re-enacts the process of mental re-enactment by which a reader gradually knits together into a coherent series an otherwise ambiguously related succession of narrated events. Thus, in order to understand the Ritual's relationship to a political 'plot' (to secure the crown until the king's son returns to claim the throne) and uncover Brunton's criminal 'plot' (to secure the precious crown for himself), Holmes must literally 'plot' the solution out, like a surveyor, on the lawn of the estate. Here, says Brooks, Doyle 'makes particularly clear a condition of all classic detective fiction, that the detective repeat, go over again the ground that has been covered by his predecessor', the criminal (25). Holmes is thus 'literalizing an act that all narrative claims to perform [. . .] a repetition and rehearsal [. . .] of what has already happened' (25). In Doyle's story, as in all narrative, concludes Brooks, 'the ultimate determinants of meaning lie *at the end*', and narrative desire 'is ultimately, inexorably, desire *for* the end' (52).

Perhaps this is so in most narratives. But it is unclear whether a 'desire for the end' is what we uniquely bring to our reading of stories of detection, as distinct from detective or crime-suspense fiction or any other imaginative narrative in general. For that matter, an inherent 'desire for the end' would seem to run counter to the pleasure we take in the sheer act of solving, or attempting to solve, the puzzle of detection. After all, when the end of the story of detection is reached, the time we are allotted for solving the crime is up: the narrative 'clock', as it were, will run out when the detective, our ostensible competitor, announces the solution and begins his summary analepsis. If anything, what we desire in reading detection is the prolongation of opportunities for induction, or, to be more precise, for imagining a variety of arrays. In fact, what we read 'for' in detection is not 'the end', but what the approach of the end makes even more urgent and exciting, namely, the exercise of our powers of imaginative invention.

In order to illustrate this point, let us examine one moment in 'The Musgrave Ritual' that Brooks singles out, where 'plotting', presumably driven by 'narrative desire' for the end, is assumed to be taking place within the reader: the moment when Holmes is given a copy of the Ritual.

This occurs just as Reginald Musgrave, last scion of the family, finishes his account of the mysterious events transpiring at his estate in the previous two weeks. Among these are the premature disappearance of Brunton, who had been discovered reading the Ritual in Musgrave's library and, for this breach of trust, was terminated with a week's notice, and the disappearance of Rachel Howells, the maid who, as we will later discover, sealed Brunton alive in the underground vault in revenge for his having cheated on her with another woman. Before she vanished, Rachel flung a bag containing the unrecognizable contents of the vault (the misshapen crown and a few pebbles) into a nearby lake. Holmes sums up, for Watson, our present knowledge of these events:

> You can imagine, Watson, with what eagerness I listened to this extraordinary sequence of events, and endeavoured to piece them together, and to devise some common thread upon which they might all hang. The butler was gone. The maid was gone. The maid had loved the butler, but had afterwards had cause to hate him. She was of Welsh blood, fiery and passionate. She had been terribly excited immediately after his disappearance. She had flung into the lake a bag containing some curious contents. [. . .] What was the starting-point of this chain of events? There lay the end of this tangled line. (535–6)

Holmes's last sentence certainly seems to confirm Brooks's theory. The 'common thread upon which' these events 'might all hang', Brooks adds, 'is precisely the interpretive thread of plot' (24).

Very good. But what is actually going on in the mind of the reader at this point? He or she is not looking to 'the end of this tangled line', but, more proximately, to what Holmes calls 'the starting-point of this chain of events'.

Faced with the evidence he or she has thus far accumulated, the reader is connecting the persons and events already conveyed by the narrative in several tentative arrays of relationship. Perhaps Brunton left in disgrace after receiving notice and the maid followed after a few days of anxiety over his new love interest, hoping to win him back. The 'curious contents' of the bag thrown into the lake could be connected with this other affair. Perhaps they are the remains of a firearm and shot belonging to a neighbouring gamekeeper, who we know is the father of the 'other woman'. Furthermore, Brunton left his clothes and belongings behind – perhaps he went out for a tryst with his new lover, who, suspecting that Rachel had won him back, killed him with this gun and then tried to destroy it. Or perhaps Rachel had somehow obtained the gun, arranged an assignation with Brunton, killed him, and fled.

All of these tentative arrays anticipate possible plot outcomes, and to that extent they all seem to be driven by what Brooks calls narrative desire 'for the end'. None of them is conceivable, however, without the meticulously constructed, richly ambiguous trail of clues and testimony that Doyle has deliberately laid down for us up to this point, and nothing like this range and proliferation of implicit arrays is typical of an ordinary work of fiction.

Here lies the true significance of Holmes's last two sentences summarizing the Musgrave case, for the 'end' we desire when reading detection is always the 'starting-point' of the master array of events gradually emerging in the narrative, and that point in the array lies *behind* us as we read even though the 'end' of the narrative always lies *ahead*. Moreover, Doyle has made these emerging events relatable in multiple ways, as if he intended to stimulate the reader to project backwards as many interconnected and overlapping arrays as possible.

Next, Reginald Musgrave hands Holmes a written copy of the Ritual. This new event helps us narrow the range of possible arrays we have projected, or, more precisely, retrojected, thus far. For instance, the contents of the bag seem to be connected with the 'it' of the first line of the Ritual, 'Whose was it?', and thus with the history of the Musgrave family, not the gamekeeper. But we cannot be sure: this might be a red herring, meant to throw us off the scent. Meanwhile, the Ritual also incites the invention of still more arrays, within a now narrower compass of possibilities and probabilities. It consists of a series of questions and answers cryptically referring, as we find out later, to the executed king, his son, the crown, and its location. There is only one question-and-answer pair that seems to have a literal rather than coded meaning and might provide us, at this point, with some concrete direction: 'How was it stepped?' 'North by ten and by ten, east by five and by five', and so on (536).

Like the 'it' in the Ritual's first line, this clue narrows our choice of possible arrays, but also contributes to their proliferation within that narrower range. Even if we connect the verb 'stepped' to a literal foot, it could still refer to dancing or dressage rather than walking, and the numerals could refer to miles or yards or furlongs, not paces. Has the butler, a former teacher, discovered that he is descended from a dancing instructor once in the employ of the Musgrave family? If so, did that ancestor perhaps carry on an affair with the Lady of the house and father a child her husband mistook for his own, thus placing Brunton in a position to inherit the estate of Musgrave in the event the current line should die out, as it might do with the death of Reginald, a bachelor? Why else would Brunton risk his position and reputation to examine a document connected with the Musgraves' ritual of succession? And why did Brunton give up teaching in the first place to seek employment as a servant to Reginald?

Many of these speculations will strike knowledgeable readers of 'The Musgrave Ritual' as absurd. And yet, any of them, or several simultaneously, could be entertained in the mind of a given reader at this particular moment in the story, considering the narrative sequence of events that has transpired thus far. George Dove is only partly correct when he says that the detection formula 'narrow[s] the field and reduc[es] the number of alternative interpretations' as the story progresses (30). The range of our speculations may tend to diminish, but their absolute number does not necessarily follow suit and might in fact multiply. In any case, it is difficult to rule some of them out entirely.

What the reader of detection desires at each step of the reading process is not its end, but its immediate continuation. He or she desires the next clue, and rarely more than the next, for each new clue brings closer the end of the narrative, which is the end of opportunities to invent imaginative, backward-looking arrays. 'Reading for the plot' of detection is not simply 'piec[ing]' events together, one by one, on a 'common thread', as Holmes puts it. That may do for ordinary reading. Detection demands that we cast backwards as many different threads as possible, and try to hang all revealed, as well as all metonymically conceivable, events on each of them, simultaneously.

This kind of proto-narrative, analeptic invention is true, active 'plotting' in the sense Brooks has in mind. While it anticipates the completed narration of a master array at the end of the tale, it is not the expression of a desire 'for' that summary array, nor for an end to the story (i.e., an end to opportunities for retrospective invention). It expresses a desire to create arrays, and its satisfaction is proximately threatened, not by the author who feeds it clues, but by the fictional detective who might at any moment interrupt the ongoing feast by reducing all possible arrays to one.

The Puzzle of the Non-Proleptic Clue

Because they are directed backwards, analeptically, the imaginative acts of invention performed by the reader of detection do not depend in any fundamental sense on what Genette calls *prolepsis*. That is to say, the emerging clues on which invention thrives do not typically appear within a distinct sub-narrative of the 'Had I But Known' variety common to much mystery fiction besides detection. The best clues are, in fact, 'simple marker[s], without anticipation', as Genette says. Since they lack anticipation, however, and assume significance only in retrospect, they are decidedly *not* proleptic, at least no more so than any other narrated event in the story.

Prolepsis in its purest form is prophecy, as in Book 6 of Virgil's *Aeneid*, when the soul of Aeneas' dead father, Anchises, foretells the glories of Rome that will follow Aeneas' defeat of the Latin peoples of Italy. Less explicit but clearly identifiable proleptic events are sometimes found in detective stories. These offer clues appearing with distinct anticipation, what Genette calls an 'advance notice', as when Holmes might call out, 'Watson, look here! There's blood on the gasogene!' Less specific but just as distinctly anticipatory are the prolepses often found in much of sensation literature.

At the end of chapter 15 in *Lady Audley's Secret* (1862), by Mary Elizabeth Braddon (1835–1915), Lady Audley's nephew Robert insinuates that he has begun to uncover her 'secret': that she is really Helen Talboys, the supposedly deceased wife of Robert's friend

George Talboys, whom she deceived into believing she had died while he was in Australia prospecting for gold:

> 'Circumstantial evidence,' continued the young man [. . .]. 'Upon what infinitesimal trifles may sometimes hang the whole secret of some wicked mystery, inexplicable heretofore to the wisest of mankind! A scrap of paper; a shred of some torn garment; the button off a coat [. . .] links of steel in the wonderful chain forged by the science of the detective officer; and lo! the gallows is built up; the solemn bell tolls through the dismal grey of the early morning; the drop creaks under the guilty feet; and the penalty of crime is paid.' (104)

At this point, Lady Audley faints in her chair.

This passage is clearly proleptic in the sense of Genette's 'advance notice'. Although it does not specify just what Lady Audley's secret will turn out to be, Robert's portentous speech will fulfil its anticipatory promise by the end of the novel. At the same time, however, the passage is not a particularly fertile source of analeptic speculation and invention. We have already learned, among other things, that Lady Audley keeps some baby clothes hidden in her room; that she has shown a marked disinclination to meet George; that upon Robert's visiting the manor house with his friend in Lady Audley's absence, George appeared stupefied at the sight of her painted portrait; and that someone has sent a telegram, which Robert finds half-burnt, informing Lady Audley about George's intention to come to Southampton to see his young son by 'Helen'.

These very first 'links of steel' in Robert's 'wonderful chain' of circumstantial evidence remain firmly in place as he augments it link by inevitable link. In the next thirty pages our suspicions that Lady Audley is Helen Talboys, George's legal wife, become all but certain, and we are never presented with clues to suggest otherwise in the two hundred pages remaining. In short, the events leading up to Robert's speech about 'circumstantial evidence' have chained us as well as Lady Audley within a tight circle of future plot developments, like a bear to a stake.

Prolepsis builds suspense, but the best clues in a story of detection are not proleptic. Rather, they are camouflaged as ordinary events, 'without anticipation'. If they seem portentous, the reader should be wary of being led astray. Indeed, the most obviously proleptic clues in stories of detection are almost invariably meant to fool us: the blood on the gasogene usually turns out to be claret. The point is that *any* event emerging in a well-crafted narrative of detection may be a significant clue. Only by inventing, at each successive narrative moment, as many retrospective arrays as possible in which that event can achieve significance will the reader of detection have a chance of guessing if it is a clue or not.

Of course, because it tells a story like any other, fictional detection cannot help but make the reader extrapolate future plot developments from current circumstances. As in any story, the reader will wonder, at every stage, 'how it will all come out'. But mere 'desire for the end', while it can heighten suspense, cannot in and of itself excite the inductive reconstruction of imaginary arrays. The difference between reading detec*tion* and reading detec*tive*, or Mystery, or sensation stories, or fiction in general for that matter, lies in the degree of intensity and variation with which a reader's analeptic invention is engaged and prolonged at every instant. That difference depends in turn on the author's degree of adherence to, and creativity in applying or even subverting (within narrow limits), the formulaic 'rules' that will stimulate the reader's desire to read for invention.

Interestingly, readers of detective fiction more often fail than succeed in solving the case before the fictional sleuth does. As Grossvogel puts it, 'only an infinitesimally small number of Agatha Christie's half-billion readers ever [. . .] expected to solve her stories in advance of Jane Marple or Hercule Poirot' (41). However, the fact that Christie's readers kept trying implies that what they truly sought in her stories was the opportunity to exercise their analeptic imaginations by inventing plot arrays. Poe put his finger on this impulse in the opening lines of 'The Murders in the Rue Morgue': 'As the strong man exults in his physical activity, delighting in such exercises as call his muscles into action, so glories the analyst in that moral activity which *disentangles*' (189).

There is no other type of fiction that is designed to induce the reader to invent, moment by moment, as many retrospective arrays to match the continuous emergence of new narrative information as is the classic tale of detection. As a static form, detection may be conceived as an author's challenge to the reader, but readers experience it as a contest with the fictional detective. The real question that arouses interest and anxiety among detection's readers is thus not 'Whodunit?' but 'Who will solve it?' as the formulaic competition staged between detective protagonists and their official counterparts in the most famous specimens of the genre seems to illustrate.

In short, limiting the reader's opponent to the author of the story is equivalent to confusing the designer of a video game with the intergalactic fighter one is trying to defeat on-screen. The writer of detection has not only done the reader a favour by creating a device for the pleasurable exercise of his or her powers of invention, but entered into an unspoken covenant that two basic rules will obtain throughout this exercise: first, that all the evidence necessary to win the game will conform to the requirements of scientific induction; and, second, that all necessary evidence will be presented before the solution is announced. As in any game, it's not just the competitors who must 'play fair', but the official in charge as well.

Having now defined detective fiction and isolated its most historically significant sub-type, detection, by examining its power to incite acts of induction and invention in its readers, we are in a better position to understand the history of detective fiction's relationship to cultural developments in its three main countries of origin, France, Britain, and America.

2

Detection and the Historical Sciences: Two Locked Rooms and Two Keys to Unlock Them

The First Locked Room: The Physical Universe

[T]he chemical laboratory . . . was a lofty chamber, lined and littered with countless bottles. Broad, low tables were scattered about, which bristled with retorts, test-tubes, and little Bunsen lamps, with their blue flickering flames. There was only one student in the room, who was bending over a distant table absorbed in his work. At the sound of our steps he glanced round and sprang to this feet with a cry of pleasure. 'I've found it! I've found it', he shouted to my companion, running towards us with a test-tube in his hand.

A Study in Scarlet, 6–7

The image of the 'scientific detective' was first popularized by Arthur Conan Doyle in the person of Sherlock Holmes, who was introduced to the world, and to his future roommate, while sitting in a hospital laboratory seeking a chemical test for human blood-stains. Holmes's work as a detective, however, does not essentially involve discovering the laws governing physical events. These discoveries are useful to his work, but the real 'science' he seeks to master is reconstructive, not experimental. That is, Holmes is not primarily interested in how the world works from day to day, but in how past events can be linked together, narratively, into a credible array. A 're-agent of Haemoglobin' (*Study*, 7) may be as useful to Holmes as carbon dating to an archaeologist, but neither is more than a means to the end of historical knowledge.

We have seen that the narrative of detection excites intense analeptic activity and a desire for priority in its readers. The physical world in general has much the same effect on scientists and historians seeking to contribute something new to our understanding of past events. The resemblance has been acknowledged by historians themselves (see, e.g., Collingwood, Ginzburg), and the great French palaeontologist Georges Cuvier (1769–1832) even boasted that his abilities in reconstructing extinct species from a single bone surpassed those of Voltaire's Zadig (Cuvier, 99). Other contributors to the world-historical narrative that has evolved as a result of work similar to Cuvier's include pioneering eighteenth-century historians; the antiquarians, collectors of 'curiosities', and 'theorists of the earth' who preceded them; and all the cosmologists, mineralogists, geologists, palaeontologists, and archaeologists who came after. The story of the development of the detective genre largely coincides with the history of narrative practice in these reconstructive sciences, and with its popular dissemination. That history is quite recent.

It is difficult for most of us today to conceive that as late as the beginning of the nineteenth century most people in America and in Europe still believed that the earth and all creatures on it were little more than six thousand years old. That was the age of the earth as calculated by Bishop James Ussher (1581–1656) of Dublin in 1650 on the basis of the number of the generations listed in the Bible from the creation of Adam to the birth of Jesus. In fact, Bishop Ussher had determined that the universe was created at precisely 1:00 a.m., on Sunday, 23 October 4004 BC.

Not everyone, of course, believed that the age of the world could be calculated this precisely. But few outside of a handful of forward-thinking Frenchmen would have conceded that the earth and the universe surrounding it were much older than six millennia, or that the events recounted in the biblical narrative were not historically factual. The Bible was the Word of God himself, the record of the miraculous deeds he had performed on behalf of his chosen people, Jews and Christians. Just as importantly, it revealed his plans for their ultimate salvation at the end of time, as indicated by the 'covenants' he made with his people in the Jewish testament; the Gospel stories of Jesus's life, death, and resurrection; and the apocalyptic Book of Revelation, which described the end of the world.

Faith in the biblical account, chronology, and direction of history persisted well after astronomers, geologists, and palaeontologists had begun to discover what most people today would consider incontrovertible evidence that the earth was not only much older than the

Bible indicated, but had also witnessed many more extinctions of plant and animal species than the one recorded in the story of Noah. That its authority lasted so long shows how deeply ingrained in Western belief systems the Bible had become. By 1800, however, the forces of secularization were eroding faith in the historical reliability of Sacred Scripture among the educated classes of Britain, America, and France.

These secular forces were primarily scientific. Beginning in 1620 with the *Novum Organum* (*New Organon*) of Sir Francis Bacon (1561–1626), which sought a new foundation for the study of nature in empirical observation, and continuing in Sir Isaac Newton's (1642–1727) breath-taking use of mathematical formulae to calculate the laws of planetary motion, 'natural philosophers' began to reconceive the behaviour of the material world in terms of physical laws – 'secondary causes' – operating independently of God's will – their 'First Cause'. Among the heavenly bodies of Newton's cosmology, as described in his *Principia Mathematica* of 1687, there was still room for a superintending hand of God to correct anomalies in the astronomical observations confirming the mathematical laws of motion. By 1786, when Pierre-Simon Laplace (1749–1827) finally resolved these anomalies, it was already widely assumed that God's intervention in the operations of the universe was no longer necessary (Russell, *Science*, 19).

The first and most obvious effect of this scientific revolution was to eliminate the hand of God from the hypotheses of all the new physical sciences, not just astronomy, but physics and chemistry as well. Inspired by Newton's triumph, scientists began to seek general and invariable laws governing the behaviour of other natural phenomena, and these laws in turn enabled humanity to control nature in predictable and useful ways. The workings of the universe were soon viewed in strictly mechanical terms, like the workings of a watch or a steam engine, in the running of which God, the divine engineer, no longer directly participated or interfered. Advocates of what was then called 'natural theology', like William Paley (1743–1805), at first viewed these developments with complacency, finding in the wondrous intricacies and regularity of the natural world evidence of an omniscient, omnipotent, and benevolent designer. At the same time, however, scientific study of the past was eroding faith in that other prop of the Judaeo-Christian religion, the revealed Word of the Bible.

As early as the end of the seventeenth century, natural philosophers were intrigued by apparent geological evidence of the early cataclysms related in the Bible. In the rugged terrain of mountains and valleys, ancient volcanic formations, and deposits of marine fossils atop the Alps, they discerned terrestrial signs of God's ancient wrath at humankind's Original Sin or its wickedness in the time of Noah. Insofar as these 'theorists of the earth', as they called themselves, sought to support rather than to undermine the biblical account of earth's origins by means of the geological evidence, they made the same assumption that Bruce Trigger has identified as basic to nearly all scientific investigations of human and pre-human history up to about the mid-eighteenth century, the assumption 'that artifacts and monuments merely illustrated the historically recorded accomplishments of the past' (72). By opening the door to empirical investigation of these past events in the present, however, early theorists of the earth helped facilitate the Deity's eventual exit from history. What was left were literal mountains of evidence pointing to violent occurrences in the earth's remote past, with no likely suspects to interrogate and increasingly unreliable 'eye-witness' testimony.

Before long, serious challenges emerged concerning the origins of earth's present-day features, based on evidence suggesting multiple deluges and serial extinctions of plants and animals over periods of time inconceivable to believers in the literal truth of Noah's flood. By the early nineteenth century, scientific narratives of origin were undergoing revision at an accelerating pace in the light of new geological and fossil evidence. Beyond terrestrial boundaries as well, as Lawrence Frank has observed, astronomers like Laplace were calling into question the very idea that the universe had a definite beginning. Laplace's 'nebular hypothesis' held that the sun, stars, and planets had condensed into their present forms out of a primordial cloud of super-heated gas, whose source was unknown. Eventually, defenders of the biblical account of creation were forced to reinterpret the Sacred Text in ever less literal terms, implicitly discounting the Good Book's claims to historical authority.

At some point during this transition from sacred to secular explanations of the past the increasing tempo of the West's reiterated crises of historical explanation began to change people's understanding of the relative priority and weight to be given to material evidence, to what we might call the physical 'clues' of history, as opposed to the 'testimony', the oral or written accounts of past events, including God's, cited to explain those 'clues'. By the 1840s, this crucial shift in evidentiary priority was all but complete, at least among the intellectual classes in Britain: the unimpeachable authority of the sacred 'testimony' that had shaped the thinking of early 'theorists of the earth' was rapidly giving way to the new authority of material 'clues' interpreted in the light of conflicting 'testimonies' that were coming to be seen as entirely human in origin.

In terms of the development of the material sciences of history, and the cultural anxieties they released concerning the origin and fate of humankind in an ever more Godless universe, the time was ripe for the emergence of a popular literature of 'detection' in which inductive inferences from material clues could be used to sift multiple testimonies concerning unknown past events. That the publication in 1841 of what is generally acknowledged as the first modern story of detection, Poe's 'The Murders in the Rue Morgue', should have coincided with one of the most important crises in the growing dispute between religion and the historical sciences of geology and palaeontology was not, as we shall see, without cultural significance.

The influence of the Bible as authoritative historical narrative continued to manifest itself in secular notions of history long after the biblical chronology of the world had been rejected by the historical sciences. Principally, as philosophers of history like Karl Löwith and Reinhart Koselleck have pointed out, it shaped the assumption that History was progressive, directed toward some 'higher' or 'better' end-point.

Judaeo-Christian history was thought to have begun with a specific intention and to have proceeded with an ultimate purpose, a 'final end' or *telos*, to use the Greek term, which was Salvation and Last Judgement. This 'teleological' or 'end-oriented' interpretation of the biblical narrative gave it a progressive direction and its early events a 'prefigurative' or anticipatory meaning. Early secular historians and philosophers of history like G. W. F. Hegel (1770–1831) in Germany and the German expatriate Karl Marx (1818–83) in England incorporated these features into their belief in material, intellectual, and moral Progress. They searched for underlying patterns and 'laws' by which the overall direction of History as it proceeded through the rise and fall of successive cultures and civilizations could be explained, and its future course predicted. In this respect, history was conceived as a fundamentally law-based empirical science, like physics, chemistry, or astronomy, and this assumption persisted, in an attenuated form, as late as the writings of Arnold Toynbee (1889–1975) immediately following World War I, when the so-called 'Golden Age' of detective fiction began.

From this brief synopsis of the secularization of Sacred History we can see that the formal similarities between detective literature and the genres of scientific history are not confined to shared methods of inductive inference in the reconstruction of past events. Like the reader of detection, the historical scientist seeks to conceive, at each moment in history's unfolding, possible arrays of past occurrences that can help him or her make sense of new clues and testimonies appearing in the present moment.

In doing so, the scientist seeks to contribute to a 'progressive' universal narrative of historical reconstruction aimed at ultimate enlightenment (although, unlike a detective story, the evolving narrative of history seems never to reach its final destination). Moreover, he or she wants to achieve priority in making that contribution, to arrive at the correct historical array of events before his or her fellow scientists do, since there is no point, let alone excitement or glory, in reiterating what has already been revealed. Finally, supernatural beings or metaphysical powers have been 'locked out' of the universe in which both literary and historical detection takes place.

In short, by the early nineteenth century the West had begun to read the history of the world in a manner later made popular by stories of detection. Ironically, the triumph of detection as a popular genre at the end of the nineteenth century occurred just as professional scientists of history were beginning to doubt that the history they were reading had a recognizable, progressive shape after all. The coincidence of these two developments seems significant. It is as though the cultural anxieties released by history's official loss of apparent purpose and direction impelled many educated readers to look for opportunities to exercise their reconstructive imaginations on more dependably purposive material. They found that material in the pages of detective fiction. Detective writers in turn began to look for ways to engage their readers' inductive and analeptic powers of invention in pursuit of this goal, instead of inviting them to sit back and watch professional investigators exercise theirs.

The Second Locked Room: The Human Mind

Not only the material but also the mental universe became an object of scientific historical reconstruction during the nineteenth century. Like their material counterparts, moreover, cultural anthropology and Freudian psychoanalysis took their rise from foundations laid some two centuries before.

With the 1641 publication of the *Meditations* of René Descartes (1596–1650), philosophers confronted directly, for the first time, the question of how the human mind, a spiritual entity, could gather sensations from and exert control over a material human body. Clearly, says Descartes, the two substances, mental and physical, are not co-extensive: the body takes up space and is subject to physical influences, while the mind has no spatial dimensions and can resist physical influences by pure acts of will. For our purposes, the Cartesian version of the mind–body problem is important insofar as, once formulated, it reflected and focused a growing practical problem for the West as a whole: in a society, indeed, a world, where traditional ways of knowing, recognizing, and identifying others were deteriorating under the pressures of urbanization, foreign exploration, and ever greater social mobility, how were the minds of strangers to become objects of knowledge?

Worldwide commercial expansion from the fifteenth through the seventeenth centuries had brought the West into contact with societies and cultures that posed this question in its acutest form. By the end of the next century the emerging science of anthropology had responded by constructing a progressive universal history of the evolution of human thought from its earliest expression in hunter-gatherer tribes, to pastoral and agricultural societies, to highly organized civilizations. Contemporary peoples 'arrested' in the earlier stages of this progressive scheme of cultural development were considered a kind of living textbook of the Euro-American past.

For the majority of British and French citizens, however, the problem of knowing other minds arose out of the daily encounter with urban crowds. The eighteenth century saw a significant rise in population throughout Europe, but especially in England, where the number of citizens rose from 5,500,000 in 1700 to nearly 8,900,000 a hundred years later. This increase in the nation's general population was accompanied by an ever-widening income gap between rich and poor, the latter of whom swelled the poorhouses and crowded the open roads searching for alms or temporary employment.

A great many of the rural unemployed migrated to cities like London, Bristol, Liverpool, Birmingham, and Manchester, where thriving international trade and industrial manufacturing were creating jobs at wages that were kept at a bare subsistence level by the large number of poor families looking for work. These rural émigrés helped to create the modern city of strangers poignantly described by William Wordsworth (1770–1850) in his 1805 biographical poem, *The Prelude*: 'How often in the overflowing Streets,/ Have I gone forward with the Crowd, and said/ Unto myself, the face of every one/ That passes by me is a mystery' (lines 595–8). The new underclasses augmenting this mysterious crowd poured into the city slums, where violent crime was nurtured by joblessness, lack of education, and the spectre of starvation.

London particularly, like its continental counterpart, Paris, swarmed with strangers deracinated – that is, 'up-rooted' – from the more stable cultural and social milieus of towns and villages, which had generally comprised multiple generations of family members living together in close-knit neighbourhoods and parishes, inheriting trades and occupations, and sharing the literal soil of the village commons. Some of these folks were moving up in the world; most were moving down. But all of them found that the familiar daily exchanges with friends, relatives, employers, and peers, through which, since childhood, they had come to know others and others had come to know them, were missing from the packed streets, marketplaces, taverns, factories, theatres, and sites of public execution in the great metropolis.

Public anonymity was further reinforced by industrialization, in which factory labourers were reduced to the uniformly mechanized status of the machines they served, and by bureaucracies in which white-collar workers – scribes, secretaries, accountants, government and sales clerks, bank tellers, and so on – were reduced to a similar status by the administrative hierarchies in which they toiled. By the late eighteenth century increasing urban anonymity had created a corresponding increase in opportunities for criminal behaviour. It also created opportunities for popular writers, who, in the later words of G. K. Chesterton, began to derive from the vast enigma of the new cityscape 'some sense of the poetry of modern life' which was to infuse the popular detective story ('Defence', 4).

Edgar Allan Poe exploited these conjoint opportunities in 'The Man of the Crowd' (1840), where an anonymous narrator describes his pursuit of the eponymous 'Man' he has glimpsed from the window of a London coffee-house. The story reads almost like a prose commentary on Wordsworth's lines from the *Prelude*. The old and decrepit wanderer's 'absolute idiosyncrasy' of 'expression' excites within the narrator 'ideas of vast mental power', 'of excessive terror, of intense – of extreme despair. [. . .] "How wild a history," I said to myself, "is written within that bosom!"' (183–4). But after twenty-four hours of trying to reconstruct that history, pursuing the man from one crowded venue to another, the narrator can come to no more definite conclusion than that he 'is the type and genius of deep crime. He refuses to be alone. *He is the man of the crowd*' (188).

The narrator describes the old man's inscrutability as a kind of illegibility, citing a German phrase concerning an obscure book, '*es lasst sich nicht lesen*' – 'it does not permit itself to be read' (179). To this extent, the old man's mysterious 'history' corresponds to that of a particularly vexing detective story, or, more precisely, to the hidden array of life events buried in the mind of its criminal protagonist.

Why that 'history' should remain obscure to Poe's narrator, however, is not immediately apparent. It is not as though he lacks the necessary skills of decipherment. He opens his story with a lengthy description and classification of the crowds passing his coffee-house window, showing his acute ability to 'read' traits of character, class, and occupation – including criminal occupations – from physical appearance and behaviour. For instance, he can identify the older office clerks from 'the right ears', 'long used to pen-holding', which 'had an odd habit of standing off on end' (181), while pickpockets are betrayed by their 'voluminousness of wristband' (181).

Poe's story seems to have registered a curious development in the interpretation of strangers occurring at about the time he wrote it. As the factual history of each stranger on the street became invisible to each stranger he or she encountered, including law-enforcement officers, that history had to be reconstructed from the immediate material clues offered by the body itself. At first this reconstruction took the form of classification, as in so-called 'natural history', which does not concern itself with the origins of individual plants or animals, but with physical appearance and grouping into species or types. As in Poe's story, the history of the individual that was 'written' within the stranger's 'bosom' remained a closed book: *'es lasst sich nicht lesen'*. Little more than four decades later, however, bodily clues – slips of the tongue, tics, compulsive behaviours, paralysis – would be interpreted by a young Viennese neurologist named Sigmund Freud (1856–1939) as signs revealing that history, apparently with more coherence and in greater detail than the stranger could, if asked, reconstruct it him- or herself.

The cultural critic Walter Benjamin thought that the skill of Poe's narrator as a natural historian of strangers corresponded to that of the nineteenth-century Parisian *flâneur* or 'dandy', whose principal pastime, according to the French poet Charles Baudelaire (1821–67), was wandering the streets and shopping arcades of the city and 'reading' the 'physiognomy of the crowd' like a botanist (Benjamin, 172). A more appropriate analogy might be drawn from early anthropology, which had already begun to classify the human species on the basis of its racial characteristics (see, e.g., Gould). More importantly for our purposes, Poe's description of this process clearly anticipates Sherlock Holmes's repeated trick of discerning the personalities and occupations of perfect strangers from their details of dress or the pattern of 'callosities' on their hands, much to Watson's repeated amazement. Unlike Poe's narrator, however, Holmes can often read the entire history of each individual's life as well. Sometimes, like his real-life Viennese contemporary, he seems to read it even better than the person who lived it, since that person remains unaware that it is even legible.

In the literature of crime as it had evolved up to 1840, identifying criminal types from physical traits was already common. The 1828 *Memoirs* of Eugène-François Vidocq (1775–1850), first head of the Parisian Sûreté (the French equivalent of Scotland Yard), contains lengthy explanations of how to identify different types of thieves, and Poe knew the *Memoirs* well. Vidocq even boasts at one point that he can describe from 'a single article of clothing' 'a thief from head to heel' more quickly 'than our celebrated Cuvier, with two maxillaries and half-a-dozen vertebrae, can distinguish an antediluvian animal or fossil man' (367). To loiter among crowds like the anonymous 'Man of the Crowd' is, according to Vidocq, the sure sign of a '*tireur*' or pickpocket, while if one entered 'shop after shop, priced nothing, and looked at all objects with a wild and vacant stare', as the narrator's quarry does at one point (185), Vidocq would immediately recognize the traits of the '*détourneur*' or shop-lifter. In short, Poe's 'Man of the Crowd' would be presumed guilty until proven innocent by nearly any of Vidocq's plainclothes subordinates, regardless of the personal inscrutability of his features.

While Vidocq did not presume to read a criminal's individual history from such outward signs, early nineteenth-century brain researchers like F. J. Gall (1758–1828) were already claiming to read individual character. The pseudo-science of phrenology purported to chart one's personality from an analysis of the bumps on one's skull, which were assumed to correspond to overdeveloped brain structures devoted to discrete cognitive abilities or emotional dispositions, like 'anger', 'friendship', or 'philanthropy'. Phrenologists located 'higher' human faculties such as intelligence and morality in the frontal lobes. Accordingly, low foreheads soon became signs of unreflective, lawless, and violent propensities. Vidocq, who had considerable experience on which to rely, dismissed phrenological evidence of criminality as useless (367). After 1860, however, professional criminologists like Cesare Lombroso (1836–1909), with less real-life experience of the criminal mind but more arrogance than Vidocq, promoted physiognomic and phrenological analyses of delinquent 'types' to an absurd degree, categorizing them, like an anthropologist, by race and nationality.

Neither Gall nor Lombroso claimed that his method could reveal a malefactor's individual history. That claim still awaited the clinical discovery of the unconscious, which was not long in arriving. For by now it was not just the face of every person passing on the street that had become a mystery. The face in the mirror began to hold its own secrets as well, as Poe's story illustrates.

Consider, for instance, how the narrator who pursues 'The Man of the Crowd' becomes himself a man of the crowd, loitering suspiciously among the very same masses of humanity as the enigmatic character he stalks. At one point, confessing to sensations of fever, he ties a handkerchief across his mouth, hiding the lower part of his face. Ostensibly, he wishes to protect himself from 'a settled and heavy rain', even though he has just said he 'did not much regard the rain' (184) and it is unclear just how a handkerchief is supposed to protect him from a drenching downpour. Later, he congratulates himself on having worn 'a pair of caoutchouc' or rubber 'over-shoes', enabling him to 'move about in perfect silence', adding, 'At no moment did he [the old man] see that I watched him' (185). Objectively considered, the man following the man of the crowd seems as legitimate a target of suspicion as his quarry. As in many other tales by Poe with unstable or unreliable narrators, such as 'The Black Cat' or 'The Tell-Tale Heart', the 'locked room' of the mind that most stoutly resists our imaginative ingress here is located in the sub-basement of the narrator's soul. And he himself seems unaware of what is down there.

The phrenological division of the mind into anatomically distinct but simultaneous functions corresponded to the growing view that consciousness itself was divided into what the narrator of Poe's 'The Murders in the Rue Morgue' calls a 'Bi-Part Soul' (194). Mesmerists, as hypnotists were then called, claimed that by directing the 'flow' of 'animal magnetism' through the brain of an entranced subject they could overcome his or her conscious memory, will, and moral judgement. Popular interest arose in experiments with mind-altering substances such as ether, nitrous oxide, and particularly opium, which tended to diminish conscious will-power and release suppressed, or 'unconscious', memories. Both mesmerism and drug-taking play an important part in the history of crime fiction. They also appear at the birth of modern psychoanalysis, in early reports by Sigmund Freud on the mental stimulant cocaine and the importance of hypnotism in the development of what he called, taking the phrase from his mentor, Joseph Breuer (1842–1925), the 'talking cure'.

Almost from its beginnings in the 1880s, psychoanalysis drew conceptually on the material sciences of historical reconstruction. Freud himself compared his methods to those of the archaeologist (*Standard*, 3.192, 7.12, 23.259) and the detective (*Introductory*, 27). Nicholas Meyer (b. 1945) has exploited the latter analogy in his bestselling Holmes pastiche *The Seven-Per-Cent Solution* (1974), where Holmes and Freud join forces in trying to break the detective's cocaine habit. Not only did psychoanalysis claim to provide access to the 'locked room' of the unconscious (with a key provided by the patient him- or herself through symbolic free association), it also claimed it could interpret with certainty what it found there: present signs of a shocking or traumatic event – something like a crime – that had been fearfully erased from conscious memory.

Thus, like historical sciences such as geology, palaeontology, and archaeology, psychoanalysis sought to reconstruct a train of unknown, often violent, past events from present clues in order to provide a complete array of those events in a single, coherent narrative: the patient's individual life-history. These clues were to be found in either the patient's speech or his or her 'symptomatic' behaviour.

Unlocking the Locked Rooms: Positivism and Historicism

Several decades ago, Marjorie Nicolson observed two 'methods' of fictional detection corresponding to two methods of scientific investigation. The first, which she called 'Baconian', was based on induction from material evidence. The second, which she called 'Cartesian', depended upon the 'intuitive' use of the imagination (126). By the early nineteenth century, historians and pre-historians, led by scholars in Germany, had begun to adopt two similarly distinct but inter-related approaches to the study of the human past. The first, positivism, depended primarily on inferences drawn from the study and interpretation of the material evidence left by past societies: coins, inscriptions, and original state documents; tombs, mosaics, monuments, and architectural ruins; and historical accounts as contemporary as possible with the events they describe. This approach has often been identified with the work of Johann Gustav Droysen (1808–84) and Leopold von Ranke (1795–1886), the latter of whom once stated that his aim was to describe the past *'wie es eigentlich gewesen'* – 'as it really was'.

The other approach, known as historicism or, in German, *Historismus*, tried to adopt a more intimate perspective on the societies of the past in order to better understand the specific purposes underlying cultural practice. Beginning with the *Scienza Nuova* (*New Science*, 1725) of the Italian historian Giambattista Vico (1668–1744), who tried to explain the cultural origins of ancient myths and legal concepts, and continuing in the work of scholars such as Johann Gottfried von Herder (1744–1803) and Friedrich Schleiermacher (1768–1834), historicism tried to interpret the past in light of the world-view, everyday outlook, and personal assumptions and prejudices of the diarists, travellers, scribes, and poets who provide the present-day historian with his or her original source material.

In practice, positivism and historicism are closely intertwined in the research of most responsible historians, even historians of the individual mind, like psychoanalysts. What distinguishes the two approaches is more a matter of attitude and emphasis than of stark methodological contrasts. Positivism generally concentrates on material relics and remains that are contemporary with the era or event or historical personage under investigation. In psychoanalysis this might mean a patient's childhood toy, a scar, or a surviving physical symptom like a tic or a compulsive gesture. Historicism generally aims at achieving imaginative identification with the 'mentalities' and motivations of historical agents and their contemporaries, a method with more obvious affinities to psychology in general. Even von Ranke, as Richard J. Evans points out, included cultural perspectives in his notion of history 'as it really was' (14). The positivist, we might say, focuses on physical retrieval and examination, the historicist on imaginative re-enactment and empathy. Neither, however, can proceed very far without the other.

As historical approaches with distinct aims, positivism and historicism also make an appearance, as Nicolson observed, in the two major crime-solving techniques of modern detective fiction. The 'Baconian' detective arrives at the solution to the mystery by comparing material clues – metonymic 'relics' of the crime or 'remains' of the victim – with verbal testimonies, preferably contemporary or eye-witness statements. Like any good positivist historian, he or she will watch for signs of prejudice or perjury in the testimonies of witnesses, and of tampering with or fabrication of the material evidence, including written documents. Often, however, the detective must resort to 'Cartesian' or historicist methods and try to identify imaginatively with the mind of the criminal. This can be achieved through empathy, as when the clues seem to resonate with criminal tendencies in the detective (and perhaps in us) that are ordinarily kept under control or beneath the level of consciousness, or through special knowledge, as when the detective recognizes a particular *modus operandi* or the 'type' of criminal (racial, ethnic, national, sexual, socio-economic) he or she is dealing with.

In rhetorical terms, historicist mind-reading demands metaphorical rather than metonymical thinking, that is to say, detection by analogy or substitution (of self for criminal or of another criminal for this one) rather than by direct connection. To catch a thief, a historicist detective might say, one must think like a thief. As we shall see in a moment, this aphorism once had a basis in fact: before the creation of a modern police force in England and France, thieves were more often than not turned in by other thieves, known as 'thief-takers'.

Romanticism and Enlightenment: The Bohemian Tendencies of the Scientific Detective

The distinction between positivist and historicist, metonymic and metaphorical, material and psychological approaches to historical reconstruction conforms to a larger distinction between two very broad attitudes emerging by the end of the eighteenth century: Enlightenment and Romanticism.

The Enlightenment refers, generally, to the prominent role accorded reason and empiricism in nearly every field of practical human endeavour in the West during the seventeenth and eighteenth centuries. Those who embraced Enlightenment values distrusted what could not be seen, touched, and measured – that is, whatever did not conform to common sense for all who had senses in common. Among the things eliciting Enlightened distrust were the waywardness of the emotions and arbitrary claims of power over others, especially when arising from superstitions or irrational traditions; the faculties of imagination and intuition; and individual obsessions and idiosyncrasies. Whatever could not be justified in rational, empirical terms had to be contained, suppressed, or, as revolutionaries in America in 1776 and France in 1789 came to see it, extirpated.

The Enlightenment bestowed many benefits on the West: democratic governments, free markets, a free press, the concept of universal human rights, and technological prowess. As Max Horkheimer and Theodor Adorno have pointed out, however, its cyclopean emphasis on material progress also gave rise to a disturbing degree of alienation in nearly every walk of life. Huge gains in administrative efficiency and productivity from the rational restructuring of government and industry soon led to the creation of an impoverished working class, ideological manipulation through advertising and propaganda, and almost continual warfare among Western nations.

Romanticism and its antecedents, such as the Sentimental and Gothic movements of the late eighteenth century, arose in large part as reactions against the Enlightenment's depersonalizing and materialistic tendencies. Romanticism encouraged emotional expression, the exercise of the imagination, spontaneity, and the placing of love before duty. Ironically, the Enlightenment and Romanticism were opposite manifestations of the same overwhelming cultural imperative: the individual citizen's growing demand for more freedom and respect. The Enlightenment sought to satisfy this demand by rationally enhancing the practical means of obtaining both. But the 'dialectic of Enlightenment', as Horkheimer and Adorno call it, ensured that these steps would also have the paradoxical effect of depersonalizing society on nearly every level, reducing each individual to an interchangeable, self-interested cog in the new political, economic, and cultural machinery of modern society, and making a great many of those individuals paupers.

The Romantic reaction promoted individual freedom and self-respect through all the channels that Enlightenment thinking had tried to shut down: not the common sense of reason, but the uncommon dreams of the imagination; not enumeration and measurement, but the innumerable and infinite; not utility, but beauty; not morality, but deviance; not conformity, but eccentricity and defiance. These were, for the Romantics, the only true expressions of individual freedom for citizens of the modern, democratic nation state, because they were the only ones that could take a unique form in each citizen.

Romantic rebelliousness and spontaneity were anticipated in the eighteenth century by the glorification of bold highwaymen, cagey thieves, and mutinous buccaneers in real-crime tales, and of virtuous but wronged outlaws and misanthropes in much of so-called 'Gothic' literature. They were also long-standing features of the 'picaresque' or 'rogue's tale', with its appeal to our love of trickery and chicanery in general. Despite his eventual identification with the powers of scientific Enlightenment, the fictional police detective began life draped in the mantle of these romantic criminal heroes, for he had been, in the role of thief-taker, one of them. For this very reason, however, his real-life counterpart was generally *persona non grata* in the homes of the respectably well-off middle and upper classes whose interests he defended. He performed a necessary, even exciting, but not very dignified service that most citizens preferred to read about rather than encounter first-hand.

This negative attitude was to change in France, England, and America not long after the establishment of the regular police force and its detective division, which was staffed with lower-middle-class professionals, and as the threat of violent crime by the dispossessed classes became an ever more serious threat to propertied well-being in the great cities of London, Paris, and New York. Nonetheless, something of the glamorous, morally ambiguous freedom associated with the Romantic side of detection clung to the detective hero throughout the century that came to identify his methods with those of Enlightened, positivist historiography. This was true especially in England, where, not long after attaining establishment respectability, he began to evolve away from his official, state-sanctioned role toward a more eccentric, amateur status, eventually splitting the difference between official and amateur detection by becoming a private professional.

As epitomized by Sherlock Holmes, this new private professional was distinguished from his rivals among the regular police by a markedly Romantic bohemianism. This term, derived from 'Bohemia', the putative Eastern European homeland of the Romany people, or 'gypsies', was applied during the later nineteenth century to artistic temperaments of all sorts. Irregular habits and colourful personalities, love of beauty, a private sense of morality (or amorality), arcane knowledge, and original genius were all considered 'bohemian' in this sense. Unlike their thief-taking progenitors, bohemian detectives like Holmes also tended to adopt the manners and attitudes of the nearly extinct feudal aristocracy, the class that, before the rise of democracy and capitalism, had legally embodied the personal prerogatives of absolute freedom illegitimately exercised by early modern criminal heroes and contemporary gypsies.

The Sherlockian detective thus tends to flout ordinary civil or moral constraints (he often operates outside and above the law he professes to defend); he does not work to live, but lives to work (his career has become his pastime and pleasure); accordingly, his interest in crime is aesthetic as well as pecuniary (murder in his view is a fine art, and he is its most astute critic); and he embraces outmoded aristocratic ideals of personal honour, especially in contrast to his salaried rivals among the members of the official police.

What is missing from this Romantic portrait is spontaneity and sexual energy. They will reappear, however, when the male detective undergoes his final metamorphosis in the hard-boiled pulp fiction of post-World War I America. There the private professional will re-emerge as a proletarian, a 'man of the people', a 'tough guy' as likely to use his fists as his head in solving crimes, and erotically responsive to, if wary of, the opposite sex. What will not have changed, as we shall see, is the genre's combined legacy of positivist and historicist methods, Enlightened and Romantic attitudes.

The evolution in the detective's social status from half-criminal, to civil servant, to amateur or private professional bohemian and aristocrat, to proletarian tough guy, reflects changes in a largely middle-class readership's projected fantasies of what true personal freedom in an increasingly impersonal, bureaucratic, and commercial society might ideally look like, short of outright criminality itself. (The 'caper' genre and its later hard-boiled variant, the crime-suspense thriller, provided, and still provide, an imaginative outlet for those interested in exploring the latter option.)

Throughout all these developments, the detective remained, with relatively few but significant exceptions, white and male, defining in the popular mind the ideal 'subject position', as Althusser might put it, from which the ordinary citizen, male or female, upper- or lower-class, white or non-white, could imagine exercising the cultural prerogative of authoritatively reconstructing history. In only one other profession was a similar prerogative freely exercised, namely, the historical sciences themselves. There, 'heroic' real-life personalities like Georges Cuvier, Charles Darwin (1809–82), and Heinrich Schliemann (1822–90), excavator of Troy, starred in non-fictional narratives of investigative adventure. These narratives, however, were not designed to encourage in their lay readers a competitive exercise of the reconstructive imagination. That task was left to their popular fictional counterparts.

Part II
The Rise of Detective Fiction and the Birth of Detection

3

From Rogues to Ratiocination

The Era of Deterrence

Crime stories in Europe predate detective fiction by two or more centuries, appearing in England as early as the rogues' tales of the high Renaissance. Modern crime fiction, however, is more nearly a product of the broadside ballads, gallows 'confessions', and purported 'last words' of condemned criminals known, collectively, as *The Newgate Calendar*. This collection of real-crime tales was named after the 'calendar' on which the Deputy Keeper of Newgate Prison in London listed the names of all inmates admitted the previous month. The *Calendar* began as a series of broadsheets published by Paul Lorraine, chaplain of Newgate from 1698 to 1719, purporting to contain the true histories of the condemned criminals incarcerated there. The broadsheets sold well. Soon, booksellers were pirating and publishing them in bound volumes, under the same or similar titles, along with other criminal accounts from the 'sessions papers' or official trial records of the Old Bailey, London's criminal court.

The 'Preface' to Andrew Knapp and William Baldwin's 1824–5 edition of the *Calendar*, in which they defend capital punishment for its deterrent effect on 'the minds of the multitude' (iii), can stand as a summary of their predecessors' declarations of editorial intent. *The Newgate Calendar*, they write, should prove 'highly acceptable to all ranks and conditions of men', because it shows 'that crime has always been followed by punishment' (iv). Indeed, as some critics have observed (Kayman, 62), there is a kind of 'Providential Plot' built into most of the stories in the *Calendar*, where the punishing hand of God is assumed to be at work in the crime-stopping efforts of the community. Typically, local citizens observe something amiss and bring it to the attention of the authorities, or undertake their own (usually brief) investigation. Arrest and punishment are foregone conclusions.

Providential arguments for the moral utility of the *Calendar* ignored the real basis of the book's popular appeal: smug condemnation of its more despicable villains, such as Sawney Beane and his cannibal clan, and perverse admiration for wily tricksters like the prison escape artist Jack Sheppard and Dick Turpin, the dashing highwayman. Knapp and Baldwin's obliviousness to the widespread popularity of such scalliwags reflected a difference between official and popular attitudes toward criminal justice that had emerged during the eighteenth century. In order to understand the reasons for this difference, we must first consider how early law enforcement worked, or didn't.

Before the establishment of modern police organizations, crimes were more often reported by witnesses or confederates than 'detected', and arrests were then made by the constable of the parish (sometimes accompanied by a deputized *posse comitatus*) on the authority of the local justice of the peace, typically a wealthy landowner. Once arrested, the accused was held in the local jail until the arrival of the presiding magistrate at the quarterly 'assize', at which time he or she was tried and, if found guilty, remanded for punishment. As Michel Foucault has pointed out in harrowing detail (32–69), the main purpose of punishment at this time was monitory. Capital punishment especially was often gruesome, prolonged, usually preceded by tortures symbolic of the type and severity of the crime, and very public, all in order to impress upon a terrified populace the excruciating consequences of breaking the laws of the realm. With few resources for preventing crime or finding criminals, the state had to scare people into behaving themselves.

The spectacle of capital punishment was a crude instrument of law enforcement made cruder over time as it was applied to an everlengthening list of offences, including petty theft, poaching, destruction of property, and vagrancy – close to two hundred offences in all by 1819. Known popularly as 'The Bloody Code', this expansion in statutory capital crimes was directed, according to Richard Kayman, at the 'criminalization of the poor' (37) by the newly monied and ever more alarmed middle and gentry classes. 'The Bloody Code' helps to explain growing popular sympathy with the criminal hero, according to Foucault: 'Against the law, against the rich, the powerful, the magistrates, [. . .] he appeared to have waged a struggle with which one all too easily identified' (67). In part, however, the widening scope of capital punishment reflected the inadequacies of an obsolete law-enforcement mechanism.

Aside from public terror, that mechanism relied on the incentives created by the Highwayman Act of 1692, which offered a bounty of forty pounds for information leading to the arrest and conviction of a thief. Few citizens other than thieves had many opportunities to benefit from this legislation, and those thieves who did so became known as 'thief-takers', often exploiting their ambiguous position on the borderline of respectability with astonishing agility. Jonathan Wild (1689–1725), for instance, was a professional thief who made a fortune by extorting money from other thieves, often coercing them into committing further robberies for his benefit under threat of betrayal, or serving as a fence for their 'swag' and making huge profits from the rewards paid by their victims.

Mike Pavett contends that Wild's activities, deplorable in themselves, did bring 'a degree of order, if not of law, to London' before his execution in 1725 (8–9). By the end of the century, however, London's criminal population was growing far beyond the control of a Jonathan Wild. Upon his appointment as magistrate of Middlesex and Westminster in 1748, Henry Fielding, the playwright and novelist, personally enlisted nine former constables to help in the investigation of suspected crimes (Jeffers, 16). Named after the street in which Fielding's office was located, the Bow Street Runners received a nominal salary and whatever else they could get by way of bounties. They also hired themselves out to investigate private cases. For nine decades the Runners in their official red vests were the only thing resembling a detective force in Great Britain, but they were vastly outnumbered by the criminal element, which in London alone amounted to some 30,000 burglars and thieves by 1822, one for every 822 inhabitants (Jeffers, 17).

The creation of an official London police force was delayed by English distrust of standing armies and centralized government. This distrust was fuelled by the hated example of France, where in 1800 Napoleon had created a 'prefecture of police' to quell civil unrest and oversee the activities of a state secret police. In general, the French Revolution and its sequel, the Napoleonic Wars, distracted England from its most pressing domestic needs, including crime, for more than twenty years, although some progress was made in 1798 when Patrick Colquon established 'The Marine Police Establishment', the first specialized police force independent of the magistrates, to guard the London wharves.

The end of the Napoleonic conflict was soon followed by economic depression, soaring unemployment, labour unrest, and agitation for government and legal reform, all adding to the pressures on public order coming from London's swelling criminal population. Finally, in 1829, the Home Secretary, Robert Peel, secured passage of the 'Metropolitan Police Improvement Bill', establishing the first governmentally administered Office of Police for greater London. Wearing blue uniforms with stovepipe hats, the new police were armed with rattles to call for help and short staffs for self-defence, but no firearms. (The Runners at least had pistols.) Their main task was to prevent crime by their conspicuous presence, not to pursue and apprehend criminals in the act. Despite their moderate success, they were initially greeted with suspicion and known derisively as 'Bobbies', after the Home Secretary who had created them. Appointment of official police detectives was another thirteen years off.

Revolution and Reaction

While the field of law enforcement slowly changed, events were also taking place in the world of ideas.

By the penultimate decade of the eighteenth century agitation for extension of the franchise, abolishing the slave trade, and ending the 'Old Corruption' of rule by the landed classes was increasing in both England and France. England watched its former colonies organize themselves into a democratically elected government, while in France what began as an effort to relieve the national debt eventuated in the bloody outbreak of revolution in 1789. At the same time, the earliest stirrings of a Romantic preoccupation with the interior life and with subjective states of perception and feeling became apparent in the rise of the Gothic novel and the 'poetry of sensibility' in England, as well as the publication of the *Confessions* (1782) of Jean-Jacques Rousseau (1712–78) in France.

In the early 1790s, before organized government terror swept through France and war was declared with England, English sympathizers with the Revolution pushed for moderate reforms at home. Among these sympathizers was William Godwin (1756–1836), a political philosopher and Deist (non-Christian theist), who in 1793 wrote *An Enquiry Concerning Political Justice*, in which he advocated democratic reforms and predicted a future for humankind, based on its continued 'perfectibility' in the use of reason, where governments would no longer be necessary. Encouraged by the enthusiastic reception of his book, Godwin went on to write a fictional critique of the corrupt practices of the English landed classes. Originally called *Things as They Are* and later re-titled *Caleb Williams* after its youthful protagonist, the book was published in three volumes in 1794, just a year after the outbreak of war between England and France.

Roughly contemporary with the Gothic mystery novels of Ann Radcliffe, which we examined briefly in the first chapter, *Caleb Williams* is often cited, along with several of Radcliffe's works, as one of the first English 'detective' novels. It features a murder, a cover-up, and the framing and execution of two innocent people by Caleb's otherwise honourable employer, a wealthy landowner named Falkland; an investigation of sorts by Caleb himself which leads to Falkland's confession of his crimes; and a thrilling series of arrests, escapes, and pursuits as Falkland seeks to ensure that Caleb will not reveal the secret he has discovered. Godwin intended to show how, given the current political situation, absolute power corrupts both those who exercise it and those upon whom it is exercised, turning the former into outright bullies or conscience-tormented hypocrites and the latter into obsequious toadies or celebrity-obsessed curiosity-seekers.

Messac was the first to note those elements of *Caleb Williams* that make it an important harbinger of things to come: the terror and mystery of crime; the obsessive nature of suspicion; the paranoid thrills of flight, pursuit, arrest, and escape; and the daring use of incognito and disguise (186–7). These are also elements of the Gothic novel as Godwin would have known it. However, rather than drawing on medieval superstitions and exotic settings to create suspense, as Radcliffe did, he turned to scenes and incidents from *The Newgate Calendar*. From the life of Jack Sheppard he incorporated several jail-breaks and Caleb's repeated attempts at disguise. From the life of Dick Turpin he borrowed the idea of the justified criminal rebel and his band of outlaws, with whom Caleb temporarily takes up lodging. The character of Gines, a thief-taker from this gang who is hired by Falkland to hunt for the fugitive Caleb after the young man is framed by his employer for theft, not only derives from the earliest models of criminal apprehension in the *Calendar*, but anticipates the ruthlessness, energy, and cunning of the fictional police detectives who will appear early in the next century.

As for Caleb himself, his detective methods consist of little more than insinuations and innuendoes designed to make Falkland betray his guilt, either by outward signs or by direct confession. Eventually these methods succeed. But there is practically no induction, or even logical inference, shaping Caleb's oblique interrogations, only suspicions that he himself admits are irrational and that do little more than incite the criminal to retaliate. Fearing exposure after he confesses, Falkland plants his personal property in Caleb's room for later discovery by the servants, creating a pretext for having his young secretary arrested.

Thus, as Michael Cohen observes, in *Caleb Williams* 'physical evidence is only misleading or elusive' (49), useful not to the detective trying to identify the criminal, but only to the rich and powerful seeking to railroad the lowly and innocent. For this reason Cohen (46–8) and several others, including Julian Symons (*Bloody*, 23), have identified the book as a distant precursor of the hard-boiled and crime-suspense stories of the early and middle twentieth century, which express an impotent cynicism toward the endemic corruption of governments and ruling classes. However, Godwin's book also reflects the general attitude toward material evidence prevailing before the rise of literary detection. The only point of obtaining such evidence was to secure conviction. 'Swag' or the spoils of theft would do for this purpose, as would a weapon or blood stains found on a murder suspect. In nine cases out of ten, the constable on the case, like the dastardly thief-taker, Gines, already knew the man or woman he was after. Gathering material evidence was important for corroboration, only rarely for detection.

The Uses of Evidence

The popularity of *Caleb Williams*, especially with its Gothic moods and tonalities, ensured its impact on writers both in England and abroad. In America, Godwin's book inspired Charles Brockden Brown (1771–1810) to write *Arthur Merwyn* (1799–1800), in which the eponymous young protagonist discovers a secret murder and is persecuted by a powerful foe. As in the novels of Ann Radcliffe, who was another important influence, Brown's point is not to challenge the reader to solve the crime by providing materials adequate to do so, but to maintain suspense by providing enough inadequate clues to keep the reader reading to the end.

Godwin kept writing well into the next century, setting an example for the 'Newgate' novelists of the late 1820s and 1830s, like Edward Bulwer-Lytton (1803–73), the young Charles Dickens, and William Thackeray (1811–63). Lytton popularized criminal heroes in *Paul*

Clifford (1830) and *Eugene Aram* (1832) by portraying them, like Caleb Williams, as victims of 'Things as They Are'. Like his mentor, Lytton was more interested in the complexities of the criminal mind than in the intricacies of induction. The same can be said for Dickens in his earliest contribution to the genre, *Oliver Twist* (1837), where the violent underworld of Fagin (a 'fence' for stolen goods), the 'Artful Dodger', Bill Sikes, and Nancy, and the devious workings of rage, cunning, fear, and guilt in their criminal minds, upstage the low comedy of the incompetent Bow Street Runners, Blathers and Duff. Meanwhile, the most atrocious crime in the book, Sikes's murder of Nancy, presents no mystery to the reader, or to a single inhabitant of Dickens's fictional London.

If detection as a challenge or even as a theme was slow to infiltrate the new genre of Gothic crime and suspense, it was not for lack of broad changes taking place in the administration of justice. As Ernest Bloch points out, by about the middle of the eighteenth century an enlightened abhorrence of torture and trial by ordeal led to the gradual introduction of evidentiary trials (246). However, it is misleading to add, as Bloch does, that 'criminal investigation arose with the detective in the foreground', or, worse, that 'the depiction of the evidence gathering work of the detective is no older than the evidentiary hearing itself'. In fact, that depiction is much younger.

As we have seen, assigning a detective to a case was not feasible until well into the nineteenth century. Moreover, little or no detection was necessary in order to secure evidence for arrest and trial, and this remained true long after the appearance of evidentiary hearings. Criminals were more often than not betrayed by confederates, discovered by accident, or caught red-handed. Thus, testimony still played a preponderant role in criminal investigations and trials.

Also working against the emergence of detection as a useful tool in the solving of crimes was the sheer number of criminal arraignments and trials processed by the courts of the day, especially in the large metropolitan centres. In 1830 one anonymous crime writer 'gave an average time of eight and one-half minutes' for each case heard in the course of a day at London's primary criminal court, the Old Bailey (Hollingsworth, 22). Under such constraints, inductive sifting of material evidence and weighing of conflicting testimony was practically impossible, and poor suspects could not afford counsel capable of performing such feats of forensic legerdemain anyway. Generally, the word of the constable and perhaps the victim or an eye-witness was all that was required to convict.

A number of other factors besides evidentiary trials had to be in place before detection and detectives could play a prominent, or even material, role in the arrest and conviction of criminals, whether real or fictional. One was legal reform. During the 1820s rational reform of the criminal laws began to make substantial headway. Several administrative changes were enacted from 1827 to 1830, some designed to reduce the number of capital statutes. After 1830 the pace of change began to accelerate: in 1832 the range of offences punishable by death was drastically reduced; in 1834, the Old Bailey became the newly reorganized and streamlined Central Criminal Court and began to meet in continuous session; and in 1836, defendants in felony trials were granted the right to legal counsel (Hollingsworth, 25).

Increasing attention to court proceedings as a forum for weighing material evidence and testimony, bolstered by the new legal assurance of counsel for the accused, was a significant factor in exciting public curiosity about crime detection in England, as well as in the emergence of criminal forensics as a distinct science. Another factor, as I have suggested, was increasing popular interest in the sciences of historical reconstruction in general, to which we shall return when we examine the earliest of Poe's 'tales of ratiocination' in the 1840s. In America, meanwhile, a young writer from a fairly well-to-do family in upstate New York had begun a literary career destined to have unforeseen consequences for crime and detective fiction in France, England, and America itself.

Parisian Mohicans and the Debut of Vidocq

James Fenimore Cooper (1789–1851) is best known to modern readers for his tales of the American colonial frontier, the so-called *Deerslayer* novels featuring an intrepid white hunter and tracker named Nathaniel Bumppo and his faithful native American companion, 'Uncas' or 'Chingachgook'. Bumppo is the frontier prototype of the American cowboy hero. A defender of civilization and ally of the white settlers and military personnel who represent its advance guard in the wilderness, he is more temperamentally attuned to the natural world that these forces are trying to subdue, and more emotionally resonant with its 'good Indian' inhabitants. His frontier sympathies tend to align Bumppo with the thief-taker detectives of early crime narratives, who are similarly positioned astride a fuzzy boundary between law and disorder.

Cooper's frontier shares something else in common with the earliest detective stories, something that proved irresistible to contemporary writers of crime fiction, particularly in France. All of his stories feature scenes of tracking and pursuit using acts of empirical induction.

Cooper's general popularity in France was no doubt helped by that country's idealization, going back to Jean-Jacques Rousseau's *The Social Contract* (1762), of the 'Noble Savage'. This concept arose from the belief that before the advent of civilization, with its inducements to hypocrisy, lying, and class oppression, human beings lived in a state of freedom, frankness, and harmony with nature and one another. In the modern city, such innocence was clearly under threat. While writers of crime fiction like Eugène Sue (1804–57) and Alexandre Dumas, Père (1802–70) drew on Cooper for their depictions of urban man-hunting, it was Honoré de Balzac (1799–1850) who made the first significant attempt to transfer such scenes of inductive pursuit from the backwoods of the New World to the back streets of the French capital. He was largely inspired to do so by the sensational *Memoirs* of Eugène-François Vidocq, the retired head of the Parisian Sûreté whom we have met in connection with Poe's 'The Man of the Crowd'.

Vidocq is unique in the history of modern crime and crime fighting, and his story is of central importance to the history of detective fiction. Born in 1775, he grew up, by his own admission, as a bully and a common thief. After running away from home and joining a travelling show, Vidocq enlisted in the army, where his confrontational behaviour drew him into frequent duels and repeated arrests for insubordination. Eventually, he deserted and began to create a life for himself on the run. During this period he was imprisoned several times, but no prison could hold him. Fraternizing with ever more dangerous criminals while in jail, he was forced, on pain of betrayal, to participate in their illegal schemes while a fugitive. Over time, he perfected the arts of escape and disguise for which he was later to achieve notoriety.

Growing weary of his unsettled life, Vidocq eventually offered his services as a thief-taker to the Parisian Prefecture of Police. For years afterward he served as a highly valued double-agent, retaining his effectiveness even after his duplicity became widely known. The *Memoirs* contains several scenes in which a dangerous fugitive brags to Vidocq, who has assumed a false identity, of his ability to spot 'Vidocq' at a glance. In one such episode, a gang leader named Antin boasts that he even knows Vidocq's secret home address, adding,

'Only yesterday I met him disguised in a manner that would have deceived any eye but mine.' Vidocq is then forced to accompany Antin and his gang on a stake-out of his own house. Not surprisingly, the quarry never shows up (207).

After several years in the pay of the Prefecture, Vidocq proposed the creation of a brigade of special agents to keep an eye on ex-convicts, chase down escaped prisoners and fugitives, and entrap suspected criminals (Stead, 57). The new detective office, ancestor of today's 'Police Judiciaire', was to be called the Parisian 'Sûreté' or 'Security' force, and Vidocq was to serve as its first chief.

Almost from the founding of the Sûreté in 1812, Vidocq got results, and for fifteen years he was the most feared man in the Parisian underworld. He was also the target of recriminations and charges of malfeasance from the regular police, who resented being upstaged by the spectacular success of this former convict. Eventually, Vidocq's official rivals got their way, and he was forced to resign from the Sûreté in 1827. He was immediately offered 24,000 francs to publish his memoirs in four volumes, and saddled with two ghost-writers in succession to help pad them. Émile Morice helped with the first two volumes, and L. F. L'Hertier de l'Ain inserted an entire novelette of his own composition in the fourth. There are many other instances of plagiarism and fantasy in the *Memoirs*, but if even a fraction of the events recorded in it are true, Vidocq's life story must stand as one of the most extraordinary in the history of crime and detection.

Central to Vidocq's self-portrait in the *Memoirs* is what Ian Ousby calls 'the myth of infallibility' (*Bloodhounds*, 47), since the book was intended to vindicate the first head of the Sûreté in the eyes of his professional enemies and the people of Paris alike. The emphasis throughout is on the traditional virtues of the picaresque trickster-figure or anti-hero, not those of the modern, intellectual detective. Thus, strength, agility, audacity, stubbornness, quick thinking, witty repartee, and unflinching courage take precedence in Vidocq's self-portrait over rational inference, although there are a handful of scenes, including one involving footprints in the sand (285) and another requiring the deciphering of an address on a torn paper fragment (337), that demonstrate his skill in this area. Nonetheless, Vidocq usually knows the person he's after and seeks material evidence only in order to draw the net tighter around the culprit. When this is not strictly the case, the reader watches Vidocq decipher the clue using his own special knowledge: the torn address, for instance, is an easy challenge, beginning with the name, 'Raoul', a wine merchant and cabaret owner familiar to Vidocq as a trafficker in contraband.

Vidocq's popularity depended largely on his personal skills, talents, and attainments. His vast acquaintance with the French underworld, not just its habits and haunts, but its individual habitués, is intriguing and arcane. His expert use of disguise, often for the sake of dramatic irony, astonishes and entertains even when his claims are implausible: at one point, he boasts that he can reduce his height four or five inches at will (181). He evinces acute powers of penetration, immediately probing the deepest recesses of the mind and personality of his opponent even when that opponent is also disguised. His patience and perseverance became legendary.

These virtues, talents, and skills reappear, in whole or in part, in nearly all of Vidocq's fictional successors, even those with a prominent genius for detection. In addition, important themes in the later history of detection make an early appearance in the *Memoirs*. One is the notion of crime as an art, although this may have been something interpolated by Vidocq's editor, L'Hertier. The criminal world, says Vidocq, 'possesses, like the literary world its classics and romances; the scheme which formerly was "deep and knowing" is now but a poor device' (366), and ostentatious displays of pick-pocketing legerdemain are as 'Rococo' as a play by Corneille or Racine (366).

Another important theme of later detective fiction first introduced by Vidocq is peer competition. Writing in 1828, he contrasts the 'frankness, [. . .] unanimity, and [. . .] cordiality' among the police in 1812, when he founded the Sûreté, with the atmosphere prevailing when he was forced to resign. 'In the present day,' he writes, 'chiefs or subalterns mistrust each other; they reciprocally fear and hate each other; a continual state of hostilities is kept up; each dreads in his comrade a foe who will denounce him; there is no longer a sympathy of action in the different departments' (192). This sense of competition among detectives, initially confined to official police investigators, will come to influence fictional relations between the official investigators and their amateur and private professional counterparts, all of whom will in turn model such competitive behaviour for their readers.

There are, finally, numerous incidents, characters, and stratagems recounted by Vidocq that were plagiarized, or at least borrowed with slight modifications, by his literary successors. Long before Holmes hired actors for a bit of street-theatre in his failed attempt to ensnare the internationally renowned actress Irene Adler in 'A Scandal in

Bohemia' (1891), Vidocq arranged for his operatives to play similar roles in order to be on hand for the delivery of stolen goods (279). And as for Minister D—'s counter-intuitive inspiration to hide the letter he stole from the Queen in plain sight in Poe's 'The Purloined Letter', could it not have been suggested by this experienced thief-taker's advice to those leaving home for an extended period of time? '[T]hink of some place of concealment, where you can hide your choicest valuables', writes Vidocq, keeping in mind that 'the place most exposed is frequently that which is not searched' (388).

Le Roman Policier

Five years after his resignation, Vidocq returned briefly to his duties at the Sûreté, then went on to form his own private detective agency in 1833. He also figured in several successful melodramas, and even wrote his own crime novel in 1844. His *Memoirs* influenced, either directly or indirectly, nearly every writer of detective fiction to come, but the most immediate beneficiaries were Honoré de Balzac, Eugène Sue, Alexandre Dumas, Émile Gaboriau (1832–1873), and Victor Hugo (1802–85), originators of *le roman policier* or the French 'police novel'.

The son of a lawyer, an avid reader of Gothic novelists like Charles Maturin (1782–1824) and Matthew Lewis (1775–1818), and an aficionado of mesmerism, physiognomy, astrology, and other pseudo-sciences, Balzac often included courtroom scenes in his works for purposes of dramatic exposition. The specific impact of Vidocq, however, first made itself apparent in *Le Père Goriot* (*Father Goriot*, 1835), with the creation of the ruthless arch-criminal, Vautrin, who would go on in later books to be appointed chief of the Paris police, just like Vidocq.

Vautrin is notorious for his cold-bloodedness, his energy, his persistence, and his mastery of disguise, as well as his cleverness in evading and manipulating the minions of the law when necessary. Bearing the mantle of Vidocq into the pages of popular literature, Vautrin inspired the likes of Javert, the relentless lawman hunting reformed criminal fugitive Jean Valjean in Hugo's *Les Misérables* (1862); 'M. Jackal' in Dumas's *Les Mohicans de Paris* (1854–5), a much more sympathetic and discerning *chef de la Sûreté* than either Vautrin or Vidocq; and flamboyant criminal supermen like the rascally Rocambole of Ponson du Terrail (1829–71), who eventually filled five volumes with his rogue-hero's adventures. Along with Arsène Lupin ('Arsène the Wolf'), the creation of Maurice Leblanc (1864–1941), such exuberant arch-criminals came to dominate French crime fiction by the end of the century, and the literary history of crime in France remained largely in their hands until after World War I.

One reason for French detective fiction's uphill fight against the growing predominance of crime/adventure tales can be traced to the 1830s, when important changes took place in the French literary marketplace. Under the pressure of tremendous growth in popular readership, the weekly and monthly journals tailored for the middle classes began to lose ground to the much cheaper, mass circulating newspapers, the *feuilletons,* whose appeal to lower-class tastes depended on the inclusion of lurid, sensational stories, both factual and fictional, which boosted circulation and, thereby, advertising revenues.

Foremost among the contents of the *feuilletons* were stories about crime. The primary aim in publishing such material soon broadened from inciting buyers to purchase the current issue to teasing them into purchasing the one coming next. The short story that had been a staple of middle-class journals soon expanded accordingly, driven by one sensational turn of events after another and with little or no planning on the part of the authors involved. Like tapeworms, these *romans-feuilletons* could grow to enormous lengths, reaching to over a million words in the course of several years. Established novelists like Balzac, drawn by the enormous sums to be made from a mass readership, soon joined the ranks of *feuilletonistes* like Eugène Sue, whose best-selling crime novel *Les Mystères de Paris,* unfolding in the slums and derelict suburbs of the capital, ran in *La Presse* from June 1842 to October 1843.

The immediate result of these developments was to create conditions hostile to the growth of the self-contained story of detection, which left nothing 'To be Continued' in the next number. But the rage for *feuilletons* impeded the growth of novel-length detective fiction as well, where the plot had to be carefully worked out in advance and the writer had to resist pressures from editors to change the intended course of events at the last minute in response to the fluctuating demands of paying readers. The deleterious effect of the *feuilleton* on the development of literary detection and the puzzle element in France would be moderated somewhat beginning in 1865, with the appearance of Émile Gaboriau's police inspector, Monsieur Lecoq, in *L'Affaire Lerouge,* but only temporarily. That event, despite the obvious nod to 'Vidocq' in the protagonist's last name, depended in turn on the signal impact made on popular French literature by a Francophile American writer's imaginary French detective.

Our journey across the Atlantic to examine the debut of Poe's Chevalier C. Auguste Dupin will, however, require us to make one more stopover in the British Isles.

The Aesthetics of Violence and the First Fictional Police Detective

The success of the *feuilletonistes* was soon emulated by British writers. George Reynolds (1814–79), inspired by Sue's popularity, began publishing *The Mysteries of London* as an eight-page, double-columned penny weekly in 1844. Part of a wave of similar 'penny dreadfuls', it ran for twelve years and eventually comprised over four million words. Reynolds was exploiting the transformation of cheap serial publications such as Charles Knight's *Penny Magazine* and William Chambers's *Chambers' Edinburgh Journal*, formerly devoted to 'improving' the lower classes with useful information, into enter-tainment media. Like the changes occurring in France, this transfor-mation was part of the turn toward a mass audience in the culture at large following the cessation of war with France in 1815. In the midst of this growth in mass entertainment, a vogue for episodic stories of city low-life was ignited by *Life in London*, an urban novel written in 1821 by Pierce Egan (1772–1849) and immediately staged under the title of *Tom and Jerry*, in which two young men tour the crowded gathering-places of nocturnal London.

That same year another curious debut took place, the anonymous publication of *Confessions of an English Opium-Eater*, by Thomas De Quincey (1785–1859). Quickly achieving fame for its baroque descriptions of the author's dreams while under the influence of the drug, the *Confessions* also contained accounts of De Quincey's Saturday night 'debauches' of opium while wandering the streets until all hours, enjoying the 'spectacle' of the London poor 'laying out their wages' in the seedier neighbourhoods and marketplaces of the labyrinthine city (2.49–50). These short narratives clearly contributed to the theme of urban voyeurism in Poe's 'The Man of the Crowd' and in Baudelaire's concept of the 'dandy' or *flâneur*. In addition, the opium-eater's specific accounts of the psychotropic and addictive effects of the drug became a source of material for more than one contribution to detective fiction over the next century.

The success of the *Confessions* ensured that the otherwise hapless De Quincey would have a fairly dependable market for his writings over the next several years. In that period he wrote his remarkable short essay, 'On the Knocking at the Gate in *Macbeth*' (1823), introducing the idea that murder might be enjoyed as an art. Linking his readers' fascination with the murder of Duncan in Shakespeare's play to contemporary interest in real-life crime, De Quincey suggested, with tongue in cheek, that we are more interested in the thoughts of Macbeth than in those of his victim for the same reason that a brutal mass murderer like John Williams draws more of our attention than the family he killed with his hammer. Williams had shown himself to be, like Macbeth, an 'artist' in his chosen profession, perhaps even a 'genius', with his 1811 '*début* on the stage of Ratcliffe Highway' (3.151).

Accordingly, argues De Quincey, the 'connoisseur in murder' who takes an aesthetic interest in such things, whether in the playhouse or on the street, naturally concentrates his or her 'sympathy of comprehension' not on the murder victim, whose thoughts have been reduced to the crudest level imaginable – 'overwhelming panic' – but on the mind of the 'artist'. In him 'there must be raging some great storm of passion, – jealousy, ambition, vengeance, hatred, – which will create a hell within him; and into this hell we are to look' (3.152).

This is a remarkable insight into the psychology of crime fiction in general, as applicable to the Newgate novels of De Quincey's day as to the psychological thrillers of our own, with their focus on the perverse motives and twisted moral logic of the criminal psychopath. It is an insight that De Quincey gained, in part, from reflecting on his own reading tastes. As editor of the *Westmorland Gazette* from 1818 to 1820, he had published transcriptions of assize court news – poisonings, robberies, stabbings, and other items of real-life mayhem – on days when his opium habit had got the better of his work habits. He went on to expand the insights of his *Macbeth* essay in a series of articles entitled 'On Murder Considered as One of the Fine Arts', which began appearing in *Blackwood's Magazine* in 1827.

'On Murder' is a facetious exposé premised on the idea that its author has stumbled upon a secret London club, 'The Society of Connoisseurs in Murder', for whom '[e]very fresh atrocity of that class, which the police annals of Europe bring up' is evaluated like 'a picture, statue, or other work of art' (6.112). De Quincey then presents the text of a commemorative lecture supposedly given at a recent gathering of the Society, the 'Williams Lecture on Murder', in which the anonymous lecturer recounts the history of the art of murder, examines its principles, and notes the artistic merits and shortcomings of some of its most famous works. The lecturer's tone throughout is wryly academic, combining brutal horror with ironic comedy and the refined diction of aesthetics, a relatively new philosophical discipline originating in Germany during the previous century. As the lecturer walks us through this 'gallery of crime', he remarks the importance of 'composition', 'design', 'grouping, light and shade, poetry, sentiment' (113), pleads for more 'patronage' (125), and condemns 'plagiarism' (130).

The lecturer's tone may be playful, but De Quincey's motives were serious. An avid student of the brilliant German philosopher Immanuel Kant (1724–1804), he was alarmed by Kant's attempt, in *The Critique of Judgment* (1790), to divorce aesthetic from moral values. True art appreciation, says Kant, is 'disinterested' – that is, influenced neither by considerations of personal 'interest', such as bodily comfort, sensual pleasure, or financial benefit, nor by universal moral 'interest', such as getting others to behave well. This amoral attitude toward art became part of the Romantic reaction against the Enlightenment's stress on pragmatism and utility, which in moral terms became personal 'improvement'. De Quincey wished to show the absurdity of taking Kant's position seriously. Facetiously defending the artistic enjoyment of murder against 'certain prigs, who affect to speak of our society [of *connoisseurs*] as if it were in some degree immoral' (113), De Quincey's lecturer asks of what use is virtue once 'the poor murdered man' is 'out of his pain'? 'Enough has been given to morality; now comes the turn of Taste and the Fine Arts' (115).

Whatever his satiric intentions, De Quincey's idea of considering murder a fine art was taken seriously by students and writers of crime fiction. While he does not give much attention to 'sympathy' with the criminal mind in 'On Murder', nor to the criminal's ingenuity in committing the crime or in getting away with it, he does emphasize the atmosphere of awe and mystery, the 'colossal sublimity' (113) conveyed by a well-planned and -accomplished homicide. Getting away with the crime can enhance this 'impression of awe, and the sense of power left behind' by the 'artist', thus making the fatal 'monument of his genius' more 'durable' (126) in public memory. But in accord with the tastes of his era, De Quincey's lecturer does not include intricate plotting among the important features of an aesthetically satisfying murder.

If De Quincey's 1827 essay can be considered a product of its place and time, *Richmond; or, Scenes in the Life of a Bow Street Officer*, published in the same year, was in many respects ahead of its time.

Attributed variously to Thomas Skinner Surr (1770–1847) and to Thomas Gaspey (1788–1871), *Richmond* is the first novel in English to feature a professional detective protagonist throughout. Indeed, it is narrated entirely by a professional detective, 'Thomas Richmond', a mischievous young man who leaves his apprenticeship to join a troop of actors and eventually falls in with a band of gypsies. He thereby acquires the skill in disguise and intimacy with how the bohemian 'other half' lives that will enable him to advance among the ranks of the Bow Street Runners, whom he joins about a third of the way through the book.

By the 1820s, the Runners were not considered the most trustworthy or competent defenders of law and order, nor were they welcome in polite company. Tom's first reaction on joining their ranks speaks to this point, but soon gives way to other feelings:

> At first, I had an indescribable notion that I was now degraded and shut out from all society, as every body has a dislike and horror at the sight of an officer. [. . .] I found the officers themselves, however, a jovial set of fellows, – free, careless, merry, and full of anecdotes of their different exploits, which exhibited a more varied picture of human life than I had hitherto met with in all my wanderings. (169–70)

Tom speaks well not only of his fellow Runners, but also of the gypsies, many of whom come to his aid as he sets about tracking down kidnappers, grave-robbers, smugglers, and con artists. At one point, he even declares his detestation of capital punishment (121). In general, Tom's attitudes are similar to those of the reformers who were trying to reduce punishment by death, put a human face on the outcasts of society, and rehabilitate the seedy image of law enforcement on the eve of the establishment of London's official police in 1829.

However, the author of *Richmond* is ahead of his time in the attention he gives to detection through inference and induction. In his very first case, what is taken by the victim's parents to be a gypsy kidnapping of their son is immediately interpreted otherwise by Tom. Responding to the assumption that the gypsies were after the young man's rich attire, he notes that the boy's pony was left standing with a 'saddle and bridle worth more than the boy's whole suit' (172). In the episodes that follow, we also encounter rogues and officers in disguise, identifications made from clothing and complexion, and what will later become a fixture of classic detection, the 'body double' switch.

These scenes of detection rarely offer the reader clues that remain undeciphered for more than a few seconds. Often, as in the case of the pony, Tom mentions the clue at the same moment he interprets it. Moreover, the correct interpretation depends, as often as not, on Tom Richmond's special knowledge either of gypsy ways or of previous cases. While the book takes the form of a series of episodes, none of them offers a single, continuous mystery for which clues and testimony gradually accumulate in a serial manner susceptible of multiple explanations, leading at last to the detective protagonist's revelation of the correct solution. In fact, detection hardly occurs in the last story, which presents a difficult situation demanding ingenious role-playing in order to outwit the obvious villains.

We are, in short, often impressed by Tom's inductive powers, but rarely placed in a position to test them directly against our own. *Richmond* thus anticipates the popular genre of detective 'memoirs', 'reminiscences', and 'casebooks' of the 1840s and 1850s, following the establishment of a formal bureau of detection in London in 1842 and leading up to the appearance of likeable but hard-nosed fictional police detectives such as Inspector Bucket in *Bleak House*. Like Richmond, these investigators are meant to impress the reader with their uncanny knack for inference, disguise, and pursuit, not to engage him or her in the game of detection. Unfortunately, Tom arrived too early to share much of their success.

Developments in the Historical Sciences

The 1820s and 1830s witnessed not only transformations in popular literary taste and in the administration of law and criminal justice, but also major developments in the sciences of historical reconstruction.

As indicated in the previous chapter, by the end of the eighteenth century the universe was becoming a 'locked room'. Its windows had already been shuttered by the physical sciences against miraculous interventions in the ordinary course of natural events, and the door standing open for the entrance and exit of a divine 'First Cause' at the far end of time was gradually being closed by the quickening pace of geological research.

That distant door was first swung on its hinges by James Hutton, who in 1785 introduced a view of geological change that came to be known as 'Uniformitarianism'. In defiance of the earlier 'Catastrophist' theorists of the earth, who thought the geological record confirmed the biblical accounts of ancient cataclysms, Hutton argued that erosion, volcanic activity, and the gradual flooding and ebbing of seas, all forces plainly at work in changing the face of the earth today, were sufficient to explain any past changes to be inferred from present geological evidence. Of course, admitted Hutton, to allow for the extremely slow, almost unobservable, pace of change implied by his theory, the age of the earth would have to be considerably greater than the Bible indicated. But he refused to speculate any further on that topic, stating only that, 'with respect to human observation, this world has neither a beginning nor an end' (28).

Hutton's theories had to struggle for acceptance given the lingering authority of the Bible among scientists as well as lay-persons. Eventually abandoning a literal reading of the Old Testament, the Catastrophists, led in England by William Buckland (1784–1856) and in France by Georges Cuvier, managed to salvage the basic features of the biblical account in the face of the Uniformitarian challenge. Noah's flood became representative of multiple deluges causing partial or complete extinctions of species present since the Creation. However, advances in geological mapping soon began to support Hutton's conclusions when it became evident that the mineral layers or 'strata' deposited on the face of the earth by flooding over successive periods contained distinct species of fossils, and that these fossils had apparently evolved, from simpler to more complex forms, over what must have been vast stretches of prehistory.

During the 1820s and 1830s particularly, writes Archibald Geikie, '[t]he petrified remains of former plants and animals ceased to be mere curiosities. Their meaning as historical documents was at last realized' (400). Quite suddenly fossils went from being minor anomalies requiring explanation in the light of divine testimony, to clues challenging that testimony. They began to stimulate scientists, and the common reader of popular science, to invent new arrays of events, and to construct new narratives corresponding to those arrays, in order to explain the sequences of different fossil species in the visible story of creation written in the layers of the earth's crust.

Hutton's Uniformitarian position was at last made scientifically respectable in 1830 with the publication by Charles Lyell (1797–1875) of *Principles of Geology*, a careful and well-argued survey of the most up-to-date research, written in a style accessible to the general public. Although Lyell had come to embrace a belief in the 'special creation' of species by God over time, like many of his Catastrophist opponents, progressive evolution was now a part of public discussion, and the biblical chronology continued to lose ground.

Meanwhile, among both amateur and academic scientists there was considerable intramural rivalry, sometimes quite vicious. Janet Browne has repeatedly remarked the 'angry atmosphere' of the university system arising from the 'intense competition' for students among professors (50–1), the ongoing disputes between 'Neptunists' and 'Vulcanists', 'Uniformitarians' and 'Catastrophists' (71), and the envy that impelled older scientists to denigrate or, worse, appropriate the new discoveries of their protégés. Young Charles Darwin himself, writes Browne, was not without a considerable 'competitive thrust' (101), and became estranged from one of his early mentors over precisely this issue of appropriation (86–7). A similar pattern of the challenging young upstart impeded by jealous superiors was already becoming a common feature of detective literature, as we have seen from Vidocq's *Memoirs*.

What is most important for our purposes is the fact that this ongoing turbulence regarding the historical accuracy of the biblical narratives offered the reading public at large an important lesson in the power of material evidence, or 'clues', to challenge or even seriously undermine the most authoritative 'testimony' in the world, that of God himself.

In this same period, as Henry Kozicki has shown, the writing of history in general was gaining a massive audience. The historical novels of Sir Walter Scott (1771–1832) were the best-sellers of the day. Biographies of world-movers like Napoleon and Wellington and narratives of the French Revolution, the Spanish conquest of the Americas, and the fall of the Roman Empire were read with the same avidity as fiction. 'Universal' histories of humanity, like the twenty-five-volume set compiled by William Fordyce Mavor (1758–1837), crowded the bookshelves of middle-class and well-to-do families and the libraries of the new private academies. In these schools, funded by the rising entrepreneurs of industry, commerce, and finance, the teaching of the modern sciences and recent history had already begun to displace the traditional curricula of the established, upper-class 'public' (what Americans would call 'private') schools, with their focus on classical languages and the events chronicled in them (Roach, 70–85; Archer, 5–24).

In short, developments in the legal system, in popular literature, and in education were combining with developments in the science and writing of history to bring into focus a new kind of public hero and to define a new kind of role for him to play: master interpreter, inventor of hypothetical arrays, reconstructor of past events. In America, meanwhile, an eccentric but highly imaginative poet disaffected with the crass materialism and pragmatic views of his fellow democratic citizens, and nostalgic for the fading gentlemanly ideals of aristocratic distinction, was beginning to turn from verse to a more lucrative career in prose.

Casebook Entry No. 1

The Ape and the Aristocrat

The Roots of Resentment

While the twenty years following the publication of De Quincey's *Confessions* in 1821 witnessed significant advances in crime fiction and in the historical sciences in England and France, the situation in America was quite different. The new nation lacked the sprawling urban milieus of its European counterparts, and aside from the contributions of Benjamin Franklin and Thomas Jefferson, it also lacked standing in the sciences. As for literature, in comparison to all but a handful of native Gothic and regional writers like Charles Brockden Brown and Washington Irving (1783–1859), best-selling foreign authors were easier for American publishers to market than their own. Since literary piracy paid handsomely before the passage of international copyright laws, foreign writers were also cheaper.

Cooper's popularity abroad began to alter the prevailing attitude, and the great writers of the so-called 'American Renaissance' at mid-century, like Ralph Waldo Emerson (1803–82), Nathaniel Hawthorne (1804–64), and Walt Whitman (1819–92), would soon eradicate it. Meanwhile, America looked abroad, mainly to the parent country, for its best-sellers and for literary models. Edgar Allan Poe was no exception to this rule, but he also paid attention to literary and scientific developments in France. He was thus familiar not only with Dickens and De Quincey, the latter of whom helped shape Poe's self-image as an author (Morrison, 'Poe's'), but also with Vidocq and Cuvier.

Poe was born in Boston in 1809, the son of itinerant stage actors and the second of three children. His parents died within days of each other two years later, and the children were sent to different families. Edgar grew up with the Allan family of Richmond, from whom he derived his middle name. He attended schools in America and England and enrolled at the University of Virginia before enlisting in the army in 1827, the same year he published his first book of poems. Another volume of poetry followed in 1829, the year before Poe entered West Point. Life there did not agree with him, however, and he was court-martialled and dismissed in 1831, just as his third volume of poems went to press.

That same year, Poe's stories began to appear anonymously in the Baltimore *Saturday Courier*, and in 1833 he won a $50 prize from the *Sunday Visitor* for 'MS Found in a Bottle'. In 1836, he began his career as a magazine editor with *The Southern Literary Messenger* of Richmond, contributing critical reviews, poems, and stories in the Gothic vein of mystery and horror still popular among middle-class American readers, but already losing its appeal in England by the beginning of the 1830s. Poe's ambivalent relationship to his American readership now commenced.

An orphan of the American antebellum North raised for most of his life in the slave-holding South, and settling as a young adult in Maryland, a border state, Poe was a strange amalgam of conflicting attitudes and inclinations. His obscure descent from theatre people, who were considered disreputable at this time, and the stigma of orphanhood drove him at first to seek distinction in the military with its ancient lustre of the warrior class. When that did not work out, as Jon Thompson and David Leverenz note, this migratory writer and editor of magazine prose began to fashion for himself the narrative persona of a cultivated and supremely intelligent Southern gentleman, a 'self-made aristocrat' (Leverenz, 223) who set himself above the sordid commercialism of middle-class publishing.

In that role, notes Thompson (53), Poe avidly followed cultural developments in the capitals of Europe while mourning the imminent disappearance of a Southern feudal ideal in the ruined gardens, decaying mansions, and perverse passions of his high-strung Gothic protagonists. The glaring fact of slavery, upon which Southern landed wealth was based, did not surface above his literary horizon. Caught between one society in the industrialized North whose materialistic values he could not accept and another in the rural South whose gentry values he could not afford to examine too closely, Poe opted to 'build a world elsewhere' (Thompson, 54), in the fantastic tales he wrote for mass consumption in order to stay solvent.

Out of Poe's self-manufactured affinity with a vanished ruling class was born his amateur Parisian detective, the Chevalier C. Auguste Dupin, a deracinated young aristocrat 'of an excellent – indeed of an illustrious family, but [. . .] reduced to such poverty that the energy of his character succumbed beneath it, and he ceased to bestir himself in the world' ('Murders', 192). Retaining 'a small remnant of his patrimony', Dupin is able to survive, barely, by taking up residence in run-down neighbourhoods and indulging in only one luxury, books, to sustain the life of the mind. Thus situated, he became the first of a long line of bohemian amateur or private detectives living at a remove from mainstream society, which was to find their adventures irresistible.

Like Tom Richmond before him, however, Auguste Dupin's time had not yet arrived. It was delayed in part, as we shall see in the next chapter, because Tom Richmond's was about to begin.

Reason and Revenge

The canon of Poe's crime and detective stories begins with 'The Man of the Crowd' (1840), and extends over the next five years to include 'The Murders in the Rue Morgue' (1841), 'The Mystery of Marie Roget' (1842), 'The Gold Bug' (1843), 'Thou Art the Man' (1844), and 'The Purloined Letter' (1844). All of these tales influenced the later course of detective fiction. 'The Man of the Crowd', with its debt to Vidocq, is almost an abstract of the detective sub-type of surveillance, flight, and pursuit; 'The Gold Bug' popularized the device of enciphered messages; and 'Thou Art the Man' tells a parodic tale of inference and entrapment leading to the exoneration of an innocent suspect, a plot too universal to require comment. The remaining three stories all feature Dupin. Of these three 'tales of ratiocination', as Poe called them (*Essays*, 573), only 'The Mystery of Marie Roget', a fictional attempt by Poe to solve the real-life murder of a New York shop girl by re-imagining the crime in a Parisian context, falls short of success: the case was solved before Poe published the end of his story, and the solution he proposed was wrong.

'The Murders in the Rue Morgue' and 'The Purloined Letter' can be said to comprise the twin fountainheads of modern crime fiction: the tale of detection that offers the puzzle of an unsolved crime (in a 'locked room', no less), and asks the reader, in effect, 'Whodunit?', and the caper or crime adventure tale that offers the problem of capturing or outwitting the person known to have committed the crime, and asks the reader, 'How is it to be done?'

Not that detection is irrelevant to Dupin's outwitting Minister D—and retrieving the Queen's self-incriminating letter from under the man's nose in 'The Purloined Letter'. Dupin must locate the letter by a process of negative inference before he can begin to hatch a scheme to steal it back. His negative inference depends, in turn, on the failure of the Parisian police to discover the letter's hiding place after probing every cubic centimetre of the Minister's home. Once he concludes that the letter must be 'hidden' in plain sight, Dupin can use his powers of 'analysis' – what De Quincey had called 'sympathy of comprehension' – to read the Minister's mind and determine how best to 'purloin' it himself. Apparently, Dupin must first walk the path of induction to its dead end, or watch others do so, before he can begin to imagine what might lie beyond.

The aristocratic lineage of Poe's cultivated amateur detective is clearly on display in 'The Purloined Letter', where we find our hero living the life of a secular monk, but at ease in the company of state ministers (indeed, he is on close terms with Minister D—, his adversary) and nonplussed by the intimate details of royal scandals. Dupin's personality stands out particularly against the cast of nonentities who inhabit this tale.

It has often been remarked that as the last of the Dupin stories, 'The Purloined Letter' managed to reduce the 'tale of ratiocination' to its bare, even abstract, essentials. With the exception of Dupin himself, its major players are either unnamed – 'a third person' writes a letter to 'a personage of most exalted station' (332) – or rendered as initials – 'Minister D—' purloins the letter to blackmail this exalted 'personage' and hides it from 'Prefect G—'. The effect is to reduce the plot to an algebraic equation or geometric proof. Only Dupin, who has a name, seems to retain a distinct personality throughout. This is grounded not only in his superior powers of detection, but also in his sense of personal honour and its need for defence.

That sense of honour is displayed by Dupin's last act in the story – indeed, his last act as a fictional character – when he scribbles an insulting message for the Minister inside the facsimile letter he leaves in the man's card-rack as a substitute for the Queen's. The Minister had, apparently, done Dupin 'an evil turn' once 'in Vienna' (348) – what, exactly, we do not know. What is important for Poe is that this 'evil turn' must be revenged. The message Dupin leaves for the Minister is a quotation from a French play by Racine about the ancient Greek royal family of Atreus. It invites Minister D—, in effect, to dine on his own offspring, as if to indicate that he who seeks power by purloining the letter will now become the victim of his own device. Dupin assumes that the Minister will not read the message until the moment he is forced to play his hand and show the Queen's incriminating letter to the King. This will happen as soon as the Queen, once more in possession of the real letter, refuses to cooperate with D—'s political schemes. The Minister's disgrace will thus be complete.

Dupin's impassioned act of revenge is superfluous to the starkly rational, schematic plot of 'The Purloined Letter' and a feudal anachronism in the age of civil litigation and modern law enforcement. Its point is to remind us that Dupin's motives, unlike those of the official police, are personal, and his right to act on them rests not on the law, but on his line of descent. Before the rise of the democratic state, the right to seek personal redress for assaults on one's honour belonged solely to the ruling class, and 'satisfaction' usually took the form of a duel. By the time Poe wrote his story, duelling had been outlawed in both America and England because it perpetuated the notion that 'gentlemen' were above the law.

While hardly illegal, Dupin's revenge is a kind of duelling with verbal weapons. Poe is showing us that Dupin adheres to a superannuated code of personal honour in an age of impersonal reason, which sees injury only in terms of the calculation of damages, as though honour could be quantified. As we shall see, Dupin has little patience with calculations and quantities.

'Cunning' vs 'Analysis'

Making Dupin a deracinated, bohemian aristocrat had several consequences for the later development of detection.

The first concerns the motive of the amateur or private professional detective. As an aristocratic atavism living outside the workaday world and moral concerns of the middle-class professions, Dupin investigates crime only for reasons appropriate to his class standing: personal honour, loyalty to his monarch, and, above all, 'mental excitement' ('Murders', 193) or intellectual 'amusement' (205). He is an 'amateur' of detection in the original sense of the word's Latin root *amator* – lover – for he 'exults' and 'glories' in 'that moral activity which *disentangles*' (189). Thus qualified for membership in De Quincey's Society of Connoisseurs in Murder, Dupin in turn helped popularize the theme of murder as a fine art or intellectual pastime, particularly among amateur and private detectives in the classical, 'whodunit' tradition. (By the time 'The Purloined Letter' was published, however, Dupin had apparently realized that there was money to be made by this 'amusement' and he is not above claiming the sizeable reward offered by Prefect G—.)

Because investigating murders for private amusement would not require the aristocratic detective to explain himself, Poe provided Dupin, on his debut in 'The Murders in the Rue Morgue', with an intimate and curious friend as confidant, one who could put questions to the detective without giving offence and then relate the answers to us. Poe's sidekick narrator is an anonymous American visitor to Paris who happens to meet Dupin at a library, where they are both looking for the same book. Stunned by Dupin's prodigious intellect and imagination, he soon proposes a common living arrangement. With Dupin's intimate friend as mouthpiece, Poe evokes in his readers a similar feeling of intimacy while keeping them at a distance from the immediate observations and conclusions of his detective hero and unobtrusively controlling, through delay and proper sequencing, access to information crucial to solving the crime. Poe's skilful use of his anonymous narrator thus illustrates nicely what Genette calls 'modality'. This sidekick device eventually became a standard feature of detection.

Drugs do not play a part in the Dupin tales, but their associated mental states do. The life that Dupin and his friend share behind closed doors resembles that of 'madmen' (193), and the way they pass their nights seems to have been inspired by the Saturday night 'debauches' of De Quincey's *Confessions*. It is a way of life that only someone with no need to work for a living could pursue. Like a pair of opium fiends, the detective and his sidekick admit no visitors and sit indoors with the shutters drawn all day, 'bus[ying] our souls in dreams – reading, writing, or conversing, until warned by the clock of the advent of the true Darkness. Then we sallied forth into the streets [. . .] roaming far and wide until a late hour, seeking, amid the wild lights and shadows of the populous city, that infinity of mental excitement which quiet observation can afford' ('Murders', 193). Dreams and altered waking states, often induced by addictive drugs and intoxicants, were soon to play an important role in the history of detective fiction as adjuncts to the unique temperament and cognitive ability of the detective or criminal genius.

Perhaps the most important consequence of Poe's sympathy for a vanishing feudalism is apparent from our first introduction to Dupin in 'The Murders in the Rue Morgue': an intense rivalry between the gifted, aristocratic amateur and the more experienced, methodical, and commonsensical official detectives working under Prefect G—, with whom Dupin will come to grips more directly in 'The Purloined Letter'. 'The Parisian police, so much extolled for *acumen*,' Dupin tells his roommate, 'are cunning, but no more. The results attained by them are not unfrequently surprising, but, for the most part, are brought about by simple diligence and activity' (204). If we have any doubt that Eugène-François Vidocq is hiding somewhere in the background of this lofty dismissal of the Prefect and his modern methods, Poe dispels it in the next sentence but one: 'Vidocq, for example, was a good guesser, and a persevering man. But, without educated thought, he erred continually by the very intensity of his investigations' (204).

Dupin scorns 'cunning', however diligent and active, because it fails to take into account the mind of the criminal. In this respect he does scant justice to Vidocq's extensive first-hand experience with felons and murderers. What Dupin means by 'cunning' is more clearly illustrated by Vidocq's fictional successor, Prefect G—. In 'The Purloined Letter', the Prefect uses excellent 'measures' (339) to examine all the invisible spaces within Minister D—'s mansion where the missing letter might be hidden, but his 'ill-admeasurement' (340) of his opponent's mind prevents him from grasping the Minister's devious train of thought.

In 'Murders', this sort of 'cunning' or mechanical calculation is closely identified with inductive reasoning. Both the Prefect and Dupin make use of it, the latter more thoroughly than the former, but Dupin's true advantage over the Prefect lies in those 'mental features' that enable 'the analyst [to] throw[ ] himself into the spirit of his opponent, [and] identif[y] himself therewith' (190). That Dupin has two opponents to contend with, one an orangutan, poses no insurmountable difficulty. In fact, the ape may be an easier target of empathy for Poe's fugitive aristocrat, as we shall see.

Both 'Murders' and 'Purloined Letter' thus promote an essentially Romantic or 'historicist' ideal of detection based on the investigator's powers of imaginative 'analysis' rather than the 'calculation' or 'cunning' of the ordinary understanding, something Poe thought his materialistic, profit-motivated middle-class readers valued entirely too much.

While his 'analytical' skill places Dupin squarely in the line of descent of De Quincey's version of Shakespeare, whose imaginative genius could identify with the complex criminal mind of an 'artist' of murder like Macbeth, it also disqualifies Poe's amateur sleuth, in the eyes of many modern critics, as a harbinger of the classical inductive or scientific investigator. According to Martin Kayman, for instance, 'Murders' is not a story of rational detection, but a study in the extraordinary, the 'monstrous', 'the mysterious which [. . .] escapes or resists [. . .] articulation in [the] totalizing language of Law, Science, and secular reason' (140). Moreover, Poe's use of a berserk ape as culprit is not only generically suspect, but unoriginal: Sheridan Le Fanu (1814–73) had anticipated Poe three years before in 'Green Tea'.

We may add to Kayman's objections several other putatively disqualifying features. Poe's title, for instance, hardly 'plays fair' with the reader. Since only humans can be charged with 'murder' (imagine sending the orangutan to the guillotine!), we are from the outset led astray in the direction of a human perpetrator by the author himself, an act of duplicity with which Dupin, our fictional rival, need not contend. Also, with Madame L'Espanaye's bed standing in front of it, the unfastened lower window sash could not have allowed the ape to enter or leave her room when raised. Finally, how Dupin could have recognized the hairs he had disentangled from the hand of the decapitated victim as those of an orangutan remains unclear. There are no pictures or descriptions of orangutan hair in the excerpt from Cuvier that the detective uses to nail the case shut, nor do we have any reason to believe that Dupin could have encountered any, let alone a live orangutan from which to gather specimens.

Perhaps the most damaging of all Kayman's criticisms is his suggestion that, far from endorsing the positivist, scientific approach to mystery-solving that later comes to define classical detective fiction, Poe holds such inductive methods up to contempt. As Jon Thompson observes, the author associates these methods with common sense, pragmatism, and utility, values dear to the hearts of the democratic masses and their hired state police (45). In his Dupin stories, concludes Thompson, Poe asks us to admire, 'not rationalism, per se, but a romanticized version or ideology of rationalism in which reason, or more properly "analysis", figures as the highest mode of apprehension' (47).

Ironically, this objection, the most serious of Kayman's and Thompson's indictments, best explains how 'The Murders in the Rue Morgue' in particular became foundational to the history of classical detection. All of Poe's other faults, the misleading title, the error in visualizing the window sash, the impossibility of identifying ape hair from an encyclopaedia entry, the borrowing from Le Fanu, the lack of realism, can be attributed either to his not 'playing fair' (which presumes the story to be, in fact, a tale of detection) or to his being unoriginal, incompetent, or careless. (There is no 'Rue Morgue' in 1840s Paris, for instance.)

Only Poe's obvious disdain for 'rationalism, per se' touches upon the single feature of his plot construction that would eventually make this story and 'The Purloined Letter' the most imitated in the history of the genre. For the point of the Dupin tales is not just to *show* readers the shortcomings of inductive detection, but to make them *experience* these shortcomings first-hand. With this aim in mind, Poe had no choice but to set his readers the task of trying to solve the mystery themselves by such methods, adding clues along the way that would encourage them to invent multiple, but ultimately inadequate, arrays of possible events demanding immediate narrative incorporation. In short, the very device Poe chose to demonstrate the futility of ordinary induction ended up making induction – or 'ratiocination' – a pleasurable and much desired generic feature of fictional detection.

Poe's minutely circumstantial description of the crime in 'The Murders in the Rue Morgue' seems designed specifically to engage the reader's inductive imagination. After the narrator's speculations on the nature of 'analysis', followed by an illustrative anecdote of Dupin's mindreading capabilities using the narrator himself as subject (194–7), 'The Murders in the Rue Morgue' leads us briskly into the puzzle of the crime announced by the news headline, 'Extraordinary Murders'. This account includes a description of the scene of the crime, the bloody razor, and the displaced bedframe; the arrest of an innocent suspect, disingenuously surnamed 'LeBon' or 'The Good'; a moneybox left behind, eliminating theft as a motive; the horribly disfigured state in which the bodies of Madame L'Espanaye and her daughter were found, indicating superhuman strength in their assailant; the windows and door of the room locked from the inside; and the several, mutually contradictory reports concerning the second of two 'voices' heard coming from inside the room just before the door was forced open.

After visiting the scene himself in the company of his roommate, Dupin reports what the police have missed, and the narrator withholds none of these discoveries from the reader: a broken nail in the window sash giving the false impression that the window was locked on the inside; a lightning-rod and shutters outside the window, but too far away for an ordinary man to reach; the pattern of fingerprints on the neck of Madamoiselle L'Espanaye, left by a hand much larger than a human's; the non-human hairs discovered in the mother's clenched fist; and the fact that the first voice of the two that were overheard was unanimously declared to be that of a Frenchman, while the second was unrecognizable as belonging to any of the modern European languages. We are allowed but a few seconds to piece all these clues together before Dupin shows his companion Cuvier's essay on the appearance and habits of orangutans. The remainder of the tale, devoted to getting the sailor to reveal himself, resembles the caper plot of 'The Purloined Letter'.

Poe did not intend to inaugurate a new genre with 'The Murders in the Rue Morgue', but only to show us that, in the words of Dupin, whenever we have arrived at apparent impossibilities in the course of ordinary induction, it is incumbent on us 'to prove that these apparent "impossibilities" are, in reality, not such' (210) by using our imaginations to think outside the locked room of common sense.

This can be accomplished, however, only on the basis of the physical clues themselves, and what they tell the detective about the behaviour of his opponent. Dupin's references to whist and, in 'The Purloined Letter', the game of 'odds and evens' show that even the most 'analytical' mind cannot identify with another's train of thought without observing his bodily movements. By matching his own facial expression with that of his opponent, the boy who succeeds at 'odds and evens' is enabled to 'see what thoughts or sentiments' have arisen in his opponent's mind (340). Similarly, in whist, one 'examines the countenance of his partner, comparing it carefully with that of each of his opponents. [. . .] He notes every variation of face as the play progresses, gathering a fund of thought from the differences in the expression of certainty, of surprise, of triumph, or chagrin' (191).

It is impossible to achieve empathy with the criminal mind, as Dupin does with the mind of his astonished roommate in the opening pages of 'Murders', without paying close attention to the physical activity displayed by the body attached to that mind. This knowledge can be either derived through direct observation – Dupin's companion stumbles on paving stones, looks up at the stars, and so on – or, as in Madame L'Espanaye's apartment, inferred from the material clues the criminal body in question has left behind.

Slavery and Shaving

Keeping in view Poe's persecutory, aristocratic anxieties can help us disentangle a particular bundle of thematic strands in 'Murders' that critics have followed, up to now, in only one culturally significant but unflattering direction. At the same time, it will help us recognize those 'mental features' – namely humiliation and rage – that enable Dupin, an aristocratic fugitive from the modern world, to throw himself into the 'spirit' of an orangutan.

Readers of an ideologically critical turn have interpreted the berserk behaviour of the ape in 'Murders' as an endorsement of the vicious racism expressed toward African Americans by the dominant white society of Poe's era, both north and south of the Mason–Dixon Line. Lindon Barrett, for instance, finds Poe's racist sympathies principally 'signalled' by Dupin's refusal to reject, categorically, the idea that the voice of the orangutan could have been that of an African (209) and his reference to Cuvier, a notorious racist, as a means of identifying the ape (159).

Poe was writing in an era when analogies between Africans and apes, especially 'chimpanzees' (a term often used interchangeably with 'orangutans'), were an intrinsic part of what Terence Whalen calls the 'average racism' of the day (18). As Stephen Gould has pointed out (32), from the late eighteenth century on, whites almost universally assumed that native Americans and blacks were inferior, their only point of internal disagreement being whether that inferiority was biological (and thus irremediable) or cultural (and thus susceptible to improvement through education).

Elise Lemire, in a study of the immediate cultural milieu in which 'Murders' was written, points out that the story appeared in a Philadelphia periodical of which Poe was editor just three years after rioting took place there in opposition to the proposed abolition of slavery, rioting inspired by fears of 'amalgamation', i.e., mixed-race marriages (190–3). Poe had moved to Philadelphia with his young wife and her mother only months before he published his story, to find the worst caricatures of sexually predatory African American males appearing in the daily press. The orangutan's invasion of the mother's and daughter's boudoir, just as they are preparing for bed, says Lemire, not to mention the particular mode of the daughter's death – stuffed up the vaginal chimney – symbolically represents black-on-white rape and is calculated to incite and exploit these racist fears.

In addition, says Lemire, the orangutan's attempts to shave itself, and then Madame L'Espanaye, seem to have been inspired by common knowledge 'in the antebellum period' that 'the tending of white men's hair and beards was typically done by blacks, for whom such labor was considered "natural"' (183). Finally, 'at the time Poe's tale was published in Philadelphia, the city's own Peale's Museum displayed stuffed monkeys dressed and arranged so as to depict the life of a barbershop' (183), an obvious 'parod[y] of black barbers' (184).

To Lemire's list we may add the lingering fear of slave rebellions, like Nat Turner's in August 1831 (Dayan, 181). The ape, after all, is about to be sold by its owner, and has been locked up in a dark closet and kept 'quiet' 'by the use of a whip' ('Murders', 222). The mere sight of this weapon drives it out into the street when, having escaped from the closet, it is caught trying to shave with its master's straight razor before a looking-glass.

The influence of the Philadephia abolition and amalgamation riots on Poe's story seems indisputable. What remains unclear, however, is what his use of this material is supposed to mean, and where, in the end, his sympathies lie. Consider, first of all, that, unlike King Kong, the orangutan is not looking for white women, but for a hiding place. It is described as a 'fugitive' (222) whose flight from the sailor has driven it, unwittingly, into a 'trap' (222).

The epigraph that Poe placed at the beginning of his tale speaks to both the fugitive and slave status of the orangutan. It also links Dupin's methods of detection to those of the historical sciences, specifically archaeology. The excerpt comes from the fifth chapter of *Urne Burial* (1658), a seventeenth-century essay by Sir Thomas Browne (1606–82) on the discovery of several dozen urns containing the cremated remains and artefacts of a vanished people. Poe quotes the passage where Browne defends the legitimacy of his attempts, however feeble, at historical reconstruction:

> What song the Syrens sang, or what name Achilles assumed when he hid himself among women, although puzzling questions are not beyond all conjecture. (quoted in 'Murders', 189)

Browne is referring to two famous events from the Trojan Wars. In the first, from Homer's *Odyssey*, Odysseus orders that his crew's ears be plugged with wax and that he be bound to the mast of his ship so that he can listen to the Sirens, whose ravishing songs often lure sailors to shipwreck on the rocks. His crew sails on, meanwhile, undisturbed by his commands or by the Sirens' songs. In the second Homeric reference, taken from the ancient legends associated with Homer's *Iliad*, the young warrior Achilles is dressed like a woman and hidden by his mother Thetis among the females of the household, in order to keep him from being sent off to fight in the Trojan War.

Martin Priestman (45) has observed the connection between the unnameable Achilles, famous for his strength, swiftness, and implacable fury once aroused, and Poe's orangutan, which cannot speak its 'name' in any manner recognizable by human beings and which hides itself among the L'Espanaye women. The fact that the ape has been wounded in the foot ('Murders', 221) further ratifies the connection, since Achilles' heel is the only place on his body where he is vulnerable. Following out the implications of Priestman's reading we recognize that, despite its ferocious tendencies, the ape, like the young Achilles, has been threatened with physical harm and, from a Homeric point of view, with something much worse: slavery. This was the inevitable consequence of capture on the field of battle in Homer's time, both for warriors and for women.

Browne's reference to Odysseus, famed for his cunning and intelligence, has never been explicated in the context of 'Murders'. However, given the story's doubled culprits, we may assume that if Poe intends Browne's Achilles to represent the ape, then he intends Odysseus to represent his owner, the sailor from the Maltese vessel who has recently arrived home after his wanderings at sea. The sailor's connection to Malta is relevant here, for Homeric Ogygia, where Odysseus was held captive by the beguiling Calypso for nine years, was reputed to be Gozo, one of the Maltese islands south of Sicily. Poe, who knew his Homer well, must also have known that 'what song the Syrens sang' is not only 'not beyond all conjecture', but actually stated by Odysseus himself, when he relates his adventures to his hosts, the Phaiakians, in Book 12. 'Come this way, honored Odysseus,' the Sirens implore him, 'for we know everything that the Argives and Trojans did/and suffered in wide Troy through the gods' despite' (*Odyssey*, 12.185–90).

The Sirens sing of Odysseus's heroic exploits in the Trojan Wars, and not only his, but those of his fellow Greeks, including, of course, Achilles. The parallel between the episode with the Sirens and Dupin's method of capturing the sailor is obvious: much as the Sirens try to lure Odysseus to shore by singing what he most longs to hear, so Dupin tries to lure the sailor to his apartment by promising him news of what he most longs to know. Dupin succeeds, however, where the Sirens fail.

It is not very difficult to see how Dupin might be able to think like a Maltese sailor, but what Poe intends by making the orangutan an object of Dupin's 'analytical' abilities remains obscure. The author's motives are not, however, as Browne puts it, 'beyond all conjecture'. Let us begin with the ape's fugitive status and work from there.

Like Achilles in drag, the orangutan seeks to hide among women, not murder or rape them. But also, grotesquely, it tries to shave Madame L'Espanaye, as it has just tried to shave itself.

Lemire argues that, since facial hair allies 'men with hairy or furry creatures' (182), shaving it off symbolically represents an attempt by the ape to become human. But if the orangutan did associate shaving with becoming human, it would never have tried to shave Madame L'Espanaye, who is human, and, besides, has no facial hair. Perhaps, then, shaving is a sign not of humanity in Poe's tale, but of the need to be recognized as human, the assertion of a claim to the freedom enjoyed by the orangutan's master, an adult white male, whom it has observed shaving through the keyhole of its closet prison.

This would explain an important reversal that Poe makes when he alludes to what Lemire contends was common knowledge about African American barbers shaving white men: the first thing the orangutan does when it escapes its dark cell is shave itself. Shaving can thus be interpreted as a symbolic gesture by which the orangutan, or the black slave it represents, lays claim to the same degree of humanity as those who would make it serve their needs, as either a provider of services or a commodity for sale. As Leland S. Person puts it, somewhat more negatively, the orangutan's attempt to shave itself reveals its indoctrination into the 'inherently unstable' 'racial signifiers' of cultural and political authority (207).

Person suggests that, having been thus indoctrinated into 'the psychological constructs of white male racism', the ape applies its patriarchal, misogynistic lesson by killing and mutilating the L'Espanaye women. But that still leaves unexplained its initial attempt to shave one of *them*. Consider the details of that scene of mayhem as reported by the sailor, who watched through the open window.

> As the sailor looked in, the gigantic animal had seized Madame L'Espanaye by the hair, (which was loose, as she had been combing it,) and was flourishing the razor about her face, in imitation of the motions of a barber. The daughter lay prostrate and motionless; she had swooned. The screams and struggles of the old lady (during which the hair was torn from her head) had the effect of changing *the probably pacific purposes* of the Ourang-Outang into those of wrath. With one determined sweep of its muscular arm it nearly severed her head from her body. The sight of blood inflamed its anger into phrenzy. (223; emphasis added)

Why would Poe, who has gone out of his way to emphasize the 'wrath' and 'ferocity' (217, 221) of the orangutan, attribute 'pacific purposes' to its flourishing of a straight-razor back and forth across Madame L'Espanaye's face? Why unless to suggest that the ape has identified the face of Madame L'Espanaye with the face it formerly saw in the sailor's looking-glass? Before this simian Achilles' 'wrath' (the first word of Homer's *Iliad*) drenches the locked room in the Rue Morgue with blood, before bodies are decapitated and stuffed up chimneys and thrown out of windows, Poe's fugitive performs what might well be called, in the terminology of ideological criticism, a ritual of solidarity and empowerment with those who have apparently sought refuge, as it has, from white male oppression.

It is important to stress that the ape identifies Madame L'Espanaye's face *with* its own, but does not mistake that face *for* its own. It has already demonstrated, in the sailor's apartment, that it knows the difference between the face it sees in the mirror and its real face. If it didn't, it would have tried to shave its mirror image. Contrarily, we may conclude that the ape has not mistaken Madame L'Espanaye's face for a reflection of its own. If it had, it would be shaving itself, as it did when looking in the mirror, and not Madame L'Espanaye.

If any symbolic meaning can be attached to this bizarre gesture, then, it must be that the orangutan is trying to bestow the only sign it understands of the freedom and authority culturally reserved for those who make second-class creatures of both slaves and women. Madame L'Espanaye's screams and struggles, however, tell this fugitive that it has found not a comrade, but a traitor, and, moreover, one who is about to reveal the hiding place they share. The result is ghastly, but the orangutan's revenge cannot negate the 'pacific' purpose behind its initial gesture of cultural kinship with the woman, a kinship registered symbolically by Poe in the testimony of those who have overheard the orangutan's voice: it is 'shrill', like a woman's, but also 'harsh', like a beast's (208).

Sympathy for the outcast, the humiliated, the insane, the marginalized, and the deviant is almost a constant of Poe's fiction, as consistent as his compensatory attraction to the traditional aristocratic prerogative of revenge. Indeed, the two go together. Achilles, after all, is not only a fugitive from physical harm and the threat of slavery, but also a prince. That is something Dupin, creature of the night, 'madm[a]n', and aristocratic fugitive from a middle-class world where everyone has his or her price, can apparently understand.

Bi-Part Souls: The Poet vs the Strong Man

The mind of Dupin, as the poet Richard Wilbur noted, seems fitted by nature to empathize with the doubled and redoubled psyches of his criminal opponents (135–6). 'He boasted to me', says Poe's narrator,

> that most men, in respect to himself, wore windows in their bosoms, and was wont to follow up such assertions by direct and very startling proofs of his intimate knowledge of my own. His manner at these moments was frigid and abstract; his eyes were vacant in expression; while his voice, usually a rich tenor, rose into a treble [. . .]. Observing him in these moods, I often dwelt meditatively upon the old philosophy of the Bi-Part Soul, and amused myself with the fancy of a double Dupin – the creative and resolvent. (193–4)

The 'philosophy of the Bi-Part Soul', as taught by the ancient Greek devotees of Orphism, took the conscious soul to be but a fragment of the unconscious principle of intelligence animating the universe, an Oversoul facilitating transmigration into other bodies. According to Wilbur, the 'Bi-Part' divisions within 'the mastermind Dupin' correspond to the individual characters of those he encounters, and Dupin's two distinct speaking voices, 'tenor' and 'treble', are meant to correspond specifically to the two 'voices' of the sailor and the orangutan, who 'may be combined and considered as a single "party"' (136). However, as we have just seen, within the orangutan itself there are also two voices corresponding to Dupin's treble and tenor, one 'shrill' or womanly, the other 'harsh' or beastly. Dupin's 'frigid and abstract' demeanour and 'vacant' eyes, meanwhile, imply that his own body has been emptied of its proper 'Soul', or, as Leverenz puts it, 'his subjectivity' (228), in order to make room for the souls he observes hidden away in the 'bosoms' through whose 'windows' he peers.

In many ways, Dupin represents what the English Romantic poet John Keats (1795–1821) called 'the Poetical character', which behaves like a 'chameleon' that 'has no self' but 'is every thing and nothing', a creature 'continually [standing] in for – and filling some other Body' (157). Peering into windows, of course, is something that the orangutan and the sailor are good at because of their physical strength and agility. If Dupin can use his imagination to peer into both of their 'bosoms', then he is in a good position to reconstruct the history of the crime they witnessed as it transpired, as well as the roles each of them played in it. To draw on the analogy between the 'strong man' and the 'analyst' with which Poe begins his story (189), Dupin's 'creative' powers of analysis can 'disentangle' the 'exercises' of 'the strong man' from the chaos he left behind in the locked room of the Rue Morgue, as well as the movements of another 'strong man' clinging to the lightning-rod outside it, just as easily as his 'resolvent' powers can disentangle and distinguish the hairs of an ape from those of an old woman.

Leverenz regards Dupin's imaginative 'receptivity to androgynous images' (228) and to 'subversive sources of intellectual power in blackness and femaleness' as a dominant form of male 'appropriation' intended to 'remasculinize his mental powers', which in Poe's case had been emasculated by 'a world that disempowered the gentry role' he had fabricated for himself (229). Considered from this point of view, Poe's 'Bi-Part' Dupin seems, again, an ominous affirmation of the cultural authority of the white male detective who, like God, presumes to know everyone while remaining himself unknowable.

And yet, in making Dupin a psychic chameleon Poe also emptied out the traditionally male role of detective, which had been occupied by the likes of Gines, Vidocq, Vautrin, and similarly hypermasculine 'strong men', and opened the door to its gradual re-occupation, first by the strong man's non-male, and eventually by his non-white and non-Western, counterparts. The figure who is barred from entry, and who will not gain re-entry until the appearance of proletarian hard-boiled fiction in early twentieth-century America, is the 'strong man' of lower-class affinities.

Assuming John Irwin (198) is correct that Dupin achieves his most important triumph not over a criminal, since technically speaking there is none in 'Murders', but over his official counterpart, Prefect G—, one might argue that with the invention of Dupin in 1841 Poe was attempting a similar triumph over the man who, up to then, had dominated the genre of detective fiction. If so, that would explain not only his demeaning references to Eugène-François Vidocq and Vidocq's fictional avatar, the Prefect, but also his hiding the first head of the Sûreté elsewhere in his story, in plain sight and, in the manner of the purloined letter, turned inside-out.

Very early in his *Memoirs*, Vidocq tells how, as a boy, he was forced to earn his literal bread in a travelling circus (5). 'One day, after having beaten me more than usual', writes Vidocq, his master said,

> Now, if you are obedient it remains with yourself to be happy: from to-day, you must let your nails grow; your hair is already of a sufficient length; you are nearly naked, [. . .] we will go through the performance. You are a young savage from the South Seas, and moreover a cannibal; you eat raw flesh, the sight of blood puts you in a fury [. . .]; you utter only broken and shrill sounds, you open your eyes widely, your motions are violent; you only move with leaps and bounds: finally, take for your model the ourang-outang who is in cage number one. (6)

Like all Poe's doubles, Vidocq comes out in reverse-symmetry in 'The Murders in the Rue Morgue': the detective becomes the fugitive, and the man trying to pass for an ape, an ape trying to pass for a man.

4

From Detectives to Detection

Dupin's First-Born: Père Tabaret and Monsieur Lecoq

'The Murders in the Rue Morgue' helped make *Graham's Magazine*, where it first appeared, the best-selling periodical in America. It had no immediate effect on the writing of crime fiction, however, at least in the United States and Great Britain, where the 1840s and 1850s belonged not to eccentric amateur detectives like Dupin but to the new official police detective. Tom Richmond's hour had arrived with the founding of London's new detective unit in 1842, which comprised twelve men at the outset and took its nickname from its location in Great Scotland Yard (Jeffers, 30–2).

Within a decade Scotland Yard's detectives had gained the public's confidence. They were helped by Charles Dickens, who in a series of enthusiastic articles appearing in his magazine *Household Words* described their activities in the seedier neighbourhoods of London. Dickens also accompanied his featured sleuths, officers Whicher and Field, on some of their nightly investigations, and later used Inspector Field as his model for Inspector Bucket in *Bleak House*. Official police detectives became the new heroes of popular crime fiction. As early as 1845 unsold copies of the original *Richmond* were being re-issued (Ousby, *Bloodhounds*, 59) and in 1849 *Recollections of a Detective Police-Officer*, by William Russell under the pen-name Thomas Waters, began its serialization in *Chambers' Edinburgh Journal*, selling well enough to be published as a single volume in 1856. Similar fictionalized 'official reminiscences' and 'true recollections' appeared over the following decade or more.

Ian Ousby notes (*Bloodhounds*, 67) that these new 'case-book' detectives, while indebted to Vidocq 'to the point of absurdity' in their use of disguise, knowledge of criminals and criminal types, and relentlessness, were much more respectable than their French prototype. Waters, for instance, who started out on the wrong side of the law, like Vidocq, was not only a married man, but enjoyed taking his family for a wholesome evening of equestrian theatre before checking in at the Yard (*Recollections*, 151).

Meanwhile, theatrical developments in England were keeping pace with those in popular fiction. In 1863 *The Ticket-of-Leave Man*, by journalist Tom Taylor (the title refers to a prison parolee), offered a sympathetic portrait of the official police detective in the character of Inspector Hawkshaw. Taylor's aims were in part reformist. He wanted to reveal how persecution by honest society and coercion by former cellmates prevented repentant ex-convicts from being rehabilitated.

Hawkshaw's task, accordingly, is not only to expose a ring of counterfeiters but also to keep the 'ticket-of-leave man', a good-hearted young 'Lancashire Lad' named Bob Brierly, from falling back into the clutches of James 'the Tiger' Dalton and his gang. Taylor's moral is summarized by Hawkshaw after he decides not to reveal Brierly's identity to his new employer: 'Poor devil, he's paid his debt' (250). In his mastery of disguise, intimacy with the criminal underworld, and physical courage, Hawkshaw indeed represents, as Ousby says, 'the apotheosis of the police detective in mid-Victorian literature' (*Bloodhounds*, 74). Despite his apparent powers of penetration, however, Hawkshaw does not star in a drama of detection: the audience knows from the first scene who is guilty and who is innocent in the events about to unfold. Taylor offers melodrama and suspense, but little mystery.

America, meanwhile, had begun to cultivate its own tradition of 'low' as well as 'high' literature. According to David Reynolds, tales of the criminal abuse of power by the rich and privileged appeared as early as the 1840s, in the writings of John Neal (1793–1876), George Lippard (1822–54), and George Thompson (1823–c.1873). Blood-drinking, cannibalism, and sexual orgies were typical features of the genre. 'The traditional trappings of horror' inherited from European Gothic, writes Reynolds, 'were quickly rejected as useless remnants of an artificial aristocracy. Republican ideology impelled the writer to look elsewhere for symbols or projections of horror', such as 'the city, with its dark slums, horrid plagues, and criminal classes' (191).

Accordingly, police detective 'reminiscences' and 'recollections' from England soon found buyers in Boston, Philadelphia, and New York, the last of which established its own organized police force in 1845. It was not long before the *Recollections* of Waters was joined by American imitators. The anonymous *Strange Stories of a Detective; or, Curiosities of Crime, by a Retired Member of the Detective Police* (1863), for instance, is set in New York City, and begins with a tale featuring a silent shooting in a locked room that anticipates by nearly forty years Doyle's 'The Empty House': the murder weapon turns out to be a powerful 'air gun' disguised as a walking stick. As in England, however, early American detective casebooks were not primarily designed to incite detection in their readers. The puzzle element was in some instances becoming more pronounced, but the solution to the mystery it presented was as often a matter of chance as of deliberate hypothesis based on carefully assembled clues and sifted testimony.

In France, Dupin drew many more admirers than in his creator's native country. Among them was a young journalist named Émile Gaboriau. In 1863 Gaboriau began a serialized novel called *L'Affaire Lerouge* (translated into English as *The Widow Lerouge*), in which he pitted the inductive intelligence of a gifted amateur, a retired pawn-broker called Père Tabaret, against the stolid, practical methods of the Chief of Police, 'the celebrated Gevrol'. Tabaret, like Poe's Dupin, pursues 'the business of the police, as others do [. . .] painting or music, for amusement' and 'the glory of success' (16), while Gevrol, who 'was really an able man', is, like Dupin's foil Prefect G—, 'liable to be blinded by an incredible obstinacy' (9). Gevrol is also famous for his 'his audacity and coolness' in the face of danger (9), virtues clearly meant to recall those of Vidocq.

From the outset, we can guess who will get the better of whom in this contest to discover the murderer of the Widow Lerouge. Standing to the side, however, is a young 'aide-de-camp' to Gevrol, 'a jolly fellow, cunning, quick, and useful in his way, but secretly jealous of his chief, whose abilities he held in light estimation. He was named Lecoq' (10). While he had little to do in *L'Affaire Lerouge*, Lecoq ('The Rooster') was featured a year later in two novels, *Le Crime d'Orcival* (*The Mystery of Orcival*) and *Le Dossier 113* (*File 113*), and finished his public career in a two-book mystery, *Monsieur Lecoq* (1868) and *L'Honneur du Nom* (*The Honor of the Name*) (1869). Père Tabaret appeared again in these last two instalments as a consultant to Lecoq, but the focus of detective rivalry had meanwhile shifted to the relationship between Lecoq and

Gevrol, the brainy, ambitious youngster and the old-fashioned police veteran.

Gaboriau is justly renowned for his simultaneous invention of Lecoq and of the full-length novel of detection, and the far-reaching influence of Gaboriau's achievement is undeniable. Still, it is not hard to see that these books represent a stage of development in detection where the puzzle element, although playing a greater role than previously, has few opportunities to engage the reader's powers of inductive reasoning. Other, more traditional techniques of investigation tend to dominate Gaboriau's detective stories, which often lapse into historical fiction.

L'Affaire Lerouge, for example, begins with a locked-room mystery and several physical clues, but the solution to the case depends less upon Tabaret's vaunted 'method of induction' (223), which leads him to conclude that the primary suspect is innocent merely because he has no alibi (270–1), than upon several coincidences, not the least of which is that the real murderer happens to be a tenant of Tabaret's whose behaviour has recently made him suspicious. As for physical evidence, it turns out to have been planted on the innocent suspect by the murderer, making it worse than useless. If there is any lesson to be learned about detection in *L'Affaire Lerouge*, it is the same as in Godwin's *Caleb Williams*: don't trust material evidence.

In the Lecoq stories to come, Gaboriau pays more attention to inductive reasoning. *Monsieur Lecoq* begins with a showpiece of empirical inference when Lecoq, assigned by Gevrol to stand guard at the scene of a multiple murder, follows some footprints in the snow. 'This expanse of earth, covered with snow', he tells his subordinate (nicknamed 'Father Absinthe' for his addiction to that dangerous concoction), 'is an immense white page upon which the people we are in search of have written, not only their movements and their comings and goings, but their secret thoughts, the hopes and anxieties that agitated them' (38). Lecoq then performs an 'analysis' that earns the admiration of Father Absinthe (who likens him to Jesus Christ), but brings down the jealous fury of Gevrol, whose permission he should have sought before proceeding. 'These would be grave accusations against him', writes Gaboriau, 'in a profession where competition and rivalry are most potent' (20).

Since the main suspect in the murders, who goes by the false name 'May', is already under arrest, Lecoq's principal task now becomes determining May's true identity, and the focus of the book shifts from detection to interrogation. Gaboriau relished the battle of nerves and cunning that transpires in these scenes as much as he enjoyed devising feats of inference. However, all of Lecoq's enquiries eventually lead to dead ends. Humiliated before Gevrol and the entire department, he is forced to let May go, but not before arranging to follow him. The book then becomes a flight and pursuit tale, until May is tracked to the mansion of the Duc de Sairmeuse. Upon enquiry, Lecoq is told by the Duc that he has seen no one fitting May's description. Meanwhile, the suspect has vanished.

The book ends with Lecoq, in despair, consulting his old mentor Tabaret, who soon explains the mystery and affirms the conclusion that Lecoq has rejected as incredible: 'May' is the Duc de Sairmeuse. Tabaret can pull this inductive rabbit out of his hat, however, because he possesses information that neither Lecoq nor Gaboriau's readers could possibly know about Sairmeuse's family history, going back to pre-Revolutionary France. At this point, *Monsieur Lecoq* comes to an abrupt close.

The book-length conclusion to Gaboriau's mystery, *The Honor of the Name*, begins by taking the reader half a century back in time, to the years immediately following the Napoleonic Wars, when the father of the current Duc returned from exile to reclaim his ancestral lands. Not until Lecoq himself is finally apprised of these events near the end of this second volume will he know enough to bring charges against Sairmeuse, at which point the pursuit resumes. Long before then, however, the reader knows almost everything there is to know about 'whodunit', how, and why. What has begun as a promising two-volume epic of detection thus devolves, less than half-way through, into a historical romance of betrayal, revenge, and reaction in post-Napoleonic France.

Gaboriau's awkwardly interrupted narrative structure in these two books so impressed Arthur Conan Doyle that he imitated it in his first Sherlock Holmes novel, *A Study in Scarlet* (1887), much to the detriment of the story as a whole. It is not hard to see how unsuitable such a device is for a full-fledged story of detection, where the point is not just to delay the solution as long as possible but also to provide continuous clues and testimony that will incite the invention of multiple plot arrays in the reader's imagination. Gaboriau did, however, fortify the emerging genre of the *roman policier* with a much higher dose of inductive reasoning and weighing of testimony than ever before.

He also fleshed out two generic prototypes of detective heroes to come: the eccentric, leisured, and enthusiastic amateur, and the young, ambitious, and up-to-date professional. It was Doyle who would eventually combine the distinctive traits of Gaboriau's two detective types into one hybrid form: professional but eccentric, inductive but artistic, the public police detective's 'consulting' private investigator, Sherlock Holmes.

Professional and Amateur Science in England

Despite Lecoq's popularity in France, the puzzle-oriented story of detection did not come to dominate crime fiction there the way it eventually did in England and the English-speaking world in general. One impediment was the continuing popularity of the *feuilletons*. Another was the lack of urgency among middle-class French readers, compared to their English counterparts, regarding the impact of the new empirical methods of historical reconstruction on 'natural theology' and the literal interpretation of the Bible. In France, religion and science tended to go their separate ways.

Just three years after the publication of Poe's 'Murders in the Rue Morgue' there appeared in England an anonymous book of popular science called *Vestiges of the Natural History of Creation* (1844). It was written by Robert Chambers, editor with his brother of the highly successful reformist weekly, *Chambers' Edinburgh Journal*, which was later to serialize Russell's *Recollections of a Detective Police-Officer*. Founded in 1832 and helped along by a burgeoning railway distribution network and the new penny postal system, the *Journal* had achieved an impressive circulation by 1840, becoming one of the primary venues for utilitarian, 'improving' material directed at the educated lower-middle- and middle-class reader. The Chambers brothers espoused pragmatic, progressive, democratic values, and their targets were Christian Evangelicals and political radicals. The *Vestiges*, which represented a popularized account of all the scientific evidence thus far adduced for progressive cosmic evolution, offered England's new mass readership the first comprehensive theory to account for the historical record of that process. It was an immediate, and highly controversial, success.

Chambers's theory of evolution embraced not only the change and descent of species over time, but (drawing on the 'nebular hypothesis' of Laplace) the beginnings of the universe and the geological changes that had taken place on earth since its formation. It was founded on a belief that all of history and pre-history was driven by forces tending to progressive development at every level of creation – inanimate, animate, and intelligent. Anticipating a fundamentalist backlash against its materialistic, mechanistic outlook (the hallmark, in English eyes, of the materialism and atheism of French intellectuals dating from the Enlightenment), Chambers took the precaution of invoking, whenever possible, the idea that this progressive development of the cosmos was ordained and subjected to natural law by a divine First Cause, while denying the possibility of direct, miraculous intervention at any step along the way, including divine creation of new species and of human beings. *Vestiges* embraced the Uniformitarianism of Hutton and Lyell, declaring that the 'sublime chronology' for the emergence of organic life from inorganic matter and of 'higher' from 'lower' forms of life could not 'be presumed to be less than many hundreds of centuries old' (23).

Despite the fury it incited among Christian Evangelicals, *Vestiges* proved tremendously popular, going through ten editions in less than ten years, and twenty editions in the United States (Secord, 38). A decade and a half before the appearance of Charles Darwin's argument for evolution, *The Origin of Species* (1859), it was a fixture in every middle-class library and debated at nearly every social gathering. The most substantive opposition to Chambers's theories came, surprisingly, from the professional scientists whose work had in many cases provided the author with the basic materials of his evolutionary edifice.

While there was a great deal of unsupported speculation in *Vestiges*, mostly concerning the specific mechanisms by which species change had occurred, this was not what motivated the professional scientists to take issue with Chambers. Like the eminent geologists Adam Sedgwick at Cambridge and William Buckland at Oxford, many of them also happened to be clergymen. They were concerned that the *Vestiges* made so good a general case for a strictly materialistic theory of evolution that the happy synthesis of religion and science achieved by 'natural theology' over the previous century was now under threat, to the detriment of religious faith in general. Strategically, Sedgwick and Buckland chose as their targets not Chambers's theological but his scientific claims, which, as 'professional experts', they could plausibly represent as misinformed. But in successive editions of the *Vestiges*, Chambers (still writing anonymously) gave as good as he got, correcting minor details and conceding lesser points while showing their irrelevance to his larger views, and even citing his opponents' previous findings and opinions against them.

Describing these tactics, James Secord suggests that another battle was being waged in the war over *Vestiges* that had little to do with the origin of the universe. This was a battle for scientific authority in the public eye. Science had been the province of aristocratic patrons and collectors, middle-class men of leisure, and curious academics until the end of the eighteenth century. These groups found common forums for discussion and information in civic clubs and 'philosophical' societies, but unlike their counterparts in Germany, France, and even Scotland, English 'men of science' were, for the most part, not connected with formal government and university departments, academies, or bureaus until late in the nineteenth century. Even the prestigious Royal Society, founded in 1662, was principally a gentlemen's club for the first two hundred years of its existence, despite the outstanding accomplishments of academic members like Isaac Newton.

Following the Napoleonic Wars, these informal arrangements were proving unequal to the challenge posed by the quickening pace of research and specialization. By 1850, the provincial philosophical societies where amateur and professional scientists had mingled were practically defunct (Russell, *Science*, 179–81). At the same time, professional science organizations had begun to proliferate, and the two major universities in England, Oxford and Cambridge, had established chairs in specific fields, like Botany and Geology.

While amateur membership declined in specialist organizations devoted to increasingly difficult sciences such as chemistry, physics, and astronomy, a two-tiered system began to develop in natural history, including geology. There, amateurs in the field continued to serve as 'humble fact-collectors' for the 'grand synthesis compiled by those with time and skill to do so: the academics and professionals' (Russell, *Science*, 191). Drawing as it did on natural history, where non-professional contributors still played an active role, Chambers's *Vestiges* appeared to the new academic professionals as 'an attempt at grand speculation by an unrecognized amateur' (Yeo, 19) who didn't know his place. Along with the appearance of new public museums, lecture series, and mass-produced weeklies like the *Edinburgh Journal* itself, scientists feared that Chambers's unprofessional views would corrupt the minds and destroy the piety of an uninformed citizenry.

Meanwhile, during the 1850s and 1860s, that citizenry was busy working out these fundamental questions of material evidence, authoritative testimony, and historical reconstruction in their own minds, and feeling increasingly justified in doing so. Evolutionary theory, proper methods of reconstructing the past, and questions of origin – planetary, geological, biological, and human – came to dominate intellectual debate throughout Great Britain.

Into this debate stepped Charles Darwin. In 1859 his *The Origin of Species* provided the first detailed confirmation of Chambers's general plan of evolution from a scientist with extensive professional training and experience, although, significantly, without affiliation to an academic institution. In effect, Darwin was a scientific hybrid: an independent professional, not unlike his later counterpart in detection, Sherlock Holmes.

Today Darwin's reputation as an intellectual pioneer is secure, but it is important to recognize the extent to which his ideas of 'natural selection' and the 'survival of the fittest' through mutation and species competition, however scandalous to religious orthodoxy, fitted comfortably into his educated, middle-class readers' faith in the benefits of competition in the marketplace and on the international stage. By the time Darwin wrote *Origin* this faith was already firmly in place with respect to the rise and fall of businesses, nations, races, and civilizations, with credit redounding to wealthy factory owners, English imperialists, the white race, and the West in general.

While Darwin himself remained sceptical of evolutionary progressivism, his book gave added impetus to this generally self-congratulatory tendency among his English and American readers. In this new scientific and popular consensus, the inherent tendency of universal historical development was ever upward, northward, and westward, and the impact of that consensus on all forms of popular literature, including detective fiction, was clearly to perpetuate racial, ethnic, and gender stereotypes. Even after Darwin's specifically biological theories went into a temporary eclipse, the paradigm of the 'survival of the fittest' on which *Origin* was based only grew stronger in the public imagination, although the specific 'fitness' of the West to survive soon became an open question.

One of the most important and lasting effects of *The Origin of Species* was the profound change it made in people's general idea of the age of the earth. Writing at the end of the century, geologist Archibald Geikie voiced the reaction of his generation when he said that the *Origin* 'produced the greatest revolution in geological thought which has occurred in my time' (439). Chambers had suggested the earth was hundreds of centuries old. Darwin was implying millions of centuries, a period of time, he wrote, that 'impresses the mind almost in the same manner as does the vain endeavour to grapple with the idea of eternity' (*Origin*, 271).

Soon after the publication of Darwin's book, the biblical chronology became extinct in the minds of most educated Britons, as impossible to resurrect as the woolly mammoth. Following in the train of Laplace and his nebular hypothesis, Darwin had transformed the universe into a locked room extending infinitely, for all intents and purposes, in time as well as space. Its many miraculous windows and single door of divine origin could no longer excite speculation among the Dupins of the reconstructive sciences, as formerly among the natural theologians and theorists of the earth. Those metaphysical apertures in the physical Creation had now vanished from the collective historical imagination.

Some two decades were to elapse, however, before locked rooms and the puzzles they posed seriously began to haunt the imaginations of English detective fiction writers and their growing readership. Several factors were responsible for the delay, the most important being a lack of cultural urgency. The methodology of the new historical sciences had been so thoroughly vindicated that the public as yet felt little need to test it in their reading practices.

Sensation and Detection

With the possible exception of the police 'recollections' and 'memoirs' of the 1850s and 1860s, detective novels and stories remained largely submerged in other types of Victorian literature, such as the Newgate novel, the historical novel, and the Gothic tale, until the stunning success of Arthur Conan Doyle's Sherlock Holmes adventures late in the century. Meanwhile, detective fiction and fictional detectives, professional and amateur, reflected the currents of popular taste running through the pages of these still dominant genres.

The 'sensation novel' of the 1860s and 1870s was particularly fertile in such characters. As in the police casebooks and memoirs, sensation novelists preferred to display acts of induction and inference rather than encourage their readers to perform them. Their principal investigators, however, were more often amateur than official. Indeed, it could be argued that Esther Summerson is as much an amateur detective in the tradition of Ann Radcliffe's Gothic heroines, ferreting out the secret of her mysterious parentage in *Bleak House*, as Inspector Bucket is in the new genre of police adventure, carrying on the same investigation in an official capacity.

But while *Bleak House* may have anticipated the vogue for sensation, it was Dickens's close friend and younger admirer, Wilkie Collins (1824–89), who inaugurated that vogue in earnest with *The Woman in White*, which began appearing serially in 1859. Collins, who travelled frequently to Paris and was familiar with *feuilletoniste* crime writing, got the basic plot of his novel from a collection of 'true crime' tales he happened to pick up at a Left Bank bookseller's while on vacation.

The Woman in White tells the tale of three half-sisters, Anne Catherick, the woman of the title, Laura Fairlie, and Marian Halcombe. Anne has been secretly committed to an insane asylum by Sir Percival Glyde because she has threatened to betray the secret of his illegitimate birth, and Laura has become the object of Sir Percival's sinister marital attentions in order to secure her money. Laura marries Sir Percival but refuses to sign over her inheritance when making out her will. When Anne dies in confinement, Glyde, with the help of a superbly conceived Italian villain, the corpulent but charming Count Fosco, has her buried under Laura's name and commits Laura to the asylum as Anne, freeing him to claim the inheritance of the apparently now deceased 'Lady Glyde'. The plot is uncovered by the intrepid Marian and Laura's secret admirer, Walter Hartright, a drawing master originally in the employ of Laura's father. Hartright is rewarded for his efforts with the hand of Laura after Sir Percival is immolated in a fire while trying to alter his birth record.

The success of *The Woman in White* helped spawn similar Gothic-style mysteries set in modern-day England, including Dickens's *Great Expectations* (1860–1), Mrs Henry Wood's *East Lynne* (1861), Mary Elizabeth Braddon's *Lady Audley's Secret* (1862), and Sheridan Le Fanu's *Uncle Silas* (1865). It was to works like these that Margaret Oliphant applied the term 'sensation novel' in 1862, likening it to an infectious disease.

Accompanying the sensation craze, as Michael Wheeler points out, was a continuing rise in the popularity of the historical novel and the sentimental romance (102; see also Secord 78, 89). The former reflected sustained popular interest in fictional period-reconstructions that had begun with Walter Scott, while the latter lent itself to hybridizations with sensation tales in which the detective role settled upon the young admirer or fiancé of an imperilled heroine, as in the case of Collins's Hartright and Laura Fairlie. Braddon exploited this pattern over the length of two fat sensation novels, *Birds of Prey* (1867) and *Charlotte's Inheritance* (1868). Here the dissolute young card-sharper and confidence man Valentine Hawkehurst, one of 'the birds of prey' who 'thrive on the flesh and blood of hapless pigeons' (*Birds*, 65), abandons his aimless, predatory existence in order to save his beloved, the unwitting heiress Charlotte Halliday, from the murderous schemes of her step-father Philip Sheldon, a former dentist well schooled in the effects of arsenic and other poisons.

Braddon had borrowed liberally from *The Woman in White* for her earlier best-seller, *Lady Audley's Secret* (1862). Returning the favour, Collins drew on the figure of Hawkehurst for his portrait of the feckless, though hardly dissolute, amateur detective and rejected fiancé Franklin Blake, in his next work, *The Moonstone*.

The Many-Sidedness of *The Moonstone*

The modernist poet T. S. Eliot (1888–1965), a fan of detective fiction from childhood, pronounced *The Moonstone* 'the first and greatest of modern English detective novels' (377). Strictly speaking, the claim of priority is untrue, unless we alter it to read 'English novels of detection', for the puzzle element is foregrounded throughout Collins's book in a fashion unknown to casebook detective fiction. 'Greatest', too, is questionable. Many chapters are padded to ridicule a favourite *bête noire*, Evangelical Christianity topping the list. Worse, Collins does note 'play fair'. The solution to the mystery of the Moonstone's theft depends upon an intimate knowledge of the (supposed) effects of opium on consciousness and will that Collins apparently expected few of his readers to possess, since he had to introduce an expert to explain them near the end of his narrative.

By 1867, however, when *The Moonstone* began to appear in the pages of Dickens's *All the Year Round*, Collins himself was very familiar with the drug, having become addicted to it while trying to relieve the pains of gout. While his public may not have known as much as Collins about opium's effects on the mind, their alarm over its addictive properties had reached the point where a law was passed the next year restricting the sale of opium and other 'poisons'.

Previously, opium had been retailed over the counter by shop-keepers, tavern owners, and nearly anyone else with the resources to buy it wholesale. It was marketed in every conceivable form and for every conceivable ailment, and was so important a prop to trade and imperial policy in the Far East that England, whose colonial posses-sions included major poppy-seed producers like Afghanistan and India, had already gone to war twice with China to secure markets there. As Barry Milligan points out, the threat of opium addiction, barely recognized when De Quincey wrote his *Confessions* in 1821, had by mid-century become inextricably entwined in the English imagination with the vague threats to Western 'civilization' posed by an imperial China and a sullen, subjugated India. This culturally reinforced, composite popular attitude toward the East has come to be known as 'Orientalism' (Said).

Featuring prominently in the opium dreams De Quincey recorded, and influential in shaping European and American popular art and imperial policy well into the early twentieth century, Orientalism envisioned 'the East' as an indiscriminate swatch of geography extending from the Islamic world, beginning at the Straits of Gibraltar, through northern Africa to the Middle East, and thence through the Caucasus and Hindu Kush to Southern and Southeast Asia, ultimately including Tibet, China, and Japan. This 'Orient' remains very attractive to the Western imagination to this day, despite, or rather because of, its supposedly unenlightened backwardness.

Excessive in their attachment to sensual pleasure, given to effeminacy and torpor, yet subject to fits of irrational violence, 'Orientals' were thought to be ruled by sweeping passions and given to treacherous, inscrutable plots and acts of unimaginable cruelty. They were governed by despots and potentates – sultans, emperors, shoguns, rajahs – who were the ideal embodiments of absolute personal freedom especially prized by middle-class, white Western males. 'Orientalism' was thus conventionally Romantic in its obsession with personal power, 'happiness', and emotional and physical satisfactions, and it represented, like Romanticism, a reaction against the constraints on personal behaviour and thought that accompanied the Enlightenment's utopic promises of better living through rational thinking. This 'Orient' was and is, needless to say, a special place in the Euro-American collective imagination, not a region on the planet Earth.

Several events occurring in Britain's Eastern possessions had conspired to heighten Orientalist fears and fantasies by mid-century. In 1857, little more than a decade before Collins published *The Moonstone*, the Indian Sepoy Mutiny had exploded in anti-colonial violence, with many atrocities committed against English settlers by the rebellious 'Sepoys' or Indian enlisted men in the British Army, and many others committed in retribution by the English. Collins invokes this Oriental complex of fears and suspicions in the persons of three sinister Brahmin jugglers seeking to restore the Moonstone to its place in the forehead of their idol, the God of the Moon. However, he does so, as we shall see, in order to mount a critique of English imperialism, along with English materialism in general.

The Moonstone was based on several sources, including the recent discovery of an enormous Indian diamond, the Koh-i-noor, and the notorious 'Road Murder' of 1861, in which a girl named Constance

Kent was accused and acquitted of murdering her younger step-brother. (She later confessed.) The evidence in the case centred on the disposal of an incriminating nightgown and the substitution of a spotless facsimile, much as in Collins's tale.

In *The Moonstone* we find, for the first time, all the essential components of the classic novel of detection deployed in proper relation to each other. Early on, a crime is committed: the precious Moonstone diamond is stolen from the bedroom of Rachel Verinder, fiancée to Franklin Blake. The clues eventually point to one and only one criminal from among a small circle of initial suspects staying at the Verinder manor house the night of the theft, but first we are led to suspect an innocent housekeeper; next, the victim of the crime herself; and penultimately, an unwitting accomplice, Blake. The mystery is not completely solved until the end, and along the way numerous clues are supplied that force the reader to invent multiple retrospective arrays of events, to reject others, and to retrieve previously jettisoned arrays in the course of reading.

As for detectives, the reader has not one, but two fictional rivals to contend with: the official police detective, Sergeant Cuff, and the amorous amateur, Blake, who turns out, in true Oedipal fashion, to be both detective and (unconscious) criminal in one. (Ezra Jennings, a medical assistant who eventually provides the complete solution to the mystery, may qualify as a third investigator.) There is even an unofficial sidekick to the official detective in the person of the Verinders' head butler, Gabriel Betteredge, who finds it hard to overcome his 'detective fever' once Cuff arrives at the scene of the crime, even when the good name of Rachel, his employer's daughter, might be jeopardized as a result.

The narrative technique Collins used in *The Moonstone* received a trial run in *The Woman in White*, which was divided into several independent narratives, ostensibly collected and arranged by Hartright, that read like a series of affidavits and documents submitted in evidence for a trial. In *The Moonstone*, Blake takes charge of soliciting each eye-witness's contribution and supplying his own, and then assembling them into a single, consecutive narrative.

Blake's dual role as both investigator and instrument of the diamond's disappearance, which he stole from Rachel's bedroom while sleep-walking under the influence of opium, reflects the fragmented nature of his own youthful, unformed personality. This Collins is at pains to emphasize in Betteredge's early description of the 'many different sides to his character' that are apparent when Blake first appears at the Verinder mansion to attend Rachel's birthday party. In his pocket is the Moonstone he will later steal. It is a birthday gift he has been entrusted to deliver from the girl's evil uncle John Herncastle, who stole it himself from the Indian sultan, Tipoo, at the siege of Seringapatam in 1799.

Blake's personality is subject to 'sudden change', says Betteredge, 'puzzling shifts and transformations'; his 'colouring' is derived from the different nations he has passed through 'before there was time for any one colouring more than another to settle itself on him firmly' (47). After learning that the Moonstone is being sought by three sinister Indians, Blake is 'in twenty different minds about the Diamond' on the morning of Rachel's birthday (65). His general indecisiveness reflects the weakness of will that has left him unsettled in life, unsure of his attachment to Rachel, and addicted to nicotine. This addiction, in turn, or, rather, his state of mind when he attempts to break the habit, makes Blake highly susceptible to the effects of the opium Dr Candy slips into his drink as a prank. As we later learn from Dr Candy's assistant Ezra Jennings, suddenly giving up his cigars as he did at Rachel's urging had damaged Blake's nervous system to the point where he had no resistance to the influence of the drug (426).

Blake's many-sided character reflects Collins's interest in exploring what Poe called the detective's fragmented or 'Bi-Part Soul', and anticipates Freudian psychoanalytic theories of the unconscious. It is clearly analogous to the many-faceted character of the diamond he carries, which shows a different 'colouring' as it is turned in different directions, toward different persons. Like Blake, the Moonstone has travelled through many lands, and the major division in Blake's personality is analogous to the 'flaw' which lies deep 'in the very heart' of the Moonstone (41). This defect makes the gem's monetary value much less than that of the sum of its parts were it to be cut up into four or six 'perfect brilliants' (42). Removing the 'flaw' of indecisiveness in Franklin Blake would, similarly, make him a more integrated and 'valuable', if imaginatively diminished, suitor for Rachel. Single-minded in his life goals, Blake would then fit the Victorian ideal of husband and father as a steady, successful bread-winner.

Cutting up the Moonstone for gain and eliminating its distinctive 'flaw', however, would destroy its incalculable value as an object of religious veneration, which is how it is seen by its Hindu worshippers. In addition, the gem would lose its sentimental and erotic significance as a birthday gift brought to Rachel, at the risk of his life, by Franklin Blake himself, who soon afterwards proposes to her. Similarly, it is clear that Franklin, flawed as he may be, is precious to Rachel in terms that transcend his anticipated value as a source of marital income. She loves him for who he is, not for what he can earn.

Several critics, beginning with Charles Rycroft, have pointed out the seduction symbolism of Blake's nocturnal theft of Rachel's precious 'jewel', which provokes her wrath and indignation while enjoining her to shameful public silence. That the theft is the ultimate result of Blake's increased susceptibility to opium from his having given up his phallic cigars at Rachel's urging links it symbolically to some form of release after sexual self-denial. Apparently, the conscious, boyish 'side' of Blake is too immature to acknowledge the 'side' containing his repressed sexual feelings toward his fiancée, thus further contributing to his present unsuitability as a proper husband.

In narrative terms, the analogy between the many-sided Blake and the multi-faceted Moonstone implies that his own integrity as a mature adult depends on his successful integration of the many 'sides' of, or viewpoints on, the Moonstone case, 'sides' represented by the testimonial fragments over which he exerts final editorial control. The single coherent array of events that emerges from this integration of disparate narratives heals the predominantly 'Bi-Part' division between the detective hero's conscious will and his unconscious desires.

Blake first becomes aware of that unconscious 'side' when he opens the tin box in which Roseanna Spearman, Rachel's maid, has hidden an incriminating paint-stained nightgown with his name on it. He manages to integrate that hidden side of personality with his conscious self, becoming fit to marry Rachel and to father her children, only after he complies with Ezra Jennings's plan to have him re-enact the theft while under the influence of opium. As in the hypnotic 'talking cure' of Joseph Breuer that later inspired Sigmund Freud's psychoanalytic method for treating victims of hysteria, reintegration of the conscious and unconscious portions of the patient's psyche depends upon his being induced to revisit a repressed trauma and incorporate it in the conscious narrative of his waking life.

The integrated detective narrative of *The Moonstone* thus represents both the end-product and the sign of Blake's efforts at self-integration as he attempts to solve the mystery that has arisen from his initial state of self-division. His success, however, comes at the expense of his official counterpart, Sergeant Cuff, a most unprepossessing figure of authority:

> [A] grizzled, elderly man, so miserably lean that he looked as if he had not got an ounce of flesh on his bones in any part of him. He was dressed all

in decent black, with a white cravat round his neck. His face was as sharp as a hatchet, and the skin of it was as yellow and dry and withered as an autumn leaf. His eyes, of a steely light grey, had a very disconcerting trick, when they encountered your eyes, of looking as if they expected something more from you than you were aware of yourself. His walk was soft; his voice was melancholy; his long lanky fingers were hooked like claws. He might have been a parson, or an undertaker – or anything else you like, except what he really was. (107)

Cuff was based on the real-life police investigator of the Constance Kent affair, Inspector Whicher, whose colleague, Inspector Field, had served as Dickens's model for Bucket several years earlier. Cuff, however, is no Richmond, Bucket, or Hawkshaw, but a human vulture, or death itself. His claw-like fingers indicate tenacity and his expectant eyes and 'hatchet' face suggest a knack for piercing deeply into the souls of suspects.

Collins is not without sympathy and admiration for Cuff, however, and we are introduced to 'the first taste of his quality' when the question arises of finding the clothing the culprit was wearing when he inadvertently smeared some wet paint on Rachel's door. Seegrave, the local superintendent, dismisses the paint smear as 'a mere trifle', to which Cuff replies, like a true champion of inductive reasoning, 'In all my experience along the dirtiest ways of this dirty little world, I have never met with such a thing as a trifle yet' (110). Cuff's special knowledge of 'the dirtiest ways' of this 'dirty [. . .] world', far removed from the cultivated rose gardens of the Verinders and their friends, reveals an unflinching attitude toward human nature. It also enables him to recognize Roseanna Spearman, now a housemaid for Lady Verinder and hopelessly in love with Blake, as an ex-convict of former acquaintance.

But while Cuff's inductive penetration is stunning and rigorously professional, he turns out to be wrong about the culprit. He assumes that Rachel pretended to steal her own gem in order to pawn it to pay off her debts, and he further suspects her of having coerced the reformed thief Roseanna Spearman into helping her. His erroneous conclusions contradict the dependable stereotype of the 'casebook' police detective. It could well be that, as Ousby suggests (*Bloodhounds*, 130), the gradual decline in police prestige during the 1870s and 1880s was already showing itself in the characterization of Cuff. But Cuff does make three predictions that come true before he is taken off the case by Lady Verinder, and when he reappears he correctly guesses the name of the real culprit, Godfrey Ablewhite, who received the Moonstone from Blake while the young man was still under the memory-erasing influence of opium.

As John R. Reed argued in 1973, however, the true crime at the flawed heart of *The Moonstone* is not the theft of the gem from Rachel's bedroom but Colonel Herncastle's original act of robbery and murder at the Siege of Seringapatam. The novel opens with this scene and ends with the brief narrative of Murthwaite, an explorer and adventurer, who describes seeing the Moonstone restored to its original setting in the forehead of the moon god at Samnauth, in India. Thus, says Reed, the book's 'unacknowledged crime', British imperialism, is symbolically expiated only with the restoration of the pillaged Moonstone to its rightful 'owners', the Hindu faithful who sent out three Brahmins and several generations of their successors to retrieve it long ago, when it was first stolen by a Muslim caliph.

Early in *The Moonstone* we are made aware of the fact that, despite their sudden, sinister appearance in the Verinders' garden on the day of the gem's arrival, the three Brahmin jugglers could not have been responsible for the Moonstone's initial disappearance, since they had been summarily locked up in the local jail, without due process, when the theft took place. And although they appear at intervals throughout the story that follows, our only first-hand account of their behaviour shows them to be far different from the berserk assassins of the English Orientalizing imagination.

That sort of blood-thirsty Asiatic maniac was epitomized for Collins's readers by the rebellious Sepoys of 1857 and the Malays who 'run amuck' (2.236) in the opium dreams of De Quincey's *Confessions*, which had just been republished in a new expanded edition in 1856. A different picture of the Brahmins emerges when the lawyer, Bruff, describes his close encounter with the leader of the trio.

> If the Moonstone had been in my possession, this Oriental gentleman would have murdered me. [. . .] At the same time, and barring that slight drawback, I am bound to testify that he was the perfect model of a client. He might not have respected my life. But he did what none of my own countrymen had ever done, in all my experience of them – he respected my time. (310)

Despite their ruthlessness in pursuing the diamond, the three Brahmins display a degree of self-control in stark contrast to the distractions and addictive obsessions that seem to divide the personalities of Collins's English characters. Thus, Betteredge's bouts of 'detective fever' (337), along with his irrational attachment to *Robin-*

son Crusoe and his pipe, often get the better of his common sense. Miss Clack's Evangelical piety screens from her conscious awareness, 'in a kind of spiritual self-forgetfulness', the erotic desires stoking her 'pure, unearthly ecstasy' (326) when in the presence of her 'Christian hero', Ablewhite. Ablewhite's abject submission to an expensive mistress overwhelms his Christian principles and turns him into an embezzler and a thief.

As for Rachel and Franklin, how else are we to take their persistent infatuation with each other, despite all that has forced them apart, other than as a form of 'being under the influence'? Nearing England again after wandering the earth in order to forget Rachel's angry rejection of him for having presumably stolen her diamond, Franklin confesses, 'her influence began to recover its hold' (325). On their first meeting, 'slowly, as if acting under some influence independent of her own will', Rachel approaches him (379). Franklin in turn 'advance[s] towards her, hardly conscious of what [he is] doing' (383). When he takes her hand, it lies 'powerless and trembling' in his. 'I was her master still!' he says (383).

None of the Brahmins display such lack of self-control in pursuing their one object of desire. Moreover, despite English hysteria about Oriental opium-fiends, Collins's Indians show no interest in the drug, acting throughout the story with deliberation, energy, and utter selflessness. As Murthwaite, Collins's putative English expert on all things Oriental, points out, in crossing the sea to retrieve the Moonstone and in disguising themselves as jugglers, the Brahmins have 'doubly sacrificed their caste. [. . .] In the land they live in that is a tremendous sacrifice to make' (79).

It is 'tremendous' because in the Hindu religion one's caste determines the worldly condition into which one will be reborn after death. To lose one's life, according to this view, cannot compare in importance with losing one's caste: loss of life is temporary because rebirth is inevitable, but beginning one's spiritual ascent all over again, from the lowest animal life to the highest forms of enlightenment, could take thousands of years. 'The sacrifice of caste is a serious thing in India,' says Murthwaite. 'The sacrifice of life is nothing at all' (81). It is in this context that Murthwaite's otherwise incomprehensible approval of the Brahmins' ruthlessness in pursuit of the Moonstone must be interpreted. In reply to Betteredge's opinion 'that they were a set of murdering thieves', Murthwaite 'expressed *his* opinion that they were a wonderful people' (81).

Unlike Murthwaite's English compatriots, the Brahmins are devoted to something that altogether transcends human life and its petty concern with personal happiness, whether in the form of love, money, opium, or tobacco. To them, the Moonstone is neither a female ornament nor a source of ready cash, but the centre of their spiritual lives. It is only appropriate, then, that the Brahmins, and not Cuff or Blake, should impose final retribution on the real thief of the Moonstone, Godfrey Ablewhite, before taking the gem back to India.

The only exception to Collins's general indictment of the West's 'addiction' to happiness is the opium addict who solves the case and brings Franklin and Rachel together again, Dr Candy's assistant Ezra Jennings. If Murthwaite represents a culturally 'Orientalized' Westerner, the mixed-race Jennings represents his biologically 'Occidentalized' Asian counterpart. Collins's sympathetic portrayal of Jennings is clearly meant to challenge his readers' prejudices against 'Orientals'. The man's addiction to opium, far from encouraging him to lose control like the Egyptian and Asian characters in De Quincey's opium dreams, becomes the settled study of his life as a man of medicine. By means of that study he alone is able to unlock the mystery of Blake's unconscious role in the Moonstone's disappearance.

Wishing to redress, specifically, the Oriental stereotypes contained in De Quincey's just republished *Confessions*, Collins uses Jennings to reconceive the one Asian character in it that epitomized the Opium-Eater's Orientalist fears and went on to tyrannize over his dreams, a wandering Malay who appeared one day, out of the blue, at the door of De Quincey's rural cottage in the English Lake District. In fact, Jennings is a racially hybridized version of De Quincey and the Malay. He has not only read the *Confessions* and enthusiastically recommended it to Blake (434–5), but he specifically resembles the English 'Opium-Eater' in several particulars. First, like De Quincey, he is a newcomer in the village where he resides; second, he became addicted only after using the drug to relieve physical pain; third, he is tormented by memories of a lost beloved; fourth, he keeps a journal of his experiences with the drug; and last, he is working on a major scientific work that he will never finish.

Jennings's combined Western and Eastern features represent not only the combined identities of the English 'Opium-Eater' and the Malay who haunted his dreams, but other hybrids as well. His piebald black and white hair suggests he is both young and old, and he confesses, at one point, to having a 'female constitution' (414). In short, Jennings is a figure of reconciliation and healing: between generations, between genders, between races and nations, ultimately between the sundered halves of each individual's 'Bi-Part Soul'.

Indeed, it is only because Jennings specifically informs Blake of his re-enactment of the theft of the diamond while again under the influence of opium that Blake can become conscious of what he has done, and how he has done it. In this sense, Jennings functions almost as an integral part of Blake's own psyche.

Jennings, like Blake, has been mastered by opium, but unlike Blake, he has an intimate knowledge of his master. He cannot overcome his addiction to it, but he can resist its power to destroy his will and help others do likewise. If, as De Quincey says of his own *Confessions*, 'Not the opium-eater, but the opium, is the true hero of the tale' (2.74), the opposite obtains in Collins's story of detection as self-detection. Here, the Orientalized opium-eater is the true detective hero, and opium the criminal 'master' of 'mind' whose divisive effect on Western consciousness, like that of all the addictions to happiness we find least acceptable in ourselves, the detective has committed himself to undo.

From Drood to Dr Watson

The Moonstone went on to influence crime fiction for many years. It did not, however, inaugurate a vogue for detection. Its most immediate impact was felt by Collins's friend Charles Dickens, who probed more deeply into the self-alienating effects of opium in *The Mystery of Edwin Drood* (1870). The principal mystery of this book is how it ends, since Dickens died while writing it, and a veritable sub-sub-genre of completed *Droods* has arisen since, some more plausible than others. Despite many theories to the contrary, however, it seems clear that the 'mystery' of Drood's disappearance was to be a murder mystery; that the murderer would turn out to be his uncle, the choirmaster John Jasper, who is an opium addict; that Jasper's motive would be jealousy over Drood's fiancée, Rosa Bud; and that the self-divisive effects of Jasper's opium habit would play a role in lowering his resistance to temptation and impair his ability to recall, when sober, what he had done while intoxicated.

This we can gather not only from what Dickens had finished before he died but also from the notes he left behind: for example 'Jasper lays his ground' (287), 'Smoothing the Way – That is, for Jasper's plan', and 'Lay the ground for the manner of the murder, to come out at last' (289). Someone who behaves very much like a detective, Dick Datchery, appears to conduct an investigation into Jasper's background and behaviour, but not much remains for him to discover that we don't already know or can't already guess. *Drood* was not intended to be a detective story, but rather another contribution to the sensation craze.

While Collins's innovative novel did not spark the creation of a distinct genre of detection, it is too much to imply, as Julian Symons does in one chapter title of *Bloody Murder*, that the ensuing decade and a half constituted an 'Interregnum', since there was no 'reign' of detection to be interrupted. Detecting continued to be displayed more often than provoked, as in the reworking of Collins's *Moonstone* plot in *The Eustace Diamonds* (1872), by Anthony Trollope (1815–82), and official detectives continued to give way to amateurs, or dwindled to the proportions of ordinary mortals. As Ousby (*Bloodhounds*) and Jeffers note, this dwindling was in part the result of a decline in the reputation of the official police and of Scotland Yard.

Ronald Thomas has described the impact on literary detection of the impressive gains made in the criminal science of forensics at about this time, which were intended to help 'control the potentially anarchic forces of democratic reform, urban growth, national expansion, and imperial engagement' (4). Nonetheless, after 1870 the competence, and even the integrity, of the London police became increasingly suspect. During the late 1860s, labourers rioted in Hyde Park for an extended franchise and Irish nationalists began a prolonged campaign of public disruption with the bombing of Clerkenwell Prison. Several well-publicized, unsolved murders occurred in the early years of the next decade, and a major corruption scandal led to the complete reorganization of Scotland Yard in 1878. Two years later another scandal arose involving an undercover sting operation against abortionists. This series of mishaps was crowned by the Jack the Ripper murders of 1888, which panicked the nation.

The public was not reassured by the failed efforts of its official police investigators, and forerunners of the bumbling, bureaucratic police detectives of the early Holmes stories began to appear in crime fiction. The height of cynicism appeared early on with the character of Paul Davies, a corrupt ex-detective featured in Sheridan Le Fanu's *Checkmate* (1870). Although Lecoq remained as popular as ever in translation, he seems to have had little impact on England's rising antipathy to its own detective officers.

Nonetheless, while gifted amateurs like Valeria Brinton in Collins's *The Law and the Lady* (1875) vied for attention with officials like Trollope's Inspector Bunfit and Major Mackintosh, and detection in general took a back seat to suspense, stories featuring detectives and detecting can hardly be said to have faded away in the 1870s. This was especially true in the United States, where detective figures became a staple of the 'dime novels' geared to lower-class audiences, and the first continuing detective in this genre, 'Old Sleuth', debuted in 1872 (Hoppenstand, 1). Soon afterwards, in 1874, Allan Pinkerton, head of the Pinkerton Detective agency, hired a ghost-writer to inaugurate his series of purportedly real-life detective novels with *The Expressman and the Detective*. Each of Pinkerton's books displayed an open eye embossed on the cover and the Pinkerton agency's motto, 'We Never Sleep', which eventually gave rise to the common term for a hired investigator, 'private eye'.

One formal difficulty in maintaining the success of *The Moonstone* style of fictional detection was the demanding length of most nine-teenth-century novels, whether published in periodical series or in full three-volume format. From the late 1870s onward, however, we find puzzle plots making headway in short stories such as Richard Dowling's 'The Going Out of Alessandro Pozzone' (1878). Part of the reason for the rise in popularity of short stories was the spread of the British urban commuter railway, which had begun to create a market for shorter entertainment in transit. With the construction of bedroom communities in the suburbs of London and other major cities during the 1880s and 1890s, short stories suitable to the dura-tion of a ride to and from the city began to replace serialized novels in the weekly magazines, providing fertile ground for the detective short story.

In America, meanwhile, Anna Katherine Green (1846–1935) pub-lished her first detective novel, *The Leavenworth Case* (1878) in a compact, single-volume format, thereby staking her claim to recog-nition as 'The Mother of Detective Fiction'.

Green has, in general, been denigrated by historians of detective fiction (see, e.g., Symons, *Bloody*, 62; Messac 578). Only Alma Murch appreciated the significance of her accomplishment, affirming that in no earlier novelist 'does the detective theme monopolize the reader's attention so completely' (159). In *The Leavenworth Case* this theme shapes the very layout of the book, beginning with section one, 'The Problem', and ending with section four, 'The Problem Solved'.

The novel opens with the discovery of the body of the wealthy patriarch of the Leavenworth family, shot through the head in the library of his stately New York City mansion. There is an initial inves-tigation by the official police detective, Ebenezer Gryce, and his amateur assistant, Mr Raymond, followed by an inquest filled with ballistic evidence and expert testimony. Material clues abound. The two Leavenworth daughters are suspected, and several other suspects soon join them, keeping our analeptic imaginations in vigorous play.

The murder takes place not only in a locked room, but in a locked house, and Green even provides a floor plan of the murder scene. Unlike Cuff, Gryce gets his man, and goes on to appear in several more of Green's books.

Anyone finishing the first chapter of *The Leavenworth Case* who is even slightly acquainted with the murder mysteries of Agatha Christie half a century later will not be surprised to learn that the queen of Golden Age detection had read and admired Green's novels since her youth.

The single-volume format first appeared in England with George Manville Fenn's *The Dark House* (1885), and might help to explain the popularity of Fergus Hume's Melbourne-sited *Mystery of a Hansom Cab* in 1886, something Symons finds 'a curiosity' (*Bloody*, 60). Just one year later Doyle's *Study in Scarlet* was published for all intents and purposes in a short novella format as well, appearing complete in *Beeton's Christmas Annual*. These developments accompanied the increasing popularity of the short-story form, which in turn helped advance the fortunes of the tall, lean private detective featured in *A Study in Scarlet*. His short, episodic adventures, faithfully recorded by his roommate, a retired army physician named Watson, began appearing in the new *Strand Magazine* just four years later.

One curious piece of evidence for the steady rise in the demand for detective fiction and stories of detection during the 1880s is a phenomenon that Murch takes to indicate a decline: parodies (143–5). Ridicule fails if its object is obscure. Stories like T. B. Aldrich's *The Stillwater Tragedy* (1880) and Robert Louis Stevenson's *The Wrong Box* (1888), while disrespectful of their targets, at least assume that those targets are visible to the public eye.

Yet despite the steady market for stories, shorter novels, and burlesques featuring detective figures, the number of writers who engaged their readers directly in acts of induction or imaginative reconstructions of events was still relatively small. Several forces had to come into play before the public began to demand such an engagement in appreciable numbers. Ironically, one of the most important factors was a loss of faith among scientific professionals in the teleological foundations of historical reconstruction itself. History was beginning to lose its aura of purpose and direction.

Casebook Entry No. 2
The Scientific Detective's Bohemian Soul

The Book of Life

In the decade or so leading up to the appearance of Arthur Conan Doyle's first Holmes story, important changes were taking place in the progressive interpretation of historical change based on Darwinian theory.

While the concept of 'natural selection' had seemed to reinforce the optimistic, forward-looking attitudes of his era, Darwin had opposed such readings of *Origin*. The very word 'selection', however, demonstrates how difficult it was for him to expunge intentionality from the evolutionary process he described. As Gillian Beer points out, in the first edition of *Origin* Darwin often represented Nature and 'natural selection' as active agents in evolution, not as impersonal processes (68).

While he tried to eradicate such tendencies from subsequent editions, some popularizers of Darwin's work not only ignored these efforts but, surprisingly, even began to read the teleology of human evolution in a retrogressive sense. Given the implicit model of individual birth, growth, and maturity used to talk about the appearance and evolution of entire species, this gloomy reading of evolution was almost inevitable: once a species had reached 'maturity', what was left except senescence and, ultimately, extinction in the face of new species 'fitter' to survive? Fears soon grew 'that decadence may be an energy as strong as development, and extinction a fate more probable than progress' (Beer, 145).

Victorians were also increasingly dismayed by the apparent randomness of the processes that Darwin described. The pervasive role of chance in species mutation and survival emphasized the contingent nature of causality in the history of the universe as a whole, a point of view inimical not only to 'natural theology' but also to its secularized, 'progressive' descendants. This challenge to the notion of a governing *telos* or intentionality directing the course of nature had been prepared for, as we have seen, by the increasing discrepancy between the divine 'testimony' of the Bible and the physical 'clues' to history and pre-history apparent in the surviving forms of nature itself. A more proximate cause of growing teleological scepticism, according to Lawrence Frank, was the lingering influence of the 'nebular hypothesis' of Laplace that had shaped the opening chapters of Robert Chambers's *Vestiges*.

Frank has traced the impact of the nebular hypothesis on the detective and mystery fiction of Poe, Dickens, and Doyle, and concludes that, along with the fragmentary and gap-riddled nature of the evidence upon which Darwin founded his theory of evolution, Laplace's hypothesis caused both writers and readers of detective fiction to question the plausibility of narrative reconstruction as a mode of scientific inquiry. In the detective stories of these three writers in particular, says Frank, we see how 'the historical imagination and the reconstructive disciplines [. . .] work with ambiguous evidence from the past to satisfy the desires of an interpreter in the present', resulting in the 'subversion of the historical imagination' (54).

While there is some truth to Frank's claims, detective fiction's principal reaction to teleological scepticism was, if anything, compensatory rather than imitative. This was true even as late as Arthur Conan Doyle's *The Hound of the Baskervilles* (1901), which Frank cites as an example of how 'fictional detection offers no satisfactory resolutions to the mysteries' (202) confronting Holmes, whose 'solutions' are, in the end, little more than provisional. In the standard detective story, says Frank, final ratification of the detective's solution comes only with the criminal's confession or acquiescence in the detective's summary of the crime. In *Hound*, however, the purported criminal, John Stapleton, disappears into the quicksand of the Grimpen Mire before he can be arrested and is thus 'not available to confirm Holmes's account' (205).

This is literally true and may prevent a complete understanding of Stapleton's motives, although they are not entirely a mystery. But Stapleton's disappearance is irrelevant to the problem of ascertaining his responsibility for the murder of Charles Baskerville, or to any of the other basic facts of the case. The ratification Frank considers 'unavailable' appears in the testimony of Stapleton's wife and in the material evidence, beginning with the carcass of the gigantic hound lying at the feet of Holmes and Watson with five bullets in it, its muzzle glowing, not with the fires of hell, but with the luminescent blue phosphorous paint found in Stapleton's hide-out in the Grimpen Mire (131–2). In addition, we have the shed where Stapleton kept the beast for use at short notice and the bones of the animals it ate.

Of course, this is largely circumstantial evidence, but the point of the Holmes stories in general is to excite in the minds of Doyle's readers that inductive activity by which narratives can in fact be constructed out of such evidence. Whether or not these narratives are confirmed by a criminal confession is beside the point, which is simply to give readers an opportunity to invent as many as they can until they arrive at one that will fit the detective's final explanation.

Frank wants to argue in general that Doyle's stories 'reflect a Darwinian world view that rejects teleological speculations, even as it finds purpose and meaning everywhere in the great chain of life' (143). But the 'purpose and meaning' that Holmes discovers in that 'great chain' are not devoid of 'teleological' intentions, only of divine ones. Every mystery in 'The Book of Life', as Holmes has entitled his essay on the enigmas of the everyday world in his first adventure, *A Study in Scarlet* (14), has a teleological explanation, for it has arisen from the actions of a human being. What Doyle offers his readers in the Sherlock Holmes stories is a carefully supervised metonymic exercise in reading intentionality, if only on a finite scale, back *into* a universe from which the Deity, along with its omnipresent but inscrutable supervisory intentions, has at last been securely locked *out*.

Frank is not the first to link the Roman Catholic Doyle's crisis of faith as a medical student with the Darwinism and scientific materialism evident in the Holmes tales (see, e.g., Carr, 35–6). Having doubted the teachings of the Church from his teenage years, says Doyle in *Memories and Adventures*, his exposure to Darwin and similar scientists and philosophers while studying at the University of Edinburgh from 1876 to 1881 destroyed the foundations of his Christian faith altogether (31). Nonetheless, Doyle considered himself an agnostic, not an atheist, and retained 'a very keen perception of the wonderful poise of the universe and the tremendous power of conception and sustenance which it implied' (32). He still found intelligent design in the anonymous 'Book of Life', even if he could not fathom its purpose or direction.

Doyle was born in Edinburgh in 1859, the year Darwin's *Origin* was published, to an artistic Irish Catholic father and a strong-willed, independent-minded, and well-read mother. He grew up big, strong, adventurous, and athletic, with a sanguine temperament, a strong sense of loyalty to family, friends, and country, and a constitutional aversion to being told what to think. His years in medical school coincided with profound changes taking place not only in scientific ideas of the history of the inorganic universe and of organic life, but in people's attitudes toward the professions and professionalism, especially in the sciences and related fields like medicine.

For one thing, the definition of the 'professions' was changing. At the beginning of the century, only four categories were legally recognized: the clergy, the military, medicine, and law (Russell, *Science*, 221). The situation was very different by the end of the 1860s, according to James Secord, as 'the supply of genteel blood in the sciences' failed to keep pace with new jobs opening up in government and industry. For ambitious young men with a scientific education opportunity beckoned. Soon there arose a 'scientific bohemia' of young male professionals looking for secure positions and circulating in a 'bohemian world of pubs, clubs, and masculine comradery' (473).

This 'new generation of careerists' largely ignored the theological implications of their work. For them, science was 'the province of a paid elite independent of the mass audience' and its pious conservatism, 'a new kind of intellectual aristocracy' based on 'expertise' (Secord, 478) rather than social connections or adherence to conventional notions of religious or moral propriety. By the 1880s, the genre of detection was similarly ready for the introduction of a professional 'scientific' detective not afraid to defy convention.

Arthur Conan Doyle, by his own admission, participated in the 'bohemianism' of outlook and life-style that characterized his generation of scientists and physicians. Indeed, with his anti-religious views, he soon become 'too bohemian' for his Catholic relatives and they, as he put it, 'too conventional for me' (*Memories*, 27). During his summer vacations from medical school he indulged his itch to wander the globe, travelling as ship's doctor on an Arctic whaler one season and on a West African steamship another. After a severe bout of malaria during this last trip, however, he gave up the roving life and took up private practice. Still, he said, his 'bohemian habits' (71) were hard to break, even after his marriage in 1885.

Stifled by the day-to-day routine of his medical practice, Doyle's bohemianism found an outlet in a second profession, writing. Indeed, writing soon competed seriously with medicine for his time. While

Doyle devoted himself mainly to historical romances like *Micah Clarke* (1889) and *The White Company* (1890), he tried his hand at a variety of genres. The fondness for historical reconstruction on display in his 'serious' novels must have found partial satisfaction in the challenges posed by the carefully plotted inductive puzzles essential to the literature of detection.

An admirer of Edgar Allan Poe, Émile Gaboriau, and Wilkie Collins from an early age, Doyle began his first detective story in 1886. In draft it featured a hawk-featured sleuth named 'Sherrinford Holmes', whose uncanny ability to decipher the personal and professional histories of ordinary citizens from clues of dress and anatomy was based on the bravura diagnostic demonstrations of Doyle's teacher at the University of Edinburgh, Dr Joseph Bell. To narrate his hero's adventures, Doyle, like Poe, invented a sidekick, 'Ormond Sacker'. The result, *A Study in Scarlet*, was published in *Beeton's Christmas Annual* at the end of 1887, with the names of the protagonists changed to 'Sherlock Holmes' and 'John H. Watson, M.D.'.

While Doyle's biographers never tire of pointing out that his first Sherlock Holmes adventure 'remained largely unnoticed' (Symons, *Conan*, 13–15) because its press run was small and reviews were few, *Beeton's* publisher, Ward, Lock & Co., reprinted *A Study in Scarlet* as a separate book the very next summer, whereupon it sold out and went into still another edition before the end of the year. Moreover, it was this story that inspired Joseph Stoddard, managing editor of the American publishing house Lippincott, to commission Doyle's next Holmes novelette, *The Sign of the Four* (known ever afterwards by its British title, *The Sign of Four*), which appeared in *Lippincott's Monthly Magazine* in 1890.

Along with *A Study in Scarlet* and Doyle's two historical novels, *The Sign of Four* helped to create a coterie of 'admirers' (Hardwick, 37). On the strength of this growing reputation Doyle hired an agent, A. P. Watt, who promptly got *The Sign of Four* serialized in George Newnes's *Tit-Bits*, a popular weekly of news extracts and entertainment with a wide circulation. It was Newnes, in turn, who gave Doyle his big break by offering him £200 for his first series of six Holmes short stories. These were to be featured in a new magazine, *The Strand*, beginning with 'A Scandal in Bohemia' in July 1891. Holmes and *The Strand* both took off from that point, intertwining their meteoric paths for the next two decades. Soon after signing his contract with Newnes, Doyle gave up his medical practice for good.

That Doyle's first two Holmes stories both sold out their press runs and were promptly reprinted indicates that the young physician was clearly on to something, and readers were responding. All he needed was publicity, and *The Strand*, with its sizeable circulation among middle-class families and suburban railroad commuters, was the perfect venue.

The remarkable fit between Newnes's periodical and Doyle's content was no accident. *The Strand* refused to publish serialized features. Each number was a self-contained collection of biographies, news, short fiction, domestic pieces, and children's stories. Taking a hint from Poe, Doyle deliberately set out to create a series of exciting stories featuring a single, continuing character that 'would bind [the] reader' to the magazine without discouraging him or her from buying future numbers if an instalment happened to be missed (*Memories*, 95–6). Holmes's compelling personality not only suited Doyle's purposes, but the detective already had a following among readers of Newnes's former magazine, *Tit-Bits*, where *The Sign of Four* had made its British début.

Having opted for a series detective hero, Doyle was now committed to devising a certain kind of plot. Fortunately, the short story format imposed by *The Strand* ensured efficiency in construction, keeping the reader's attention focused on the mystery at hand and providing a quick pay-off. But Doyle saw from the beginning that something besides mystery and suspense *per se* was needed to write a good detective plot. As he later put it, 'The first thing is to get your idea. Having got that key idea one's next task is to conceal it and lay emphasis upon everything which can make for a different explanation. Holmes, however, can see all the fallacies of the alternatives, and arrives more or less dramatically at the true solution by steps which he can describe and justify' (*Memories*, 106–7).

Doyle was the first writer of detective fiction to conceive the plot of detection specifically in this way, as a device for uncovering a hidden narrative 'idea' through the imaginative projection of analeptic arrays invoked by 'lay[ing] emphasis on everything' suggesting 'alternative' explanations. Only one of these, the one arrived at by the detective, would turn out to be correct. The rest would be 'fallacies' (or 'red herrings'). This uncovering, he implies, must proceed in 'steps' and be 'justif[ied]' in light of the clues and testimony made available in the course of the narrative. While it is possible to fault his execution of this aim in any number of stories, Doyle established a pattern of consistently foregrounding the puzzle element for all the literature of detection to follow, down to the present day.

The Mystery of Holmes, the Use of Watson

The most common criticism of Doyle's use of the puzzle element is that crucial evidence or special information known only to Holmes is often withheld from Watson and, thereby, from the reader. For this reason, Martin Kayman calls Holmes's claims to method 'fraudulent' (216), 'a false democratic promise' suggesting that inductive ability is available to everyone.

In fact, says Kayman, 'what is at issue is the power of accumulated knowledge of individual criminals and of criminal London', 'specialized training', and hidden information, not skills in common (220). Holmes thus became 'the site [. . .] for mastery itself' (221), something to admire rather than imitate. His infallible demonstrations of 'empiricist' skill, says Jon Thompson, helped to reassure the middle classes benefiting most from the capitalist system that 'abstract quantification, domination, and use of resources, human or natural, in the name of progress or profit' (66) were not only rational but right, especially when it came to exploiting labourers at home and colonized peoples abroad. In creating Holmes, says Thompson, Doyle became 'one of the great apologists of empire' (68).

Doyle's middle-class and imperialist attitudes would be difficult to deny. He was a strong supporter of Queen and country and a firm believer in the value of hard work and self-made opportunities. But his representations of profit and of empire, far from 'push[ing] to the margins almost every potentially disruptive subject imaginable – racism, imperialism, class conflict, even women', as Thompson claims, brought these topics into the immediate, personal orbit of everyday late-Victorian men and women. As we shall see, the outcomes of his characters' direct engagements with these 'disruptive subjects' are not as predictable as critics like Thompson assume, nor is the obvious moral of the Holmes stories, when there is one, invariably simple and self-congratulatory. Finally, the point of these tales, as of the Golden Age fiction to which they eventually gave birth, is not to ensure that the reader will always reach the correct solution on his or her own, but to incite him or her to make the attempt.

Let us start with the question of special or withheld knowledge, and begin at the beginning.

In *A Study in Scarlet* Doyle's most glaring omission is the information Holmes obtains from the Cleveland police after telegraphing to ask about the married status of the murder victim, Enoch Drebber. Specifically, he is told that Drebber had asked for protection from a rival in love named Jefferson Hope and that this rival was now in Europe (102). Other withheld evidence includes the narrow gauge of the wheel tracks in the street, indicating the presence of a cab at the murder scene, and their wandering character, which showed that the driver had left the cab at the kerb for a few minutes (100, 102); previous cases of forced poisonings in Holmes's files and the contrasting *modus operandi* of political assassinations, which this forced poisoning superficially resembles (101); and the correlation of the bloody trail at the scene with the track of the murderer's shoes, which confirmed Holmes's hypothesis that this blood was the assailant's (101–2).

Examining the story carefully up to the end of Part One, when Holmes springs his trap on the murderer, Jefferson Hope, we discover that some of this information is already embedded in the partial conclusions Holmes has announced immediately after examining the evidence at the scene of the crime.

For instance, a process of elimination indicates that the blood found near the unwounded victim must have come, as Holmes states, from the murderer (there are only two sets of footprints in the dusty unoccupied house and one matches the shoes of the victim). We don't need to track the blood around the room to arrive at this conclusion (27). Much of the rest of the evidence is to be inferred from the way Holmes behaves and the questions he poses at the scene of the crime. Thus, the first thing he asks Inspector Gregson upon arriving at 3 Lauriston Gardens and inspecting the roadway in front of the house is, 'You did not come here in a cab?' and the second, 'Nor Lestrade?', referring to Gregson's fellow investigator (22). Clearly, we are to infer that Holmes found wheel tracks in the road indicating, in some way, the presence of a cab rather than of a private carriage. Our next question should be, not 'How did Holmes know this was a cab?' but 'Where was the cab-driver while the murder was being committed?'

In short, much of the mystery we are invited to solve in *A Study in Scarlet*, as in nearly every other Holmes story, concerns the nature of what Holmes himself is thinking at any given moment. Using Watson to control our access to the material evidence of the case, although it enables Doyle to pace and direct the reader's invention of imaginative arrays at each step in the unfolding of his narrative, does occasionally lead to the withholding of direct evidence for the sake of suspense: not only does the good doctor often 'see' without 'observ[ing]', as Holmes puts it in *The Sign of Four* (1890) (211), but at times he doesn't even see what there is to observe. In nearly every instance of this kind, however, Doyle takes pains to have Watson describe how Holmes behaves and what he says while in the process of investigating. The mystery we are to solve thus depends in part on our solution of the mystery of Holmes himself, the supreme master at deciphering others' thoughts, motives, and identities from signs of dress, anatomy, and behaviour.

In short, while Holmes may be 'a site [. . .] for mastery itself', as Kayman contends, he is not there just to be admired. That may have been true of predecessors like Richmond, Vidocq, Waters, and Inspector Bucket. Holmes is also there to pose a challenge to the reader – to be deciphered, anticipated, and, if possible, bested. He is there as our opponent and rival, to give our reconstructive imaginations a thorough work-out, and this, above all, constitutes his creator's greatest contribution to the detective tradition Holmes did so much to revitalize and refashion.

Doyle made these aims known at the very beginning of the Holmes saga, starting with the title of the first chapter of *A Study in Scarlet*, 'Mr Sherlock Holmes'. Before encountering that human enigma, however, we are presented with another that is somewhat easier to penetrate, if no less difficult to appreciate fully in light of Doyle's disingenuous workmanship: 'John H. Watson, M.D.'.

Few scholars of the Holmes canon appreciate the strokes of genius evident in Doyle's creation of Watson, whose name appears as author of the 'Reminiscences' we are about to read. He borrowed the concept of the sidekick narrator from Poe, of course, but made it serve more specific narrative and thematic purposes. These were deliberate from the first, as he implies in *Memories and Adventures*, where he indicates his early realization of the need for 'a commonplace comrade as a foil – an educated man of action who could both join in the exploits and narrate them' (75). But in order to be in a plausible position to narrate them, Doyle's 'man of action' would have to be sedentary enough to spend a good deal of time writing up the 'exploits' in which he participated. He would also have to be living in close proximity to the detective protagonist to whom he was to serve as, in effect, a 'Boswell', as Holmes himself puts it ('Scandal', 213), alluding to James Boswell (1740–95), biographer of the eighteenth-century essayist and lexicographer, Samuel Johnson (1709–84).

In short, while Doyle's narrator was partly to serve as a 'foil' to set off the detective's eccentric genius, he had to have enough in common with the hero to make a plausible long-term companion. Moreover, the narrator would have to be someone inherently trustworthy in the eyes of Doyle's readers, since all the fun of the game of detection in which the author was inviting them to participate depended crucially on their unquestioning acceptance of his narrator's candour and reliability.

Consider how Doyle solved these problems. First, he made his narrator a veteran of the Afghan war, patriotic defender of Crown and Empire and a wounded one at that. Second, he made him a doctor, one of the most respected and trusted of professionals, a compassionate healer of the sick and, by the end of the century, a member of a highly scientific confraternity. This last qualification, particularly with its diagnostic emphasis, makes Watson a natural choice of roommate for the superlatively 'scientific' detective whom Doyle has in mind, as does the good doctor's deracinated, bohemian tendencies, which the author is at pains to stress in these early tales, along with those of his protagonist.

Watson's bohemianism is partly a consequence of his war-related disability (a bullet in his shoulder, according to *A Study in Scarlet*, and in his leg, according to *The Sign of Four*), which serves several other purposes as well. First, it prevents him from reassuming his professional duties upon returning home. Having 'neither kith nor kin in England', Watson thereby becomes, in his own words, one of the 'loungers and idlers of the Empire' draining into the 'great cesspool' of London (*Study*, 4) at its centre.

Doyle seems to have conceived Watson as a displaced and even disillusioned veteran now living in the shadowy margins of respectable, middle-class society. This would make him a tepid forerunner to the embittered anti-heroes of World War I found in the fiction of American writer Ernest Hemingway (1899–1961), such as Harold Krebs in 'Soldier's Home', a story from *In Our Time* (1925), and Jake Barnes of *The Sun Also Rises* (1926). Like them, Watson leads a 'comfortless, meaningless existence' after his discharge, spending his pension money at an 'alarming' rate and drinking the day away at the Criterion Bar. So isolated is he in 'the great wilderness of London' that even 'young Stamford', a junior acquaintance from his medical school days who 'had never been a particular crony', is hailed 'with enthusiasm' (4).

Despite their differences in temperament – Watson is sentimental and affectionate, Holmes the epitome of cold, clear reason – the disabled doctor's 'idle' life-style makes him a particularly suitable companion for Holmes, to whom Stamford introduces him as a prospective flatmate. Watson's limitless free time, respectably earned by personal sacrifice, can now be spent with and on Holmes. Sharing the great man's living and professional quarters (their common room is Holmes's consulting room) gives him ample opportunity to do so. Most important, however, is the perfect fit that Doyle has conceived between the two men's interests and needs at this particular juncture of their lives. For into the ex-professional Watson's 'meaningless' and uprooted existence there comes a man just starting out on his professional career, one to whom every detail of life is as meaningful as if it had appeared in a book, specifically, 'The Book of Life' (14).

Watson's disparagement of the essay that appears in his morning newspaper under this title introduces the scene in which Holmes first reveals to his new roommate the nature of his profession and reveals to him, and to Doyle's readers, the 'Science of Deduction' (the title of Doyle's second chapter). Carefully prepared for, this moment brings to a head what amounts to a competition in detection between Holmes and Watson that begins even before their first meeting in the chemistry laboratory of 'Bart's', better known as St Bartholomew's medical college. 'A medical student I suppose?' Watson asks Stamford of Holmes. 'No,' Stamford replies, 'I have no idea what he intends to go in for' (5).

Holmes is first encountered in the medical laboratory just after he has isolated the 're-agent' of 'Haemoglobin' that will enable detectives the world over to identify human blood stains. His detection of this tool of detection (accompanied by cries of what amounts to an English translation of 'Eureka') is immediately followed by another act of detection performed on the 'Dr Watson' to whom Stamford introduces him: 'You have been in Afghanistan, I perceive' (7). To Watson's astonished query as to how this information was deduced, Holmes replies, 'Never mind. [. . .] The question now is about haemoglobin' (7), as though the two questions – of personal identity and chemical composition – were in the same category of 'scientific' inquiry.

Reciprocally, however, as the weeks pass, Watson cannot deduce a thing about Holmes's past or profession. When he first expressed his eagerness to take on the 'mystery' of Holmes, he was warned by Stamford that he'd find his new roommate 'a knotty problem' and that Holmes would 'learn[] more about you than you about him' (9). The good doctor's bewilderment leads him to keep detailed notes of Holmes's appearance, habits, talents, studies, and fields of knowledge (as well as of ignorance), all with the aim of solving the 'little mystery' of what Holmes does for a living (11).

Having methodically tabulated the categories of his roommate's apparent expertise ('Astronomy. – Nil', 'Sensational Literature. – Immense', and so on), Watson finds himself completely at a loss. His dismissal of Holmes's unsigned essay 'The Book of Life' as 'ineffable twaddle', however, finally forces Holmes, in defending it, to reveal his profession: 'I'm a consulting detective' (15).

Detective Rivalry

The essay that Watson denigrates proposes that it is possible 'to distinguish the history of [a] man, and the trade or profession to which he belongs' by his 'finger-nails, by his coat-sleeve, by his boots, by his trouser-knees, by the callosities of his forefinger and thumb, by his expression, by his shirt-cuffs' (15). Using these diagnostic methods, Holmes had been able to 'distinguish the history' of Watson on first meeting him (as he explains to his roommate in due course), while Watson has signally failed to discern 'the trade or profession' to which Holmes belongs after weeks of living with him.

In short, Doyle uses the two opening chapters of *A Study in Scarlet* not just to introduce us to Holmes and his 'science of deduction', but also to inaugurate a theme he will particularly emphasize in this and the next Holmes tale, *The Sign of Four*, namely, rivalry. This theme will recur often in the series of Holmes stories running in *The Strand* from 1891 to 1893, before the ten-year publication hiatus following the detective's apparent death at Reichenbach Falls in 'The Final Problem', while locked in combat with his arch-foe, Professor Moriarty. After his resurrection and return to duty in 'The Empty House' (*The Hound of the Baskervilles*, published in 1901, is a pre-Reichenbach adventure), Holmes will no longer be the target of official envy.

From the beginning of the Holmes canon we are made aware of Doyle's intention to place Watson, our reader surrogate or stand-in, in direct competition with his detective protagonist. Similarities between the skills required in their respective professions, namely, medical diagnosis and criminal detection, help to point up this note of competition. Of course, Watson is invariably defeated in these jousts, which is what encourages us to think that we might stand a better chance in the lists and leads us to read the stories with the aim of testing that assumption.

What most readers don't recognize in these early skirmishes between Watson and Holmes, however, is Doyle's implicit warning that if one is not able to figure out the mystery of Holmes, 'to fathom' his 'inmost thoughts' (14) as well as Holmes can fathom the thoughts of others, one will be placed at a distinct disadvantage in the ensuing competition. Holmes's improvisatory violin playing, which Watson takes to reflect 'the thoughts which possessed him', obscurely symbolizes for both reader and roommate the tantalizingly indecipherable inner workings of Doyle's 'calculating machine' (117).

While Holmes handily defeats his most intimate rival and even wins his admiration and affection, the battle with his professional competitors is much more difficult and prolonged. In *A Study in Scarlet* Inspectors Lestrade and Gregson, or their official colleagues at Scotland Yard, play a part, directly or indirectly, in every chapter where Holmes himself appears, except for the first. Doyle even devotes one entire chapter to Gregson's false lead and half of the next to Lestrade's.

The two have already consulted Holmes on several particularly difficult cases, as have many 'private inquiry agencies' (15), for that is the conceit with which Doyle begins his tale: Holmes is secretly consulted by other detectives who are 'at fault' (a hunting term meaning they've lost the scent) in their investigations. After merely listening to the evidence, however, Holmes can 'unravel' the problem without ever leaving his room (20). At the urging of Watson, he agrees to visit the scene of the Lauriston Gardens murder himself (20). Watson's influence must have been long-lasting, for in all his future investigations Holmes shows himself to be similarly extramural and energetic.

The main reason why Holmes is initially reluctant to help Gregson and Lestrade with the murder of Enoch Drebber directly reinforces Doyle's theme of rivalry: 'What does it matter to me?' he asks Watson. 'Supposing I unravel the whole matter, you may be sure that Gregson, Lestrade, and Co. will pocket all the credit' (20). Indeed, the Scotland Yarders 'have their knives into one another', says Holmes, and 'are as jealous as a pair of professional beauties' (19). Not that Holmes himself is above petty vanity. At his first meeting with Watson he is so taken with his own brilliance at having devised what he calls 'the Sherlock Holmes test' for blood stains that he 'bowed as if to some applauding crowd conjured up by his imagination' (8). Later, Watson's fulsome praise makes him 'flush up with pleasure', as 'sensitive to flattery on the score of his art as any girl could be of her beauty' (29).

In *A Study in Scarlet* Doyle takes pains to spotlight Holmes's vanity and love of fame and to display the bare-faced hypocrisy of his official rivals, who privately flatter Holmes to secure his help while sneering publicly – and especially in each other's company – at his unconventional 'theories' and methods. Like their official predecessors, Vidocq, Prefect G—, and Gevrol, Gregson, Lestrade, 'and Co.' are 'conventional – shockingly so' (19). 'I am his superior,' Holmes says of Gregson, 'and he acknowledges it to me; but he would cut his tongue out before he would own it to any third person' (20). Nonetheless, the great 'consulting detective' must swallow his pride in order to receive the mental stimulation he craves, not to mention the fees that keep him in shag tobacco and cocaine.

Holmes agrees to visit Lauriston Gardens intending only to 'have a laugh' at his competitors (20), and in the end that is all he gets, for the daily newspapers bestow all the detective 'credit' on Gregson and Lestrade. Securing for Holmes the recognition he deserves in the face of his rivals' unfair claims is, in fact, the original *raison d'être* of Watson's published 'reminiscences', as Doyle calls them in his subtitle:

> 'Didn't I tell you so when we started?' cried Sherlock Holmes with a laugh.
> 'That's the result of all our Study in Scarlet: to get them a testimonial!'
>   'Never mind,' I answered; 'I have all the facts in my journal, and the public shall know them.' (103)

Despite his repeated sniping at Watson's sentimental style of writing up his cases, Holmes knows that he is 'lost' to fame without Watson's faithful record of his successes ('Scandal', 213).

Doyle makes the rivalry between Holmes and the obtuse official police, as well as the futile challenges tirelessly posed by Watson, the amateur, a staple feature of the early stories, as if he wished both to model such rivalry for the reader and, by the patent ineptitude of Holmes's fictional competitors, to open up a nameless space among his *dramatis personae* for the reader's imaginative self-projection as a worthier opponent. That space was illuminated by what Harold Perkin calls 'the professional ideal' of universal opportunity culturally prevalent at this time (8–9): just as anyone, presumably, could learn the methods and skills necessary to rise in the putative meritocracy of a trained profession, so any reader, presumably, could learn the Holmesian 'methods' of observation and deduction and rise in the meritocracy of fictional detection.

Only as Holmes achieves real fame in the eye of his reading public and begins to attract a corresponding fictional clientele of royalty, heads of state, and celebrity plutocrats does the jealousy of Lestrade, Gregson, Athelney Jones, and their peers begin to moderate. By 1904, one year after his resurrection from the dead, Holmes is paid the ultimate compliment by his old rival, Lestrade, in 'The Adventure of the Six Napoleons': 'We're not jealous of you at Scotland Yard. No, sir, we are very proud of you, and if you come down to-morrow, there's

not a man [. . .] who wouldn't be glad to shake you by the hand'
(825).

By this time, however, Doyle's readers had been taught how to step
– respectfully – into the boot-prints that Holmes's competitors had
left behind, and they had developed a distinct taste for the contest.
Doyle had almost single-handedly made the challenge of the puzzle
element an eagerly anticipated feature of detective fiction.

Decadent Detection, the Science and the Art

When Holmes reveals his profession to Watson in *A Study in Scarlet*
he also explains his methods, which depend upon 'observation',
'deduction', and 'special knowledge' (15–16). The usefulness of the
last item is not hard to understand, and it is contained in his extensive files on previous criminal cases and learned monographs on
everything from tobacco ash to the forensic uses of plaster of paris
(110). However, not until the first chapter of *The Sign of Four*, whose
title, 'The Science of Deduction', repeats that of the second chapter
in *A Study in Scarlet*, does Doyle specify what Holmes means by
'observation' and 'deduction'.

In reconstructing a trip Watson made to the post office and his
reason for it, Holmes shows that 'observation' and 'deduction'
involve distinct types of inference (110). 'Observation shows me that
you have been to the Wigmore Street Post-Office this morning,' he
tells Watson, 'but deduction lets me know that when there you dis-
patched a telegram' (110). Specifically, Holmes has observed that a
'little reddish mould' on Watson's shoe matches the 'peculiar reddish
tint' of the earth thrown up by construction workers in front of that
particular post office. Since Watson's morning activities did not
include letter-writing and he did not need to purchase stamps or post-
cards, by a process of elimination Holmes can conclude that Watson
sent a telegram. 'Eliminate all other factors, and the one which
remains must be the truth' (111), he says, echoing Dupin.

Thus, 'observation' seems to mean metonymical inference and
'deduction' an inference from negation, in the almost mathematical
sense of 'deduction' as the subtraction of alternative possibilities. But
of course, in the real 'Book of Life' where all of us live, such neat
categorizations are impossible to make. Holmes's 'deduction' that
Watson sent a telegram depends on his 'observation' that Watson
wrote no letters and that there were still plenty of stamps and cards
in his desk.

As for observation itself, Thomas Sebeok has pointed out its close affinities with what the logician Charles Peirce called 'abduction', or a perceptual inference proceeding from a 'rule' that is not axiomatic or self-evident (8). Here, one unspoken 'rule' underlying Holmes's inference is that excavation work exposing red earth to the tread of pedestrians is 'peculiar' in London. If true, this means Watson probably received the red dirt on his shoes at the construction site in front of the Wigmore Street post office. But in fact there could be other sites unknown to Holmes nearby, some excavated that very morning.

Doyle seems to have been prepared for comments like Sebeok's. Right after this lesson in 'observation' and 'deduction' Watson decides to test Holmes by offering an old watch for analysis. The accuracy with which Holmes identifies the owner as Watson's deceased older brother, describing in detail the rather sordid life of 'H. W.', outrages the younger sibling, who assumes that Holmes has been making inquiries about his brother and using the knowledge thus obtained to perform a piece of 'charlatanism' (112). This Holmes denies.

> 'Then how in the name of all that is wonderful did you get these facts? They are absolutely correct in every particular.'
>
> 'Ah, that is good luck. I could only say what was the balance of probability. I did not at all expect to be so accurate.' (112)

Doyle, however, encourages his readers to expect such accuracy every time. Although rare stories like 'The Yellow Face' show that Holmes can be completely wrong and 'A Scandal in Bohemia' suggests that his axiomatic assumptions (in this case, about women) sometimes needed revising, his career success rate is far beyond what the probabilities of real life would allow. It is certainly beyond that of most real-life professional detectives or historical scientists using similarly 'abductive' methods for reconstructing past events.

Like his haughty remarks on the absurdity of fictional detectives such as Dupin and Lecoq (*Study*, 16–17) and his assertion that 'all fiction with its conventionalities and foreseen conclusions' is inferior to the '*outré* results' of real life ('Identity', 251), Holmes's avowed reliance on 'probability' helps give the contrived infallibility of his methods a sheen of verisimilitude. The avowal is ironic, however, because Holmes considers the probable and expected not worth investigating. As he tells Watson in *The Sign of Four*, 'I abhor the dull routine of existence' (108).

Holmes 'cannot live without brainwork', but his chosen profession seldom offers him any. 'Crime is commonplace, existence is commonplace, and no qualities save those which are commonplace have any function upon earth' (*Sign*, 113). Because the probable and the commonplace offer insufficient nutriment for Holmes's prodigious intellectual appetite, this manic-depressive detective must turn to an artificial mental stimulant, cocaine, whenever the tedium of this 'dreary, dismal, unprofitable world' (113) becomes too much to bear.

'*Outré*' and 'bizarre' and 'queer' (230) cases, however, are much better than cocaine. Athelney Jones, Holmes's official rival in *The Sign of Four*, calls him a 'connoisseur of crime' (204), a phrase that points once again to the far-reaching influence of De Quincey's 'Murder Considered as a Fine Art'. What Doyle attempted from the very beginning was to unite into a single and, to use one of his favourite words, 'singular' profession what C. P. Snow later termed 'the two cultures' of science and the arts, which were already beginning to go their separate ways by the turn of the century. 'Bohemianism', in Doyle's view, is what makes the most brilliant men of science truly artistic, for it represents an outlook that is fundamentally at odds with the 'commonplace' attitudes of middle-class life that restrict genius and, thereby, impede progress.

Doyle advances in numerous ways this bi-cultural view of what he calls Holmes's scientific but 'Bohemian soul' ('Scandal', 209), which 'loathes every form of society' and seeks refuge from tedium in 'alternating' bouts of 'cocaine and ambition'. Take for instance Stamford's initial comments on Holmes's 'scientific [. . .] cold-bloodedness' in *Study in Scarlet*: 'When it comes to beating the subjects in the dissecting-rooms with a stick, it is certainly taking rather a bizarre shape' (6). The laboratory is to Holmes what the studio is to the sculptor, but where the latter makes 'life studies' of beautiful nude bodies, Holmes makes death studies of hideous cadavers. His violent attempts to 'verify how far bruises may be produced after death' (an impossibility, by the way) were meant to be as scandalous to Victorian middle-class pieties regarding the handling of corpses as the dalliances with female models carried on by a sculptor like Auguste Rodin (1840–1917) to similar notions regarding sexual decency.

The 'art' that most stimulates Holmes's intellectual curiosity is the art of crime, and he is its foremost 'scientist', the keenest interpreter and critic of its 'artists' and their traditions. It is most unfair of Holmes, therefore, to accuse Watson in *The Sign of Four* (108) of inventing an artsy title for his first recorded adventure, *A Study in Scarlet*, with its echo of works by the American impressionist James McNeill Whistler (1834–1903), when he made it up himself (33).

Thinking along these lines, Reginald Hill has cited the intriguing links between the publication of *The Sign of Four* (1890) and *The Picture of Dorian Gray* (1891), a novel by the decadent homosexual writer and public wit Oscar Wilde (1854–1900), describing the moral decline of the beautiful but narcissistic young man of the title. Doyle and Wilde first met at a lunch to which they were invited by Joseph Stoddart, editor of *Lippincott's*, who commissioned both books on the spot. Surprisingly, the two writers got along quite well, and many have supposed that the character of Thaddeus Sholto in Doyle's novelette is a good-humoured parody of Wilde's exotic, sybaritic lifestyle (see, e.g., Baring-Gould, 1.625). The deeper connection between Doyle's bohemian tastes and the Decadent Movement of which Wilde was a leading light appears, says Hill, in the character of Holmes himself: 'This languid, violin-playing, cocaine-addicted intellectual [. . .] could have been one of Dorian Gray's own circle' (22).

But the magnitude of the difference between the effete Dorian Gray and the energetic Holmes can be estimated by comparing Holmes to Sholto, a wealthy, kind-hearted, but pusillanimous hypochondriac stranded with his Oriental vases, hookahs, tiger-skin rugs, and 'quack nostrums' (131) on an 'oasis of art in the howling desert of South London' (123). That very 'desert' is the work of art that intrigues Holmes most. To him it is a 'labyrinth' (122, 157) every bit as intricate and subtle as the original labyrinth constructed by the master artist, Daedalus, for King Minos of Crete, in order to hide the minotaur, a monster who is half-man and half-beast.

Doyle drew on Poe's composite minotaur-figure, the sailor and the orangutan, for his own version in *The Sign of Four*: lurking at the heart of his metropolitan labyrinth are Jonathan Small and his savage Andaman Island companion, Tonga.

Love is the Drug: The Sign of One and Two

The Sign of Four is among Doyle's finest accomplishments, although, compared to *A Study in Scarlet* and the shorter tales upon which his reputation rests, it offers fewer sustained opportunities for readers to engage with the puzzle element. Instead, as in most of its crime fiction predecessors, Doyle's second Holmes tale invites us to watch the detective hero going about his business, introducing many of its clues and testimony almost in the same instant that the scientific detective tells us what we are to make of them.

This is not to say that the puzzle element is lacking entirely, of course. By the time we reach the end of chapter 6, for instance, when Holmes informs his Scotland Yard rival Atheney Jones that the man who escaped with the treasure following the murder of Major Bartholomew Sholto, Thaddeus's twin brother, is a sunburned wooden-legged ex-convict named Jonathan Small, sufficient evidence to this effect has been introduced upon which Holmes has made no comment, leaving the inferences, and imaginative reconstructions, up to us. This evidence includes the fact that Major Sholto and Captain Moran had been stationed in the Andaman Islands, a tropical penal colony; that a piece of paper with a map, four linked crosses, four names including that of 'Jonathan Small' (the only Englishman), and 'The sign of the four' written on it was found in Captain Moran's effects; that Major Sholto was morbidly afraid of Englishmen with wooden legs; that he apparently died of fright at the sight of a strange face at his window; and that only 'a single footmark' (could a two-legged man have jumped to the ground below and left only one such mark?) was found in the flower-bed afterwards (128). Put all of these facts together and, as Holmes would say, the inferences should prove '[c]ommonplace' (19).

From this point on, however, the story reverts to the flight-and-pursuit and 'caper' formats of the Adventure type of story popularized by the police 'memoirs' and 'reminiscences' from earlier in the century. In larger terms, *The Sign of Four* conforms to the genre of the quest-romance, not least in the way it incorporates the dream-material of myth and medieval legend into the waking lives of its protagonists, while suffusing the cityscape of the imperial capital of Western Progress with the lurid aura of its primitive archetypes.

The 'labyrinth' of South London where Small and Tonga have hidden themselves with the Agra treasure was a working-class neighbourhood across the Thames from the city's major shopping areas, business districts, and posh residences. Its Asian counterpart, lying on the banks of another river, the Yamuna, in India, is the Agra Fortress, where Small and his three Sikh conspirators originally hid their treasure after murdering the merchant Akhmet during the Indian Mutiny. Located among the 'narrow, winding streets' of the city, this 'enormous' fortress, 'acres and acres' in size and full of 'winding passages, and long corridors twisting in and out', comprises 'a labyrinth' where, says Small, 'it is easy enough for folk to get lost' (188–9).

The ancient, impenetrable fortress of Agra seems to have figuratively surfaced in the quotidian present of Doyle's South London, transforming its 'commonplace' events into the turnings and culs-desac of a correspondingly baffling maze. As his allusions to the Greek legend of Theseus and the minotaur suggest, the thematic cement Doyle uses to laminate the Agra treasure's exotic Oriental past to his readers' familiar Occidental present is mythological. In this way Doyle anticipates the incorporation of myth and legend as shaping thematic elements in modernist poetry and fiction, such as T. S. Eliot's *The Waste Land* (1922) and the novel *Ulysses* (1922), by James Joyce (1882–1941).

Another legendary theme serving the same purpose is announced by Mrs Forrester, Mary Morstan's employer, after Watson 'amaze[s]' the two of them with the tale of his and Holmes's adventures:

> 'It is a romance!' cried Mrs Forrester. 'An injured lady, half a million in treasure, a black cannibal, and a wooden-legged ruffian. They take the place of the conventional dragon or wicked earl.'
> 'And two knights-errant to the rescue,' added Miss Morstan with a bright glance at me. (164)

Looming behind these allusions to knight-errantry is the legend of the Arthurian knights of the Round Table and the oath of loyalty that bound them together. *The Sign of Four* is full of episodes, characters, and events that focus on the choice between loyalty to or betrayal of one's fraternal 'mates', from the original 'Four' – Small, Mahomet Singh, Abdullah Khan, and Dost Akbar – who swear not to betray the secret of the treasure or each other, to the 'brother officer[s]' (115), Sholto and Morstan, to the twin brothers, Bartholomew and Thaddeus Sholto, to Holmes and Watson themselves, and even to Small and the vicious Tonga, his 'faithful mate' (201). Doyle thus continues to play the changes on the theme of rivalry he introduced in *A Study in Scarlet*, but in a contrapuntal fashion.

Given the number of 'brothers' who 'go bad' or have a falling out in *The Sign of Four*, Holmes's deduction of the unhappy fate of Watson's impecunious and alcoholic older brother from the evidence of his watch appears prophetic. The break-up of Holmes and Watson at the end of the story is a result of their contrasting personalities, which are based on different Arthurian prototypes.

Holmes is a pure-hearted Galahad in quest of the Holy Grail of detection, the Truth. His superiority to the temptations of the flesh is indicated early on, when Mary Morstan, Holmes's new client, first leaves 221B Baker Street. Watching her go, Watson exclaims, 'What a very attractive woman!' 'Is she?' responds Holmes. 'I did not observe' (116). Here Watson's congenital inability to 'observe' what he 'sees' is turned into a Holmesian virtue: the detective deliberately blinds himself to whatever detracts from his professional quest. In response to Watson's charge that he is 'an automaton – a calculating machine', Holmes eagerly acquiesces: ' "It is of the first importance", he cried, "not to allow your judgement to be biased by personal qualities. A client is to me a mere unit, a factor in a problem. The emotional qualities are antagonistic to clear reasoning" ' (117).

In stark contrast to Holmes's cold-blooded indifference to feminine charms, Watson is a well-travelled ladies' man, 'with an experience of women that extends over many nations and three continents' (114). Watson is the Lancelot of this knightly pair, and Mary Morstan is his Guinevere. The motive driving him toward the centre of the 'Agra' mystery – 'here indeed was a labyrinth' (146) – is thus an ulterior one, like that of Theseus himself, who first conquered the mystery of the Cretan labyrinth and slew its fearsome inmate to win the hand of a princess, Ariadne.

Doyle elaborates this love theme at the most implicit symbolic levels of his tale. Nearly any of his readers familiar with the name of Agra, for instance (and there were no doubt many of them), would have associated it with a far different 'treasure' to be found there located almost directly across the river from the Agra Fortress, namely, the fabulously expensive tomb known as the Taj Mahal, which a grieving sultan built for his Moghul princess. This allusive spatial juxtaposition of the ruined labyrinthine fortress, a monument to the ephemeral vanity of worldly grandeur and wealth, and the perfectly preserved Taj, a monument to the lasting power of love and loss, captures the irony of Watson's position as wooer. His quest to restore to Miss Morstan a share of the Agra treasure will, if successful, make her the equivalent of a princess, 'the richest heiress in England' (130), but place her permanently beyond his reach as a marriage partner. No wonder Watson's 'heart turned as heavy as lead' when he heard of her prospective good fortune.

As in *The Moonstone*, where the curse of an Oriental treasure also stands in the way of true love, the Agra treasure must disappear before love can triumph. Doyle takes a leaf from Collins and places the treasure safely beyond recovery, not by whisking it off to India but by having Small scatter it along the Thames estuary. The way is now clear for Watson to propose to Mary Morstan.

In doing so, however, Watson becomes still another brother in this tale who has betrayed his fraternal companion. To the news of his roommate's betrothal, Holmes's first response is 'a most dismal groan' (204). Not anticipating the future triumphs of his two knights-errant, Doyle thus inadvertently created a recurring impediment to their continuing adventures together, forcing him to contrive ever flimsier excuses for Watson's truancy from his new bride and medical practice in order to chronicle Holmes's future cases for the readers of *The Strand*. 'You have done all the work in this business,' Watson tells Holmes at the end of the tale. 'I get a wife out of it, [Athelney] Jones gets the credit, pray what remains for you?' 'For me,' Holmes replies, 'there still remains the cocaine-bottle' (205).

Doyle book-ends his fantastic amalgam of 'scientific' detection, chivalry, romance, treasure-hunting, and bizarre crime with scenes of Holmes injecting himself with the only drug that will save him from the mental tortures of the 'commonplace' when no case is pending. His doing so suggests that the Morstan case and the pharmaceutical stimulant are for Holmes fundamentally interchangeable methods of overcoming boredom. The suggestion is highlighted by Watson's asking Holmes, just before Mary Morstan appears at their door, whether Holmes has 'any professional inquiry on foot': 'None,' replies Holmes. '*Hence* the cocaine. I cannot live without brainwork' (113; emphasis added).

Doyle seems to imply that *The Sign of Four* is intended to have the same effect on his readers, offering us a spate of artificially induced, disengaged 'brainwork' to relieve the tedium of our own 'hopelessly prosaic' (113) lives. This suspicion is borne out by Doyle's motivic play with genre-specific terms like 'case' and 'solution' in *The Sign of Four*, especially in its early chapters.

On the first page we are introduced to the 'neat morocco case' in which Holmes keeps his hypodermic syringe filled with 'a seven-per-cent solution' of cocaine. Doyle's description of Holmes's self-injection anticipates his chivalric themes: Holmes 'thrust[s] the point home' (107) as though he were delivering the *coup de grâce* to an opponent. Later chapter titles play on the double associations of 'case' and 'solution'. Thus chapter 2, 'The Statement of the Case', begins with the entrance of Miss Morstan and her complimenting of Holmes on his handling of Mrs Forrester's 'little domestic complication'. 'The case', replies Holmes, 'was a very simple one.' '[Y]ou cannot say the same of mine,' says Miss Morstan, adding, 'I can hardly imagine anything more strange, more utterly inexplicable.' At these words Holmes's 'eyes glistened' as if responding to a chemical stimulant. 'State your case,' he says (114).

Holmes has already told Watson that in many 'cases' 'the work itself, the pleasure of finding a field for [his] peculiar powers', is his 'highest reward'. Within two pages of opening her 'strange' and 'inexplicable' 'case' (114), a 'singular case' as Holmes calls it (115), Miss

Morstan also opens a literal case, the 'flat box' (presumably resembling the shape of Holmes's 'neat morocco case') containing the six pearls she has been sent during the previous six years by, as it turns out, Thaddeus Sholto. 'Your statement is most interesting,' Holmes immediately replies (116), as though her 'statement of the case' and her presentation of the flat box for examination were one and the same.

At a single stroke, Doyle thus connects the woman (in her grey turban), the Agra treasure, the box of pearls, and the 'case' of *The Sign of Four* into a composite Oriental symbol of all that the men in this story desire: Watson, love; Small, wealth; and Holmes (like us), the mental stimulation of a criminal 'case', without which he must settle for what comfort he can find in the 'neat morocco case' (also of Oriental manufacture) on his mantelpiece.

Watson deplores Holmes's cocaine use and urges him to stop, but is himself subject to comparable bouts of mental stimulation whenever he is in the presence of his sole object of desire. For Watson, however, these experiences are inevitably disorienting.

Riding in the cab with Miss Morstan to their rendevous with Thaddeus Sholto, Watson is 'so excited' that his attempts to 'cheer and amuse her by reminiscences of [his] adventures in Afghanistan' become (as she later tells him) nonsensical. When he next says that he has 'lost [his] bearings' in the maze of South London (122), Doyle presumably means us to take Watson's geographical bewilderment as an symbol of his mental and emotional confusion. Later, Watson's disorientation is exacerbated by the news of Miss Morstan's antici- pated share of the Agra treasure. In response to Sholto's hypochon- driacal complaints immediately after receiving this information, he 'dreamily' recommends 'strychnine in large doses as a sedative' (131), among other odd prescriptions.

Thus Watson becomes the prime example of what Holmes takes to be the deranging effects of the softer emotions on 'that true cold reason which I place above all things' ('Scandal', 205). By the end of *The Sign of Four*, love has become Watson's drug, and it can't be found in any 'case', morocco, iron-clasped, or otherwise. Marrying Miss Morstan will, in fact, impede Watson's easy access to Holmes's future 'cases', and create an ongoing problem for his creator. It is a problem, as we shall see, that Doyle will confront head-on in his very next Holmes story, his first for *The Strand*, where Holmes will meet his own female 'match'.

5

From Holmes
to the Golden Age

The Holmes Revolution

With the success of Doyle's first series of Sherlock Holmes short stories (1891–3), detection as a distinct sub-genre of detective fiction began to overtake other categories of crime and mystery fiction in popularity.

Soon after Doyle sent his hero plunging into Reichenbach Falls in 1893, an ordinary, unassuming detective named Martin Hewitt took his place in the pages of *The Strand*. The creation of Arthur Morrison (1863–1945), Hewitt was an 'Everyman' detective meant to challenge the detective-as-superman that Holmes represented. But Hewitt and his predecessor had more in common than not, because Morrison knew he couldn't push the envelope of his readers' newly shaped expectations too far. Like Holmes, Hewitt keeps a scrapbook of odd and famous cases ('Ivy', 362), and his abstruse meditations can make him insensitive. Forgetting to offer his condolences to the brother of a murder victim, Hewitt tells his unofficial sidekick, Brett, 'The work very often makes me forget merely human sympathies' ('Ivy', 351).

Among other writers boosted by Doyle's success were M. McDonnell Bodkin (1850–1933), creator of private investigator Paul Beck; Ernest Bramah (1867–1942), author of tales featuring Max Carrados, the blind detective; A. E. W. Mason (1865–1948), whose Inspector Hannaud of the Sûreté made his first appearance with his sidekick Mr Ricardo in *At the Villa Rose* (1910); and the Baroness Emmuska Orczy (1865–1947), whose 'Old Man in the Corner' series (1905–9) drew on Doyle's original conception of Holmes as a strictly 'consulting' detective by featuring the eponymous Old Man solving cases entirely by brain-power while sitting in a tea-room. Even more abstract and cold-blooded was Professor Augustus S. F. X. Van Dusen, a.k.a. 'The Thinking Machine', a version of the Holmesian 'reasoning machine' devised by American newsman Jacques Futrelle (1875–1915). Van Dusen's brain capacity is so prodigious that in 'The Problem of Cell 13' (1907) he manages to escape from a high-security prison using nothing but the material between his ears. More ostentatiously scientific in practice than Van Dusen was chemistry professor Craig Kennedy, the creation of Arthur Reeve (1880–1936).

   In folksy contrast to both Van Dusen and Kennedy, but every bit as acute at inductive analysis, was the antebellum Virginian back-woodsman 'Uncle Abner', who was featured in stories by Melville Davisson Post (1869–1930) and served as precursor to Mississippi county attorney Gavin Stevens, protagonist of the stories in *Knight's Gambit* (1939) by William Faulkner (1897–1962). Humorist Mark Twain (b. Samuel Langhorne Clermens, 1835–1910) took a less respectful view of scientific detection and its progenitor than did many of his compatriots. In Twain's 'A Double-Barreled Detective Story' (1902), Sherlock Holmes appears at a California mining camp to defend his nephew, Fetlock Jones, from a charge of murder and makes a complete mess of things, to the point where he is threatened with lynching.

   Holmes parodies appeared in other countries besides America, including the detective's homeland. Conan Doyle's brother-in-law, E. W. Hornung (1866–1921), created a topsy-turvy version of the Holmes–Watson partnership in the gentleman safe-cracker Arthur J. Raffles and his worshipful school chum, Harry 'Bunny' Manders, who first appeared in 1899 in *The Amateur Cracksman*. By 1909 Holmes was famous enough to be introduced as the renowned 'Holmlock Shears' to French readers of Maurice Leblanc's Arsène Lupin adventures, which had been inspired by Hornung's success. In *The Blonde Lady*, Shears and his imbecilic sidekick, 'Wilson', provide endless amusement for the exuberant Lupin, whose *élan vital* makes Shears's 'methods' look as pedestrian and obtuse as Prefect G—'s.

   Some anti-Holmesian detectives, like the artist and amateur investigator Philip Trent of *Trent's Last Case* (1913), by E. C. Bentley (1875–1956), appeared in stories deliberately intended to reveal the unlikelihood of the detective's arriving at the true solution to the crime, given the human limitations of the investigator and the exigencies of real life. Others conformed to the Paul Davies type, the evil detective who commits the crime and may even (mis)lead the investigation himself. The most famous bad detective of the early

Holmes era was retired Inspector Grodman of *The Big Bow Mystery* (1891) by Israel Zangwill (1864–1926). Summoned to examine a man assumed to be dead, Grodman murders his sleeping victim for no other reason than an artistic ambition to pull off the perfect crime.

The Holmes model of detection, often with sidekick attached, influenced popular literature beyond the boundaries of crime fiction. The racist Fu Manchu spy novels written by Sax Rohmer (b. Arthur Sarsfield Ward, 1866–1959) re-created the Holmes–Watson investigative team in the partnership of British agent Nayland Smith and his narrating sidekick, Dr Petrie. Rohmer also drew on Doyle's archvillain Moriarty for Smith's Chinese nemesis, 'the yellow peril incarnate in one man' (*Mystery*, 15), with 'the brains of any three men of genius' (14).

Of all Holmes's legitimate successors, Dr John Thorndyke came closest to replicating the 'scientific' aura of the great detective. The brain-child of R. Austin Freeman (1862–1943), himself a physician, Thorndyke first appeared in *The Red Thumb Mark* (1907). Based like Doyle's Holmes on a real-life medical instructor, Dr Alfred Swayne Taylor, Thorndyke is a medico-legal expert with a home laboratory for the analysis of forensic evidence and a faithful lab assistant, Nathaniel Polton, to maintain it. Dr Jervis, a former fellow medical student, tags along on his hero's adventures and writes them up for our edification.

Thorndyke is what one can imagine Holmes having become if Doyle had never let him out of the chemistry laboratory at St Bart's. Nearly every Thorndyke case turns on a question that can only be answered by a sophisticated physical analysis, usually chemical or microscopic in nature. These were carefully tested in advance by Freeman himself, who, like his protagonist, kept a home laboratory for the purpose. Many of the forensic advances appearing in the Thorndyke stories were even adopted by real-life police investigators.

Ironically, the arcane nature of Thorndyke's 'scientific' investigations works against any serious attempt to engage the reader in solving the puzzle of the crime. In Freeman's stories the special knowledge required to crack the case is not only withheld, but is almost impossible to convey without giving away the entire mystery. In *The Red Thumb Mark*, for instance, everything depends on knowing that fingerprints can be forged, and, moreover, on exactly how they could have been forged in this particular case. In 'The Old Lag' (1935), not only fingerprint technology, but the microscopic peculiarities of camel's blood figure in the solution to the crime. Unlike Holmes's behaviour when handling or inspecting evidence, Dr Thorndyke's gnomic demeanour tells us little more than that he knows something we cannot possibly guess. When he visits the Royal Zoo to have a casual talk with the camel-keeper, we have no idea he has discovered that the spot of blood on a suspect's handkerchief belongs to the species of *camelidae*, and we haven't even been told that he's tested it yet.

The Thorndyke tales were, nonetheless, very successful, largely I would argue for the same reason as the famous innovation that Freeman introduced with 'The Case of Oscar Brodski'. This was the first of a series of 'inverted' tales published in *The Singing Bone* (1912), where the reader witnesses the crime at the outset and then watches as the detective sets about trying to solve it.

Freeman's highly technical 'scientific' detective stories and his 'inverted' variations both use deft and compelling devices for exciting curiosity and wonder, particularly with respect to the miracles of modern science, and his skill in portraiture, scene-setting, and pacing is excellent. His 'inverted' tales, a return to the earlier, Hornung-inspired 'caper' style he adopted when writing as Clifford Ashdown in *The Adventures of Rodney Pringle* (1902), later provided a model for the 'inverted' novel-length experiments of Anthony Berkeley (1893–1971, writing as Anthony Iles) in *Malice Aforethought* (1930) and *Before the Fact* (1932). These two books, in turn, helped popularize the modern psychological thriller focusing on the thoughts and behaviour of the criminal.

Ironically, it was a very unscientific, decidedly anti-Holmesian investigator, the inspiration for Bentley's amateur sleuth, Trent, who was to prove the most important transition figure between Doyle's popularization of the puzzle element and the rage for inductive detection in the Golden Age.

The Empiricism of Father Brown

Father Brown, the creation of G. K. Chesterton (1874–1936), has long outlived many of his pre-Great War contemporaries. Chesterton was a devout convert to Roman Catholicism and something of a Christian socialist. His defence of faith in a materialistic, mechanized, and sceptical age, his belief in conversion and redemption, and his concern to preserve the dignity of the overlooked man and woman of the crowd shape much of the plotting, and nearly all of the allegory, of the elegant little mysteries he wrote to showcase his soft-spoken cleric.

With this unprepossessing man of the cloth, who has acquired from his experience in the confessional as intimate a knowledge of the criminal mind as any Holmes or Thorndyke, Chesterton set out to challenge the idea of the detective as a reasoning machine. Impatient with men of science in general because their faith in pure reason undermines their moral affections, he much preferred the simpler, unreasoning immorality of ordinary criminals, which proves less resistant to the transforming grace of Christian forgiveness. Thus, the French arch-thief Flambeau, a big, strong, cunning culprit in the tradition of the pre-Sûreté Vidocq, is eventually inspired by the example of Father Brown's meekness and charity to throw over his criminal life and become a private detective himself. By contrast, Flambeau's godless nemesis, Parisian Police Chief Aristide Valentin, is driven 'mad' ('Secret Garden', 38) by reason in only the second of Chesterton's parables, to the point where he can commit a gruesome murder in cold blood and, when found out, take his own life with equanimity.

When we meet Flambeau in the first Father Brown story, 'The Blue Cross' (1911), he has disguised himself as a French priest in order to fall in with the good padre on his journey to Westminster for a Eucharistic Congress. Flambeau intends to steal the precious, jewel-encrusted relic of the title, which the priest is bringing with him wrapped in plain brown paper. In the end, the fiery Frenchman discovers that this dim-looking cleric has decoyed him with a facsimile package. Before Flambeau can tear the priest to pieces, he is seized by Valentin, whom Brown has cunningly led to his rendezvous with Flambeau by leaving a trail of apparently random acts of absurdity and disorder: overturned fruit displays, soup thrown at a wall, a broken window.

Chesterton's point here, and in many of the other Father Brown stories, is that the apparent randomness of everyday life is in fact part of a larger pattern of significance overseen by God but beyond the finite cognitive powers of humanity to comprehend. In Chesterton's mind, the unforeseen or unreasonable event is precisely the form in which miracles occur, and 'the most incredible thing about miracles is that they happen' (11). His intended moral is that there is a divine *telos* at work behind the purposeless, mechanical workings of the universe as modern science understands it.

For Chesterton, godless rationality carried to extremes was a kind of lunacy. True reason, like a ship's mainmast, requires the ballast of faith in order to keep pointing heavenward. At the end of 'The Blue Cross', Father Brown reveals how he knew Flambeau was not a true priest: 'You attacked reason [. . .]. It's bad theology' (23). After his suicide in 'The Secret Garden' (1911), Brown's detective arch-rival Valentin is replaced by other proud scoffers, usually professional doctors, lawyers, or academics, who embrace the illusion of scientific mastery, of getting '*outside* a man and studying him as if he were a gigantic insect' ('Secret of Father Brown' [1927], 465), at the expense of moral reason, which is what enables Father Brown, in his Christian modesty, to get inside the criminal mind and heart. 'I am a man,' says Father Brown, 'and therefore have all devils in my heart' ('Hammer', 130).

Father Brown's detective philosophy reaches all the way back to Auguste Dupin's contempt for inductive 'diligence' and facility at reading minds by 'analysis'. But for all his criticism of secular reason and championing of everyday 'miracles', Chesterton's Father Brown solves his cases largely by induction, not divine inspiration or moral hunches. Just as invariably, crimes in Chesterton's tales that initially appear miraculous are shown to have quite commonsensical explanations, just as the apparent randomness of Father Brown's trail of 'unforeseen' vandalism in 'The Blue Cross' turns out to have a perfectly reasonable human purpose behind it, namely, Father Brown's. Often in such cases, the miraculous appearance of the crime has an allegorical meaning. 'The Hammer of God' (1911) is a case in point.

The story opens with Vicar Bohun and his dissolute brother, the Colonel, arguing in the yard of a smithy next to the cathedral, where Colonel Bohun is loitering for the purpose of carrying on an affair with the blacksmith's wife. After they quarrel, the vicar enters the cathedral to pray. Moments later, the colonel is discovered lying in the yard with his head pulverized by a tremendous blow from one of the blacksmith's hammers.

There is reason to suspect the burly blacksmith, of course. But he has an airtight alibi, and it begins to look as though God himself must have reached down from heaven and punished the miscreant for his sins. No one else in the village has the strength to have delivered such a devastating stroke, except the blacksmith's nephew, the village 'idiot', whom the vicar singles out as the prime suspect because his mental impairment would explain the murderer's choice of an inappropriately light hammer.

What catches Father Brown's attention, however, and should catch ours, is what the vicar says by way of preface to this accusation: 'I am a priest . . . and a priest should be no shedder of blood. I – I mean that he should bring no one to the gallows' (126). The nephew, because of his mental condition, cannot be executed for the crime if convicted. The vicar's slip of the tongue about priests 'shedd[ing] blood' and his 'curiously happy smile' (126) at realizing that his accusation cannot result in harm to the young man both point to the correct solution to the crime. As it turns out, the hammer was thrown from the parapet of the cathedral next door to the smithy by the vicar himself, infuriated at his brother's insolence and shameless debauchery. Watching the wastrel strutting about far below him 'like a poisonous insect', the vicar succumbed to the sin of pride: he decided to play God. 'Then something snapped in your soul,' Father Brown tells him, 'and you let God's thunderbolt fall' (130). The hammer is a small one, but its momentum gives it crushing power, not just physically, but symbolically.

Chesterton is compellingly impressionistic in his use of colour and light, and close to surrealistic in his architecture, which conforms improbably to the demands of his physical conundrums: cathedrals cheek-by-jowl with smithies; odd T-shaped country houses with exitless conservatories; mansions built like silos topped by concentric circular rooms and surrounded with flower gardens and walls of electrified steel. His landscapes and cityscapes are clearly intended to convey spiritual realities. And yet, perhaps more consistently than any other detective writer of the pre-Great War period, Chesterton worked hard to engage his readers in the imaginative effort to solve the crime in question by continuous and recurrent analeptic reconstruction. His tales require no special knowledge, not even of Catholic doctrine, ritual, or history. For all his talk of the inherent 'reason' of faith, Father Brown solves cases by appealing to the known laws of the modern, scientific, common-sense universe. Moreover, Chesterton almost never withholds information from the reader that Father Brown himself has in his possession.

In 'The Hammer of God', for instance, we are made aware from the outset of the two brothers' hatred of each other, of the vicar's love of praying alone in remote, high places in the cathedral, and of his hunched-over posture after confronting his brother in the blacksmith's yard, 'with bowed head, crossing himself', a gesture he adopts not out of piety, but in order to hide the hammer he has just snatched up. Reading carefully, we see Chesterton going out of his way to feed us clues without making things too easy. Just a line or two before the vicar slouches into the cathedral, his brother explains why he is wearing such a 'queer round hat covered with green': 'It was the first to hand,' he tells his brother (120), just like the small, light hammer – too light for the purposes of murder in the hands of an ordinary mortal walking the earth – that the vicar impulsively snatches up next.

What Chesterton deliberately avoids mentioning throughout the tale that ensues is the towering height of the cathedral looming over the smithy yard where the body is discovered. Perhaps that, too, has its allegorical purpose. Just so, Chesterton believed, does the saving grace of God loom over us in our ordinary, 'insect'-like lives: massive, heaven-pointing, and ignored.

Bohemian Souls of Steel

When Doyle first grew tired of Holmes and (apparently) killed him off in the death-embrace of Moriarity, all of England mourned. Men went about in black arm-bands and women wore black veils. Doyle was flabbergasted but 'fully determined' to lay Holmes to rest, 'even if I buried my banking account along with him' (*Memories*, 99). As 'The Empty House' and dozens of later stories attest, Doyle eventually found 'the temptation of high prices' impossible to resist (*Memories*, 100), much to the delight of Holmes fans everywhere. That just as many women as men seem to have welcomed the great detective's resurrection says a great deal about the undeniable appeal that Holmes had for readers of the opposite sex, despite his misogynistic pronouncements on the distracting nuisance posed for 'clear reasoning' of 'emotional qualities' like love (*Memories*, 117). This appeal has endured. Of fictional males whom women readers recently chose as favourite hypothetical dinner partners, Holmes was among the top ten (Anonymous).

When Doyle took Watson from the hearth-side of his fraternal and professional 'mate' and placed him in the arms of a sexual one at the end of *The Sign of Four*, he could not have anticipated the large female readership that *The Strand*, a family magazine, would bring to his next instalment of the Holmes saga. 'A Scandal in Bohemia', his first *Strand* tale and first Holmes short story, raises the question of finding a corresponding match for the human reasoning machine, indicating Doyle's canny awareness of his new, female reading demographic.

That Holmes's 'match' – both in the sense of a worthy opponent and of a possible heterosexual partner – should take the form of a woman who belongs to a profession distinguished for its accomplishments in acting and disguise, as well as notorious for its bohemian, independent females, reflects the author's belief that the art and science of detection are best left to private professionals, not state-sponsored officials or unskilled amateurs. Moreover, that Irene Adler, '*the* woman' (209), should defeat the great detective by dressing as a man represents not only Doyle's recognition of the socially constructed basis of gender identity, but also his positive view of the talents and abilities to be expected of women newly seeking admission to the traditionally male professions, including, presumably, that of detection.

At the time Doyle wrote his story, women in record numbers were entering professions previously closed to them, though in absolute terms those numbers were still small. Long relegated to nursing and education, for which they traditionally did not require certification, women were denied admission to British universities until 1869. The Education Act of 1870, guaranteeing elementary schooling for all British children, helped improve girls' chances for success at colleges and professional schools. Once there, young women began to push for corresponding opportunities in the fields for which they had been trained. Similar pressure was applied in sports and the clerical workforce. As Patricia Craig and Mary Cadogan note, the so-called 'New Woman' was becoming 'a force to be reckoned with', and stories featuring 'women and girls in challenging situations proliferated' in weekly and monthly magazines and in books (23).

Increasing feminization of the professions and the appearance of professional women in the mass media accompanied growing agitation for women's property and voting rights. The first women's rights convention in the English-speaking world took place in Seneca Falls, New York, in 1848, and John Stuart Mill's ground-breaking essay defending women's civil liberties, *The Subjugation of Women*, appeared in England in 1869. Before long, changes were enacted in the British common law granting married and divorced women control over their own property for the first time. It took almost four decades after passage of the Second Married Women's Property Act of 1882, however, for British women to win the right to vote in national elections.

Professional women detectives began to appear in popular crime literature as early as 1864, with the publication of *The Female Detective*, by Andrew Forrester, Jr, and an anonymously authored collection of tales, sometimes dated to 1861, entitled *The Revelations of a Lady Detective*, featuring the female sleuth 'Mrs Paschal'. By 1901, notes Michelle B. Slung, 'no fewer than twenty women detectives [had] made their appearance' (xix), in America as well as England, including the Pinkerton operative Mrs Hugh Lawton in Allan Pinkerton's *A Spy of the Rebellion* (1883) and American dime-novel heroines like the eponymous protagonist of *New York Nell, the Boy-Girl Detective* (1886), by Edward Wheeler. The pace of female professional debuts increased appreciably in the immediate wake of Sherlock Holmes. None of these heroines was particularly feminist. In fact, as Kathleen Gregory Klein notes, early female professional detectives almost invariably tended to reinforce rather than challenge the 'conventional sex/gender bias' (*Woman*, 2) of their readers, both male and female, abandoning their jobs for marriage with dismaying enthusiasm whenever the opportunity arose.

Klein takes a jaundiced view of fictional female detectives in general, seeing an irreconcilable contradiction between the liberationist agenda of the late twentieth-century women's movement, which she endorses, and the masculinist assumptions that have shaped traditional fictional detectives into defenders of a social order oppressive to women. She does not comment on '*the* woman' of 'A Scandal in Bohemia', Holmes's female nemesis, since Irene Adler is not, technically, a detective. But if she had, Klein would no doubt have cited Adler's retirement from the stage and her marriage to Godfrey Norton, a lawyer, as 'undercutting' the actress's distinction as a worthy opponent of Holmes by taking away her means of maintaining an independent livelihood and 'reestablishing [her] in her traditional place' after the dust of detection has settled (*Woman*, 58). Doyle's mixed score-card with respect to women's rights would tend to support that judgement.

Doyle was opposed to unconditional women's suffrage and increasingly unsympathetic to the suffragists as their tactics became more militant after the turn of the century (Stashower, 294). He endorsed the chivalric ideal evident in his serious historical fiction and his first two Holmes adventures. It is no surprise, therefore, to find so many of Holmes's female clients conforming to the stereotype of the damsel in distress. But Doyle was no male chauvinist. He strongly advocated giving women control over their own property and reforming the divorce laws to make it easier for women to leave abusive husbands. This advocacy is a consistent theme in the Holmes stories, where crimes against women are often motivated by the desire of a male guardian or step-father to get his hands on the female client's personal wealth.

Nor did Doyle feel threatened by the New Woman. Handsome and sturdy Mrs Westmacott, the middle-aged heroine of his social comedy, *Beyond the City* (1891), scandalizes her suburban neighbours by her outspokenness on behalf of women's rights – 'I say that a woman is a colossal monument to the selfishness of man' (629) – as well as her taste for dark beer and dumbbells. Doyle's portrayal, notes Daniel Stashower, 'wavers between admiration and comedy' (130), but admiration must have sounded the predominant note in the ear of one American publisher, for he took the author to be a young woman (Stashower, 130). As for women professionals, 'The Doctors of Hoyland' (1894) tells of the competition between a male physician and his female counterpart, who is a far better doctor than he (Stashower, 123). The story ends with Dr James Ripley proposing marriage to his fair rival, only to be rejected because his incompetence would harm their joint practice!

The retired American opera singer Irene Adler, purported blackmailer of the King of Bohemia, is another such strong, independent-minded woman. Holmes is defeated by Adler, first, because she is far better at one of the cardinal skills of professional detection than he is, and, second, because there is a fatal flaw in his 'method' when it comes to a woman like her, who possesses, as his client the King of Bohemia puts it, 'a soul of steel'. Being her former lover, the King should know: 'She has the face of the most beautiful of women, and the mind of the most resolute of men' ('Scandal', 216).

Holmes, however, who has presumably never been intimate with a woman, decides to outwit Adler by relying on his stereotyped ideas of how women behave. Since '[w]omen are naturally secretive, and they like to do their own secreting' (223), Holmes decides, rightly, that the incriminating photograph of Adler and the King must be in Adler's house. He counts on the natural compassion of women to compel Adler to receive him into her home under the impression that he has been injured trying to defend her from ruffians outside her door, men he has hired to play the part. And he is not disappointed. Finally, Adler succumbs to her womanly 'instinct' to 'rush to the thing that she values most' – the photograph – when she hears Watson's cry of 'Fire!' and sees the smoke from his plumber's rocket. 'It is a perfectly overpowering impulse,' says Holmes, 'and I have more than once taken advantage of it' (226).

Holmes, a typical Victorian male, sees Adler as a 'natural' woman, governed by emotion, instinct, and impulse. But as he soon learns, she stands so far in advance of this Victorian stereotype that she blocks it from view, 'eclips[ing] and predominat[ing] the whole of her sex', as Watson puts it (209). Lulled into a false sense of security by Adler's initial conformity to his predictions, Holmes underestimates both her professional competence and her unconventionally masculine resolution.

On a professional level, Holmes fails to anticipate Adler's keen eye for the disguises and performances of other actors, as well as her ability to disguise herself and fool them with her own. 'Male costume is nothing new to me,' she says in the letter she leaves for Holmes after her escape. 'I often take advantage of the freedom which it gives' (228). On a personal level, Holmes fails to anticipate the degree of quick-wittedness and resolve that enables Adler, disguised as 'a slim youth in an ulster' (226), to follow him home in order to confirm her suspicions of his true identity. Nor could he possibly credit her audacity in addressing him as she passes his very doorstep with 'Good night, Mister Sherlock Holmes'. ' "I've heard that voice before," said Holmes, staring down the dimly lit street. "Now, I wonder who the deuce that could have been" ' (227). Smitten with his own genius, Holmes hears but does not observe.

'[S]he was a lovely woman,' Holmes tells Watson earlier, after his first, clandestine glimpse of Adler as she left for St Monica's church to be married, 'with a face that a man might die for' (220). This statement is sometimes taken to indicate that Holmes has let Adler's physical charms addle his 'cold, precise, but admirably balanced mind', and that Watson is wrong when he states that the detective felt no 'emotion akin to love for Irene Adler' (210). But in fact Doyle has again placed a clue to what Holmes is thinking right under our noses, and again we are on the verge of failing to recognize it.

The 'man' that Holmes has in mind here is not himself, but the clergyman he will later play in the operatic scene he choreographs in front of Adler's fancy townhouse in the West End. 'He is dead!' cry several (carefully coached) voices when the Nonconformist minister who has rushed to defend Adler is struck down in the midst of 'a little knot of flushed and struggling men' outside her door. Meanwhile the opera singer, having hurried up the steps, stands and watches 'with her superb figure outlined against the lights of the hall' (224). It is a scene worthy of Puccini's *La Bohème*, 'The Bohemian', a role Adler herself might have sung had Doyle not invented the New Jersey nightingale before Puccini created it. The scene, however, could well have been inspired by *Scenes de la vie de bohème* (1851) by Henri Murger (1822–61), which was Puccini's source. Watson is reading the book at one point while waiting for Holmes to return home in *A Study in Scarlet* (38).

Holmes does not love Irene Adler. He cannot afford to, if he wants to stay at the top of his game. He admires her just as he would admire any other professional rival he considered worthy of respect, and that admiration was no doubt one source of the appeal he had for women imagining themselves in similarly emancipated roles.

The professional rivalry in which Adler proves herself every bit a 'match' for Holmes, and more, is that of disguise. Holmes's 'soul' is 'Bohemian' because it is consummately theatrical. When Watson first sees him in his clergyman's get-up, he states that this was more than a change of costume: 'His expression, his manner, his very soul seemed to vary with every fresh part he assumed. The stage lost a fine actor, even as science lost an acute reasoner, when he became a specialist in crime' (223). These sentiments echo similar praises uttered throughout the Holmes canon regarding the great detective's unique battery of professional skills. Based on comments made in *The Sign of Four* alone, we could substitute for 'actor' or 'scientist' in the sentence above 'boxer' (132), 'criminal' (140), and 'acrobat' (148), as well as medievalist, musicologist, religious historian, and nautical engineer (171–2).

The 'Bohemian soul' of the detective is that of a professional chameleon. But one cannot master all trades without occasionally proving a jackass in at least one. The 'King of Bohemia' is he who can master the art of disguise, but this king has been mastered by Bohemia's queen, whose 'soul of steel' retains its stubborn integrity beneath its duplicitous changes in outward form. The real 'Scandal in Bohemia' is Holmes's defeat by '*the* woman', whose maiden name, 'Adler', is German for 'eagle', the imperial emblem of the Habsburg Empire to which the real Kingdom of Bohemia was originally subservient. Adler is, in short, a perfect 'match', in character and expertise if not in marriage, for Sherlock Holmes, the monarch of bohemian professional detectives. In her retirement from the stage, as Watson might put it, the world lost a fine private investigator.

Many other women soon sprang up to take her place in the pages of popular detection. Not long after Holmes's defeat by Adler in July 1891, the readership for female detectives, professional and amateur, increased markedly. While this development was as much due to the prominence of the New Woman in the public eye as to Holmes's and Adler's influence, Doyle's impact was not inconsiderable, as is shown by the frequent appearance of Holmesian details in the female detectives of this decade and the gradual falling-off in demand for such characters as the novelty of Holmes faded in the decade following, at least in England.

As early as 1894, two anonymous Holmes pastiches published in *The Student: A Journal for University Extension Students* featured

Mrs Julia Herlock Shomes, widow of a former 'Private Enquiry Agent', and her sidekick Mrs Lucilla Wiggins (Craig and Cadogan, 19). That same year saw the publication of *The Experiences of Loveday Brooke, Lady Detective*, by Catherine Louisa Pirkis (?–1910), whose industrious heroine works for Ebenezer Dyer's private detection agency, and one year later *The Fatal Finger Mark*, by Milton Danvers, introduced Rose Cortenay, a female operative working for the firm of private investigator Robert Spicer. Cortenay went on to appear in five subsequent novels, while Dorcas Dene, heroine of *Dorcas Dene, Detective: Her Adventures* (1897), by George R. Sims (1847–1922), proved so popular that a second series of adventures soon followed. Deane is a former actress, like Irene Adler, and has her own Watson, a dramatist friend named Mr Saxon.

Dora Myrl, the Lady Detective (1900), by M. McDonnell Bodkin, introduced a male professional, Paul Beck, as rival to Bodkin's female private investigator. Unlike Holmes's female 'match', however, Myrl later married her male counterpart in *The Capture of Paul Beck* (1909). By this time, the British demand for female professional detectives was beginning to taper off. The last significant addition to the sub-genre before the outbreak of World War I was *Lady Molly of Scotland Yard* (1910), by Baroness Orczy, which reflects in its detective heroine's supercilious attitudes toward the lower classes much of the Baroness's own aristocratic prejudices. Lady Molly's Watson-like sidekick and narrator is her maid, Mary.

Lady Molly would have had difficulty working an international case with most of her plebeian American counterparts. In the United States, female detectives had for the most part arisen in the context of the cheap dime novels and detective weeklies of the 1870s, venues in which the tradition of the action-filled urban detective adventure lingered well into the twentieth century.

As in England, the Holmes craze helped fuel the demand for female sleuths, although they had already appeared more often in the flourishing 'dimes' than in the pages of English popular fiction. Klein identifies *The Lady Detective*, by Harlan P. Halsey (1839?–1898), as the first of the dimes to feature a female professional sleuth, Kate Goelet, but gives no date (*Woman*, 36–41). (The title appears as number eighteen in the series of *Old Sleuth Library* monthlies and quarterlies that began in 1885.) While Klein counts only forty out of more than 2,500 pulp detective titles as mentioning female investigators, titles alone are not an accurate guide to the frequency with which women detectives appeared in the dimes. The 'Co.' in Halsey's *Old Sleuth, Badger, and Co.* (1891), for instance, turns out to be 'The

Lady Detective, Maggie Everett' (Hoppenstand, 141), and in *Secret Service* (1909), by Francis Worcester Doughty (1850–1917), 'Miss Alice Montgomery' (Hoppenstand, 201) is an important undercover operative employed by Old and Young King Brady.

Whenever they first appeared, American female investigators were more than just languishing sidekicks of the male detectives flooding the pulps, and their popularity did not diminish, like that of their English sisters, after the first wave of the Holmes mania in the 1890s. Right through the First World War American female detectives kept appearing in books like *Miss Madelyn Mack, Detective* (1914), by Hugh C. Weir (1884–1934), *Constance Dunlap – Woman Detective* (1916), by Arthur B. Reeve (1880–1936), and *The Green Jacket* (1917), by Jeanette Lee, featuring female sleuth Millicent Newberry. Meanwhile, amateur American woman detectives like Anna Katherine Green's Miss Amelia Butterworth in *That Affair Next Door* (1897) and *Lost Man's Lane* (1898), as well as Green's teen-aged ingénue sleuth Violet Strange in *The Golden Slipper and Other Problems for Violet Strange* (1915), were gaining English as well as American readers.

The Great War and the Golden Age

The First World War (1914–18) was known to contemporaries as 'The Great War' for good reason. It was the most costly in lives and materiel in the history of the world to that time, and its traumatic effects persisted long enough to cause the outbreak of a Second World War two decades later. According to Paul Fussell, eight and a half million soldiers died on both sides of the conflict, five million among the Allied forces (19). In England, after a burst of initial enthusiasm among a generation of young men wholly unfamiliar with the realities of mechanized trench warfare (21–2), national conscription had to be enacted by early 1915.

In July 1916, at the Battle of the Somme, also known among enlisted men as 'The Great Fuck-Up' (Fussell, 12), new working-class recruits in the 'War to End All Wars' were sent marching senselessly, repeatedly, in broad daylight, into raking fusillades of machine-gun fire. Of 110,000 men attacking on the first day of action, 60,000 were killed. A similar disaster at Passchendaele the next year left 370,000 men dead and wounded after three and a half months of fighting in the rain-soaked fields. Thousands of them had literally drowned in bottomless pits of mud (16).

These and other fiascos in the early years of the war led many English enlisted men to resent the privileged class of officers commanding them and the political leaders back home who had gotten them into this débâcle, creating a high degree of cynicism toward social privilege and political authority among returning veterans. Home-front naïveté regarding the brutal reality of the war also tended to alienate these men from civilian life, leaving the post-war governance of the nation in the hands of the Conservative old guard.

As Charles Mowat points out (9), the officer class itself had suffered heavy losses among its younger, front-line members, enfeebling the political leadership among their demographic cohort. Called 'The Lost Generation', most of these veterans had little say, or even interest, in the post-war running of the government. The worse-off among them withdrew into insular domesticity or listless unemploymment, while the better-off joined 'The Bright Young Things' who had come of age after the fighting was over, devoting themselves to partying with their 'flapper' girl-friends, driving fast motor-cars, and getting high on heroin and cocaine. Left to themselves, writes Mowat, the older Conservatives now sought to create 'a better society by returning to the prewar order purged of its former inequalities' (8). Their hold on power was reinforced by the tremendous increase in governmental bureaucracy caused by the war effort itself. By 1931, however, after two years of world Depression and with Fascism on the rise, it was clear that these efforts to 'return to the world of 1914, with the illusion of time standing still' (8), were doomed to failure.

Meanwhile, as Colin Watson points out, the middle- and upper-middle classes anticipated the 'secure continuance of the old order and its gradual enrichment by the innovations of progress' (35). Watson notes that such middle-class complacency was starkly at odds with the social turmoil at the bottom of the economic hierarchy during these years, including the General Strike of 1926, workers' riots, mutiny, and, in the 1930s, hunger marches. But British society had become highly stratified, not only by income, but also by recreation and community (36). While unemployment among workers and servants was a chronic problem well into the mid-1930s, average national income for those who had jobs rose by some 40 per cent from 1920 to 1940. Steady growth in sales of consumer goods and services continued throughout the two decades (Mowat, 451), while any possibility that working-class dissatisfaction might burst into outright revolution, as had happened in Russia in 1917, was foreclosed by increasingly liberal and extended government unemployment insurance, also known as 'the dole' (Mowat, 31).

For those with some disposable income the interwar years were devoted to getting things back to normal. It was to this group of readers – white-collar clerks, retail employees, professionals and academics of both sexes, conservative politicians and middle-class housewives, all of whom were relatively well educated and well placed to advance in the post-war economy – that detective fiction in the Golden Age most directly appealed. With its reliable evocation of order out of disorder, its respect for the rule of law in defence of life and property, and its faith that a rational intention informs even the most baffling acts of violence, the new genre of detection seemed tailor-made to allay the anxieties that lingered below the superficial complacency of British middle-class life.

For despite their affirmations of faith in the future, writes Watson, '[p]eople were aware in their hearts that the 1914–1918 war had solved nothing, and that the public optimism of the politicians masked their impotence and perplexity' (82). Accordingly, the cultural nostrums of fictional detection were artificially enhanced with pre-war sweeteners: sprawling country estates, tidy villages, and townhouses populated by comfortable eccentrics. Here was a world embodying the values of the vanishing gentry class and prominently featuring members of the four most ancient and honourable professions: retired military officers, local clergy, lawyers, and doctors.

Above all, detective fiction offered the glittering promise of 'scientific' historical reconstruction to a generation that considered the Great War 'a hideous embarrassment to the prevailing [. . .] Idea of Progress' (Fussell, 8) and had, as a result, lost faith in 'a seamless, purposeful "history" involving a coherent stream of time running from past through present to future' (21). Among historians themselves, notes Richard Evans, rancorous disagreements arose over the causes of the war, heightened by nationalistic grievances.

A new generation of historians, including Benedetto Croce (1866–1952) in Italy and R. G. Collingwood (1889–1943) in England, incorporated into their philosophies of history the relativity of viewpoint that had been popularized by the new physics of Albert Einstein (1879–1955). His General Theory of Relativity, first announced in 1915, portrayed the very fabric of the universe, both the mass of its objects and the time within which they moved, as expanding or contracting relative to the motion of the observer. In a similar manner, Croce and Collingwood argued that all reconstructions of the past depended upon the historically determined cultural prejudices and presuppositions of those making such reconstructions in an ever-moving present.

'Scientific' or 'objective' historiography was now impossible, since history itself seemed to have been broken, like Humpty Dumpty, into as many pieces as there were historians to study it. While detectives like Agatha Christie's Hercule Poirot and Dorothy Sayers's Lord Peter Wimsey could not put history back together again, they did offer its middle- and upper-class readers the flattering illusion that, on a small scale at least, the task was not impossible, and that people like them were capable of doing it.

The perfect fit between the Golden Age plot formula and a relatively affluent and conservative middle-class readership led to classical detection's dominance of the interwar best-seller lists. According to Julian Symons, the annual number of crime and detective publications quintupled between 1914 and 1926, and doubled again by 1939 (*Bloody*, 124). At the end of the 1930s, writes Watson, one of every four novels sold in England was a work of detective fiction, and demand had outstripped supply to the point where nearly anyone who wrote a detective story could find a publisher for it (96).

Critics like Symons and Watson tend to divide the Golden Age into two stages corresponding roughly to its two decades. The twenties saw the rapid displacement of the short story as the primary venue of detection in favour of the short, one-volume novel. There were several reasons for this: increasing leisure time for reading and rising income to spend on books in middle-class households, especially among women; a boom in circulating libraries that loaned books on subscription for pennies through newsagents and stationers' stores; and the popularity of travel by automobile rather than railroad, reducing the demand for short fiction to be read *en route* (Symons, *Bloody*, 95–6).

The twenties were a decade of relative generic naïveté in England, where detective fiction was dominated by the tight timetables, explicit floor-plans, multiple suspects, and exotic weaponry found in the works of G. K. Chesterton, R. Austin Freeman, Agatha Christie, Freeman Wills Crofts (1879–1957), Dorothy Sayers, and Anthony Berkeley. Their classical American counterparts, such as Willard Huntington Wright (a.k.a. S. S. van Dine), Earl Derr Biggers (1884–1943, the creator of Charlie Chan), and Ellery Queen, the pseudonym of cousins Frederic Dannay (b. Daniel Nathan, 1905–82) and Manfred B. Lee (b. Manford Lepofsky, 1905–71), were just as formulaic. As we have seen, detective writers like these soon became interested in devising 'rules' to ensure 'fair play' between their fictional detectives and the readers whom they were challenging to guess 'whodunit?'

The so-called 'rules' were anything but firm. Before the end of the decade, Christie had radically undermined one cardinal assumption of generic purists in *The Murder of Roger Ackroyd* (1926) – namely, that the detective narrator was never to be considered a suspect – and Berkeley had published *The Poisoned Chocolates Case* (1929). Here, a fictional 'Crime Club' of four writers, a lawyer, and one ordinary reader of detection is presented by gentleman amateur Roger Sherringham with a real-life case to solve. Each member's solution, ingenious and persuasive at first, is shown to be inadequate to the complexities of real life.

Some of the more forbiddingly erudite Golden Age detectives seemed to annoy as many readers as they charmed. Van Dine's sleuthing art connoisseur Philo Vance drew from humorist Ogden Nash (1902–71) the acerbic couplet, 'Philo Vance/ Needs a kick in the pance'. Far from appearing irrelevant during the economically depressed 1930s, however, the brittle superficiality of most classical detection seemed to enhance its appeal as a genre of distraction and escape, even as a more cynical, putatively more realistic type of crime fiction called 'hard-boiled' was fast gaining popularity in America.

Many of the Golden Age writers who got their start in the twenties continued to do well in the thirties, though some, like Dorothy Sayers, began to experiment with longer plots in which detection shares the spotlight with, or is even pushed into the shadows by, more complex character development and interpersonal relations. Despite continuing sales, however, writers like Sayers, Christie, and Queen now had to compete with some of the best-selling and most durable detective writers of the interwar years. These included John Dickson Carr (1906–77), master of the locked-room mystery, whose Dr Gideon Fell was based on the real G. K. Chesterton; Michael Innes (pseudonym of John Innes Mackintosh Steward, 1906–94); Margery Allingham (1904–66), Ngaio Marsh (1895–1982), Nicholas Blake (pseudonym of Poet Laureate Cecil Day Lewis, 1904–72), and Rex Stout (1886–1975), creator of the corpulent and irascible Old World expatriate Nero Wolfe and his wise-cracking, fast-talking, up-to-date American personal secretary, Archie Goodwin.

The books written by these authors reveal a profound indebtedness to Arthur Conan Doyle's influence and example, informed by each writer's personal expertise and embroidered with his or her personal obsessions. However, notes Martin Priestman, while Doyle's tales and those of his pre-Great War contemporaries were still 'capable of handling current ideas with some sophistication', the 'politically questioning edge seems largely to disappear' among their post-war successors, whose characters remain isolated from contemporary historical reality in all but the most superficial ways (134). Golden Age writers also tended to flatten out fictional personalities in order to enhance the motivic rationale of the puzzle element, frequently resorting to racial, ethnic, and class stereotypes, along with corresponding epithets, that can make Doyle's generation seem 'politically correct' by comparison.

The interwar authors perfected the technique of multiplying their readers' opportunities for analeptic invention by a careful selection and narrative sequencing of events, both clues and testimony, capable of arrangement into several overlapping arrays. Their detective heroes were usually distinguished by Holmesian penetration and acumen, along with one outstanding hobby or eccentricity and, typically, a sidekick – perhaps the most obvious of all Holmesian debts. Only one Golden Age detective besides Chesterton's Father Brown went on to achieve widespread, lasting fame without the aid of such a sidekick: Agatha Christie's Miss Jane Marple.

Detection by Metaphor

Agatha Christie Mallowan (1890–1976) was not only the most prolific and popular author of detective fiction in the twentieth century, but the world's best-selling writer, ever. More than half a billion copies of her works have appeared in more than a hundred languages since the publication of her first book, *The Mysterious Affair at Styles*, in 1920. Before her death she had written 76 novels, 158 short stories, and 15 plays, and many of these have never gone out of print.

Christie's two most famous continuing series detectives are the dapper, egg-headed Belgian private eye, Monsieur Hercule Poirot, who first appeared in *Styles* with his ingenuous chum, Captain Hastings, and Miss Jane Marple, who debuted in a series of short stories in 1928 featuring the members of 'The Tuesday Night Club' of amateur detectives, and graduated to her first novel, *The Murder at the Vicarage*, two years later. Poirot, relying exclusively on his 'little grey cells', is the more famous of the two.

Styles epitomizes the form, and formulae, of the classical tale of Golden Age detection. Christie herself stated that in writing the book she consciously set about imitating Arthur Conan Doyle (*Autobiography*, 242–3), and the influence is not hard to see: a brainy, eccentric, and inordinately vain private professional detective; a slightly dim-witted, demobilized, wounded war veteran as amanuensis; and a plot designed to wring every ounce of effort from the reader's reconstructive imagination. Set at a country estate during the Great War, the book almost immediately introduces the reader, via Hastings's narrative voice, to a closed circle of suspects all living together as guests, retainers, or relatives of a wealthy and philanthropic widow, the former Mrs Cavendish, and her new husband, the sinister Alfred Inglethorpe.

Christie wastes no time conveying the reasons – nearly all pecuniary – that each of these characters has for wishing the new Mrs Inglethorpe dead and, not surprisingly, the woman soon is. Poirot's investigation, related to us by Hastings and interspersed with his own false speculations, uncovers numerous subtle details of the crime scene and elicits a great deal of conflicting testimony. Like her early detective muse, Anna Green, Christie offers us maps, diagrams, and facsimiles of writing fragments in order to clarify the metonymic possibilities for our ongoing invention of retrospective arrays. Right up to the end we are kept in the dark as to the real culprit, despite the exonerations of two apparently guilty parties. In the final scene, Poirot assembles and addresses all the suspects, explains his deductions, and reveals the actual murderer, crystallizing the analeptic ritual of classical detective fiction for decades to come. The only formal flaw in Christie's inaugural venture into detection is Poirot's undisclosed discovery of the chemical formula – written in Latin! – that enabled the murderer to kill Mrs Inglethorpe while she slept.

As she matured in her art, Christie became more attentive to the demands of 'fair play', skilfully revealing, or hinting at, vital information in the course of the story without giving too much away. She also became less dependent on esoteric means of murder, turning more often to standard weaponry – household toxins or food poisoning, knives, guns – in counter-intuitively complicated circumstances. She was generally more adept in the handling of opportunity and motive than of means, and much of her appeal to her largely female audience lay, as Stephen Knight has observed, in her use of metonymic clues taken from everyday domestic life (*Form*, 108–9).

It should come as no surprise to find that the Golden Age was indeed a golden age for women writers of detective fiction like Christie, whose sensibilities were attuned to their women readers, of whom there were many. In the aftermath of a conflict that had killed one in every seven eligible men and injured as many more (Lewis, 58), the proportion of middle-class young women to young men, both married and single, rose throughout England, and the 'surplus woman problem' even came to be seen as a threat to the institution of marriage (54). Detective fiction shifted accordingly, away from the adventure elements that had traditionally appealed to male readers and toward plots of ratiocination and inspired observation verging on 'intuition', capabilities which most women at the time were more inclined to admire.

What is surprising, however, particularly after the advent of the New Woman, the widespread feminization of male occupations during the Great War, the winning of women's voting rights, and their increased opportunities for economic independence, was how long it took for Golden Age authors, especially in England, to conceive or think of popularizing female characters as professional detectives rather than as amateurs. Only one professional exception leaps out, Miss Maud Silver, a private 'sleuthess' (34) who made her first appearance in *Grey Mask*, by Patricia Wentworth (1878–1961), in 1929.

Christie's amateur sleuth, Miss Jane Marple, appeared almost simultaneously with Miss Silver, and, like Wentworth's creation, Christie's draws on the precedent of Anna Green's New York spinster and snoop, Miss Amelia Butterworth. Silver and Marple are single women, exemplary survivals of pre-war Victorianism, with a strong sense of the distinction between good and evil, but with little of the stereotypical Victorian squeamishness about sex. In 'The Tuesday Night Club' stories, Marple's Victorianism is a bit overdone: she spends each tale working hard at her knitting, dressed in black lace like Whistler's Mother, before popping out with the correct, and unexpected, solution to the problem of the evening. From Marple's first book-length appearance in 1930, however, in *Murder at the Vicarage*, her clothes become more modern and she spends more time in outdoor settings, usually her garden. There she can observe all the doings of the village of St Mary Meade, which could lay claim to the highest homicide rate for middle-class citizens of any borough in England.

In Christie's Marple adventures, a shameless disregard for the old values has unleashed a heartless degree of selfishness among the younger, post-war generation that threatens the social foundations established by elder, wiser heads. The very titles of Christie's first two Miss Marple novels, *Murder at the Vicarage* and *The Body in the Library* (1941), reveal the intimacy of the threat to the old order now coming from below: violence has erupted at the sacred sites of religious piety and gentry respectability. Innocence can be restored only by identifying and casting out the upstarts who would dare such desecration, and in each case the malefactors turn out to be greedy members of the ruthless, restless, and rootless younger crowd.

Marple solves her cases by means of an acute power of intuitive insight. While the detective's subconscious processing of evidence goes back at least as far as Sherlock Holmes, one of Christie's most important models, Doyle implies that this apparent power of 'intuition' is simply another form of metonymic induction, Holmes's 'brilliant reasoning power' speeded up by repetitive training ('Red-Headed', 243; see also *Study*, 16). At first glance, Miss Marple's version of intuition appears similar. 'It's really what people call intuition and make such a fuss about', she says in *Murder at the Vicarage*. 'Intuition is like reading a word without having to spell it out. A child can't do that, because it has had so little experience. But a grown-up person knows the word because he's seen it often before' (76).

Marple's appeal to the power of lifelong 'experience' and the wisdom concerning 'Human Nature' (*Murder*, 192) that is accumulated with age reinforces the pre-war Victorian values that Christie wishes to uphold throughout her work: the inexperienced 'children' of the new post-war generation cannot 'read' human nature without 'having to spell it out' step by step, while members of the older generation, like Miss Marple, can do so at a glance, because they've seen it all 'before'.

In practice, however, Miss Marple's version of intuition does not much resemble the Holmesian concept of accelerated induction. The vicar, Len Clement, gives us some idea of the difference when he replies, 'You mean that if a things reminds you of something else – well, it's probably the same kind of thing' (76). In Jane Marple's case, intuition has nothing to do with metonymic connections. It is a species of almost purely metaphorical thinking unrestricted to any particular type of activity, criminal or otherwise. Thus, in *The Body in the Library*, an important associative clue turns out to be Marple's memory of a schoolboy prank by a youngster named Tommy Bond, who hid a frog in the classroom clock.

Miss Marple announces her 'mission statement', as it were, late in *Murder at the Vicarage*. When living alone, she says, one needs a hobby, and hers is 'Human Nature'. She goes on to describe her hobby in horticultural terms (she is, after all, an expert gardener): 'So varied – and so very fascinating [. . .]. One begins to class people, quite definitely, just as though they were birds or flowers, group so and so, genus this, species that. [. . .] You'd be surprised if you knew how very few distinct types there are in all' (192–3). Marple's village laboratory is her database, as it were, as essential to her methods as Holmes's true-crime files are to his.

Christie is not willing, however, to sacrifice metonymical reconstruction on the altar of metaphorical intuition, however informed by 'village parallels' the latter may be (*Murder*, 74). Marple's 'intuitive' analogies are only the starting-points of her investigations, which invariably proceed, like those of Father Brown, by a series of rigid inductions, both positive and negative. Motive, means, and opportunity – who wants what, what the murder was done with, and who was where when it happened – are still, for Marple as for Poirot, the sole sure means of arriving at the truth. 'The point is', says Miss Marple as she and the vicar peruse the 'schedule' of events surrounding the murder of Colonel Protheroe, 'that one must provide an explanation for everything' (195).

Meanwhile, however, readers are tantalized by the almost infinite, sometimes poetic, associative possibilities opened up by Jane Marple's resort to 'Human Nature'. It is a method unique in classical detection not because it is intuitive, but because it is based ostensibly on metaphor rather than metonymy, while never abandoning the metonymic basis of all classical detection.

Casebook Entry No. 3
Of War and Wimsey

To Be of Use

Before Miss Marple – one year before to be precise – there came Miss Climpson. Katherine Climpson makes her first appearance in Dorothy Sayers's third Lord Peter Wimsey novel, *Unnatural Death* (1927). She is a tall, lean, energetic single woman, loquacious, middle-aged, and Evangelical, quite conventional but possessing 'great acumen' (40). Along with several other women in similar circumstances, she works as an 'inquiry agent' (43) in Lord Peter's unofficial investigative agency, the 'Cattery' (as he calls it).

The Cattery's female employees, who pretend to be typists, are actually paid to answer personal ads directed at vulnerable single women in straitened circumstances in order to entrap possible male predators. They are Wimsey's response to the increase in sexual victimization brought about by the so-called 'surplus women' problem of the 1920s, and a tentative solution to the problem itself. As he explains to his friend and future brother-in-law, Inspector Charles Parker of Scotland Yard, unmarried female operatives like Miss Climpson, with their 'magnificent gossip-power and units of inquisitiveness' (42), are a wasted national resource that can be turned to important public service rather than remaining the butt of bad jokes. By finding a way to make them useful to a society that ridicules them, Wimsey offers these women both a means of self-support and a source of pride.

Miss Climpson and her companions are never the central focus of Sayers's books, and their 'professional' status is somewhat ambiguous, since, like Wimsey's valet and detective factotum, Mervyn

Bunter, they work at the sufferance and behest of their private employer, as though they were part of Wimsey's household staff. Whatever we may feel about Sayers's stereotyping of 'catty' 'spinsters' like Miss Climpson, the feminist themes of social usefulness and dignity advanced by the 'Cattery' resonate throughout Sayers's relatively small but richly textured collection of detective novels and stories, colouring her representations of class and gender relations in the post-Great War era.

These themes are especially pertinent to Lord Peter Wimsey himself, a shell-shocked veteran officer of the Great War who is driven by his sense of guilt for the deaths of his men, as well as by his old-fashioned adherence to the code of *noblesse oblige*, to make the society they died to defend worth their sacrifice. Despite appearances, Wimsey deliberately defies the post-war stereotype of the vapid, dim-witted, aristocratic playboy – a role he will not hesitate to adopt if it will advance his investigations – by trying hard to right wrongs as an amateur detective.

Sayers's interest in the problem of making oneself useful, of fulfilling one's social responsibility while maintaining one's self-respect, was a personal one. Born in 1893 to an upper-middle-class Oxfordshire family, Sayers imbibed her religious faith, generally conservative outlook, and respect for intellectual achievement from her father, a Church of England parson. An only child, Sayers developed a rich imaginative life and a love of books from an early age. She found her adult métier when she matriculated at Oxford's women's college, Somerville, in 1912. Though a brilliant student who went on to win First Class Honours in Modern Languages, Sayers was forced to defer her academic ambitions upon leaving college in 1915, since Oxford did not grant women academic degrees until 1920.

Meanwhile, Sayers worked as an editor for the academic publisher Blackwell and in a student exchange programme abroad, ending up as a successful copy-writer for an advertising agency, an experience which she later mined for *Murder Must Advertise* (1933). Although she was granted her MA in 1920, and achieved some renown as a medievalist and translator of Dante before her death in 1957, Sayers's international reputation is founded upon her Lord Peter Wimsey novels and stories.

During her immediate post-college years, Sayers also had three love affairs. The last, with an auto mechanic (Sayers adored cars and fast driving), left her pregnant with a son, who was born in 1926. Although she named him her heir, Sayers could not bear to scandalize her devout family by revealing her indiscretion and sent the boy to be raised by a distant relative, never acknowledging him as her own child. This decision, cold-blooded as it is, says much about her fierce attachment to an independent life.

Sayers's adulthood, in short, had clearly acquainted her with the difficulties, both professional and romantic, that faced intelligent, independent-minded, single women in the era immediately after the war, when the ratio of eligible women to men had substantially increased and the jobs that women had rushed to fill during the years of mobilization reverted to the hands of returning veterans. The decline in post-war female job openings must have been especially difficult, not to say ironic, for educated and talented young women like Sayers. As Sandra Gilbert and Susan Gubar point out, while the war had sown alienation and cynicism among the men who fought it, it had empowered women in both salaried professions and wage occupations to the point of exhilaration, lending them a new confidence in their abilities that often spilled over into their personal lives, including sexual relationships, for the next decade (264).

Sayers did not let her literary talents lie fallow for long after receiving her degree in 1920. That same year she began her first Lord Peter Wimsey detective novel, *Whose Body?*, which was published three years later. By 1925 she was making enough money from royalties to leave advertising altogether. She continued to write Wimsey novels until 1937, although, much like Doyle, she professed little interest in her detective protagonist except as a source of income. It wasn't until 1930, in *Strong Poison*, that she thought to introduce a female counterpart and love interest for Wimsey, the detective novelist Harriet Vane, and then only for the purpose of getting rid of her monocled mastermind by sending him down the aisle at the end of the book. Again like Doyle, Sayers had tired of her hero.

She found, however, that she could not dismiss Lord Peter so easily, and the Wimsey–Vane relationship became the focus of three subsequent novels, *Have His Carcass* (1932), *Gaudy Night* (1935) (which ends in Vane's betrothal to Wimsey), and *Busman's Honeymoon* (1937) (which follows their marriage). Along the way, the books became longer, less centred on detection, and more taken up with those difficult issues of sexual and professional identity, independence, and interpersonal relations with which Sayers had had to cope in her own life.

Predecessors to Lord Peter Wimsey have been cited, among them Franklin Blake and Philip Trent (see, e.g., Murch, 216), but Wimsey is unique. He is wealthy beyond the dreams of avarice, with a fashionable address in Piccadilly, expensive automobiles, a valuable collection of rare books and art works, a taste for fine wines and Parisian mistresses, and the resources and leisure to indulge his every 'whim', as his name suggests. In appearance, he seems nothing more than a rather lightweight and superficial Jazz Age playboy, with all the possessions (a monocle, a cane, a valet) and locutions (the dropped 'g', the interjected 'Eh, what?') appropriate to the type. Julian Symons finds Wimsey unbearable, 'a caricature of an English aristocrat' whose speech 'strongly resembles that of Bertie Wooster' (113), the hilariously air-headed young man-about-town popularized in the comic novels of P. G. Wodehouse (1881–1975).

Symons misses the point of Sayers's broad-brushed exaggerations of Wimsey's mannerisms, which the amateur sleuth has no difficulty shedding whenever he has something serious to say and someone trustworthy to say it to. In conversations with Inspector Parker, his official counterpart and unofficial colleague, for instance, Wimsey speaks only the King's English (*Whose*, 72–3), whereas disarming the suspicions of a local police superintendent requires laying on the expected role with a trowel while handing around a few choice cigars (*Clouds*, 76). At one point in *Unnatural Death* (1927), Wimsey himself notes his physical resemblance to Wodehouse's Bertie (66), almost as though it were a deliberate imitation.

Despite his flippant style and appearance, however, Wimsey is intelligent, virtuous, and dutiful. The monocle he affects is 'a powerful magnifier' used in investigations (*Unpleasantness*, 32) and his cane is marked off in precise increments for taking measurements at the scene of a crime. Wimsey's playboy act serves the same purposes as some female sleuths' conventional femininity: it lulls those around him, especially other males, into a false sense of superiority. It is also, as Terrance Lewis points out, a defensive reaction against having to take seriously the often fatal consequences of the 'game' of detection that Wimsey 'plays' as a service to society. His 'hobby', as he calls it in accordance with the family motto, 'As my whimsy takes me', often leads to someone being hanged by the neck until dead.

Lewis is quite perceptive about Wimsey's professedly 'whimsical' interest in detection. Feeling guilty for having sent so many of the men enlisted under him to their deaths during the war, Wimsey suffers recurrences of the shell-shock that left him for months afterward debilitated and catatonic. He is never more vulnerable to these attacks than when he is forced to confront the fact that his investigations may result in the death of another human being, no matter how just the culprit's deserts. Whether soldiers or criminals, says

Lewis, '[a]ll represent[] people sacrificed to social principles which Wimsey felt bound to enforce' (10).

Wimsey's commitment to do good despite its personally devastating consequences is based on more than lingering guilt from the war. While specific incidents have left him with mental wounds – nightmares, depressions – that will not begin to heal until after his marriage to Harriet Vane, the incidents themselves have the impact they do because he takes so seriously the aristocratic obligations traditionally placed upon the ruling class to which he belongs. His sense of responsibility to his society is rooted in a rationale for the privileges of the landed, warrior classes that goes all the way back to Homer's *Iliad*, where Sarpedon preaches to his companion, Glaukos, on the obligations that attend nobility:

[Y]ou and I are honoured before others
with pride of place, the choice meats and the filled wine cups in Lykia[. . .].
Therefore it is our duty [. . .] to take our stand, and bear our part of the
  blazing of battle,
so that a man [. . .] may say of us: 'Indeed, these are no ignoble men who
  are lords of Lykia.' (12.310–18)

Inheriting wealth, property, and infinite leisure, Wimsey has also inherited a strong sense of the duty that goes with them: to lead his people in their fight against the common enemy, whether foreign or domestic. After the Great War, this would be an uphill battle. England's young lords were little respected in their own country, except, perhaps, as a source of income for society columnists, who filled the rotogravure pages of the daily newspapers with their celebrity hi-jinks. Sayers's aim in creating Wimsey was, in part, to rehabilitate the idea of social responsibility for her own 'lost generation' by embodying it in a member of England's ostensibly least responsible and currently most superfluous class.

Carrying On

Whatever we may think of such aims, or of her degree of success in achieving them, Sayers held up a broader mirror to interwar British society than did most of her Golden Age counterparts. As Lewis points out, the impact of the war on middle- and upper-class mores is reflected in the Wimsey novels in ways both obvious and subtle. In *The Unpleasantness at the Bellona Club* (1928) Sayers takes the more obvious route.

The Bellona Club is an officers' club to which Wimsey belongs. On Armistice Day, old General Fentiman, an octogenarian veteran of the Crimean War, is found dead of apparent heart failure in his favourite armchair before the fire at the Club. Wimsey is asked to investigate the time of death to settle a disputed question of inheritance and uncovers a deep-laid murder plot implicating both of the General's grandsons: Captain George Fentiman, an embittered, unemployed, mentally disabled survivor of the Great War, and his resilient, blustery older brother, Major Robert.

In many ways, notes Lewis (3), *Unpleasantness* offers a more thorough and nuanced portrait of the impact of the war on veterans, their families, and their society than some better-known contemporary novels like Ford Madox Ford's *The Good Soldier* (1928) or Robert Graves's *Goodbye to All That* (1928). Unlike its mainstream counterparts, however, it lays the blame for the morally destructive effects of the war at the doorstep of the younger generation of veterans, and specifically those who were not professionally trained for combat. As Colonel Marchbanks concludes, following the discovery that General Fentiman's murderer is himself a greedy, ambitious younger member of the Bellona Club, 'Sometimes, Lord Peter, I think that the War has had a bad effect on some of our young men. But then, of course, all are not soldiers by training, and that makes a great difference' (335). Class and training tell for Sayers, and virtue in the ancient Greek sense of *aristoi* ('excellence') or Roman *virtus* ('power') means carrying out the duties attendant on one's position in society effectively and thoroughly, in war or peace.

Although Wimsey is a detective amateur, he brings to his investigations all the talents and skills of the professional, aristocratic officer class to which he belongs. A leader of men in combat, a gifted tactician and strategist with experience in foreign intelligence, including disguise and code-breaking, Wimsey finds a peacetime use for these skills in the 'hobby' of detection. In addition, like 'analytic' predecessors stretching back to Auguste Dupin, he enjoys detection as an art. For him a criminal 'with inspiration', capable of 'real, artistic, finished stuff' (*Whose*, 42), is 'a poet of crime' (45).

At first, detection is simply Wimsey's escape from the trauma of war, not a way of giving something back. Contrasting his amateur status with Inspector Parker's professional commitment, Lord Peter admits he took up his 'hobby' because 'the bottom of things was rather knocked out for [him]' at war's end. '[I]t was so damned exciting,' he tells Parker, 'and the worst of it is, I enjoy it, up to a point'

(*Whose*, 156). That point is when the hobby begins to have fatal consequences. 'It *is* a game to me, to begin with,' Wimsey continues, 'and I go on cheerfully, and then I suddenly see that somebody is going to be hurt, and I want to get out of it' (158). To his credit as a member of the warrior class, Wimsey does not retreat once he commits himself, but accepts the mental self-punishment of fulfilling his inherited obligations.

Lord Peter's own war experiences do not surface in *Unpleasantness*, but Sayers had already woven them into the fabric of her first Wimsey novel, *Whose Body?* (1923), the very title of which evokes the ubiquity and anonymity of death between the trenches at the Somme, Verdun, and Passchendaele.

In *Whose Body?* Wimsey suffers a recurrence of his old malady when he realizes that the murderer of Sir Reuben Levy is a prominent researcher famous for his contributions to science and his personal generosity toward the needy. When his manservant, Bunter, who formerly served as his sergeant at the Front, discovers Wimsey in a state of nervous collapse, he attends to his master throughout the night and accompanies him to the country for a few days' rest in the care of his mother, the Dowager Duchess. Before Wimsey leaves London, however, he sets in motion the machinery that will eventually lead to the exhumation of Sir Reuben's heretofore anonymous remains and the eventual suicide of his murderer. The nocturnal exhumation scene, for which Wimsey returns, represents the final test of his nerves, evoking as it does, particularly in its features of cold and fog, the terror and disorientation of night-fighting in No Man's Land. Sayers's inspired use of second-person narration conveys an appropriately eerie sense of the self-alienating effects of combat at the Western Front: 'You could not see your feet, you stumbled in your walk over dead men's graves. [. . .] You floundered in a mass of freshly turned clay' (223).

The milieu of the Wimsey novels occasionally includes country estates, hunting lodges, and rural villages, but most cases unfold within and around London, where Sayers can display Lord Peter's sophisticated taste in first editions, burgundy, escargots, Daimlers, and Bond Street tailors without much strain. Wimsey is also at home in, if a bit detached from, bohemian London, among whose artists and composers and would-be anarchists he has a considerable acquaintance. Along with Sayers's occasional use of untranslated French, such settings and characters are meant to appeal to an educated, middle-class, status-conscious audience curious as to how 'the other half' – whether aristocratic or artistic – lives.

The author's own middle-class limitations appear in her persistent denigration of the modernist avant-garde, with writers like D. H. Lawrence (1885–1930) reduced to 'animal squeals' (*Clouds*, 142) and James Joyce ironically hailed as our liberator 'from syntax' (142). Her casual placement of racist epithets such as 'dago' and 'nigger' in the mouths of protagonists we are supposed to admire, such as Parker (*Unnatural*, 239) and even Wimsey himself, not to mention her tediously conventional anti-Semitism, reveal an embarrassing narrowness of mind reflecting the parochialism of Sayers's life-experiences. Toward left-wing movements her attitude was not so much alarmist as condescending and dismissive. Her most committed Communist, George Goyles in *Clouds of Witnesses* (1926), is outspoken but ineffectual and, worst of all, a cad to boot.

Sayers was not very interested in puzzle plots that ask 'whodunit?' In most cases, the likeliest suspect by the story's midpoint becomes a cinch for hanging well before the end. Even an exception like *Clouds of Witnesses* seems to move from suspect to suspect in a perfunctory manner, raising evidence against one person only to dismiss it in favour of the next. This does not diminish the analeptic energy of Sayers's plots, however, which vigorously stimulate speculation regarding questions ancillary to identifying the criminal, such as 'How?' 'When?' and 'Why?' The four books devoted to the meeting, courtship, marriage, and honeymoon of Harriet Vane, professional writer of detective novels, and Lord Peter Wimsey, amateur detective, deviate little from this pattern. If anything, they devote ever less attention to the puzzle element as Sayers broadens her social canvas and deepens her characters' personalities in more traditionally novelistic ways.

Just two years before publishing the first book of the Vane–Wimsey tetralogy, in her introduction to *The Omnibus of Crime* (1928), Sayers had expressed her opinion that the love sub-plot had become a 'fettering convention' in tales of detection ('Omnibus', 103) and was better avoided. She may have had in mind several of Agatha Christie's novels, including those featuring the Tommy and Tuppence Beresford duo, or the Charlie Chan novels of Earl Derr Biggers, which began to appear in 1925 and invariably featured a sub-plot involving two young lovers.

At least, that's what is suggested by Harriet's frustrated attempts to contrive a bit of lovemaking dialogue at the request of her editor in *Have His Carcase* (1932): ' "Betty – darling – I suppose you couldn't possibly –" Harriet came to the conclusion that she couldn't – not possibly' (165–6). Overcoming similar qualms, Sayers used the troubled love relationship between Wimsey and Vane to introduce a 'potential for change and development' into her oeuvre, writes Gayle Wald. She 'reinstates doubt, reasserts progression over regression, and makes possible the revelation of some of the "mysteries"' of ordinary life (108). Along the way, the criminals become more difficult to indict, the crimes less clearly illegal, and the narratives longer and more open-ended.

The character of Harriet Vane, a literary denizen of London's artistic Bloomsbury community, was anticipated by that of Marjorie Phelps, a close friend and casual lover of Lord Peter's in *Unnatural Death*. Marjorie is no pioneer of the avant-garde, but a level-headed, pragmatic sculptor specializing in personalized porcelain figurines, the sales of which provide her with enough money to get by. For Sayers, who took pride in making her own way, whether as editor, author, or advertising sloganeer, the marketing of one's professional talents and expertise is nothing to be ashamed of. She was, she frankly said, drawn to writing detective fiction because it paid well, and she did her homework before getting started, reading widely in the work of predecessors like Doyle, Poe, and Collins (Durkin, 19). Like Sayers, Marjorie Phelps uses her talents to create art that will sell, making herself useful and securing financial independence by creating things that people want and appreciate enough to pay for. What Marjorie earns from her art does not cheapen it; rather, her income as an artist both supports and signifies the extent of her personal freedom, especially as a woman.

Detection as Courtship

Early on in *Have His Carcase*, the second of the Vane–Wimsey mysteries, Harriet observes some ballroom dancers and overhears a conversation in the lounge of the Resplendent Hotel, a coastal watering-spot, that brings into sharp focus Sayers's interest in 'The Woman Question'. Noting the retro-Victorian fashions then popular among the dancers, along with the requisite 'imitation' coyness, Harriet doubts whether contemporary men are 'really stupid enough to believe that the good old days of submissive womanhood could be brought back by milliners' fashions' (35). They may 'like the illusion that woman is dependent on their approbation and favour for her whole interest in life', but only until her age begins to show, reflects Harriet. Then, 'if she doesn't find something to occupy her mind, always supposing that she has a mind', she will turn into a desperate 'predatory hag' (35), like the woman at the next table. During Harriet's musings, three stout matrons at another table nearby are 'engaged in an interminable conversation about illnesses, children and servants' – ' "And these," thought Harriet, "are the happy ones, I suppose" ' (36–7).

The coyly countenanced and attired maidens on the dance floor, the three stout matrons, and the 'predatory hag' represent for Harriet, as for Sayers, the three inevitable stages of life awaiting the modern woman, with brains or without, who lacks an independent income. Harriet, fortunately, has income as well as brains, thanks to the notoriety she has gained as a result of her having been tried for the murder of her former lover, as recounted in *Strong Poison*. This book ends with an acquittal won by the sleuthing efforts of Wimsey, who has in the process of investigation fallen in love with the accused.

Far from reciprocating his affection, however, Harriet has tried to put as much distance as possible between the two of them by undertaking a walking tour of the coast of southwest England, near the fictional resort of Wilvercombe. By the end of the first chapter of *Have His Carcase*, that tour will bring her to the top of a rocky tidal outcrop called the Flat-Iron and the corpse of a professional dancer at the Resplendent, the Russian émigré Paul Alexis, whose throat has been cut with a straight razor found gripped in his gloved hand.

Harriet has been impelled to the scene of Alexis's death, as it were, by her need to escape Wimsey's attentions, which painfully remind her of her indebtedness to him for saving her life. The situation is complicated by the fact that she does feel attracted and grateful to him. Stumbling upon Alexis's corpse only makes matters worse.

Hearing the news of Harriet's discovery, and fearing that she might again become a murder suspect, Wimsey drives down to Wilvercombe to be of assistance, a gesture that Harriet interprets as another attempt to secure her affections by placing her in his chivalrous debt. '[D]o give me a little credit for intelligence,' he replies angrily. 'Do you think it's pleasant for any man who feels about a woman the way I do about you, to have to fight his way along under this detestable burden of gratitude?' (154). Of all the men in her life, it is Wimsey who seems to understand Harriet best, especially in the aftermath of her bitter break-up with the lover she was accused of killing: 'You don't want ever again to have to depend for happiness on another person' (155), says Lord Peter. But without the ability to accept, gratefully, what another gives, reciprocation, and thus true love, is impossible.

Wimsey seeks to overcome Harriet's aversion to dependence not by persuading her to suppress her desire for independence – that would result in the sort of desperate, one-sided relationship that Harriet has just seen acted out in several ways in the lounge of the Resplendent – but by seeking opportunities for her to cancel her self-imposed 'debt of gratitude' with reciprocal gifts of her own. The Alexis case offers many such opportunities.

Unlike *Strong Poison*, where Wimsey assumes the active role of investigator and Harriet the passive role of damsel in distress, in *Have his Carcase* the two cooperate in solving the mystery of Paul Alexis's death. Wimsey brings to the case his innate intelligence and charm, along with his acquired talents and wealth. Harriet brings her experience as a writer of detective stories, which includes a sympathetic imagination, a talent for play-acting when required, and an eye for forged documents, as well as a nose for incoherence and implausibility in hypothesized solutions.

Thus, when Wimsey, Superintendent Glaisher, and Inspector Umpelty have reached the point of contriving dozens of untested and improbable contingencies in order to fit the apparent facts of the case, Harriet bursts out, 'I don't believe a word of it' (296).

> Glaisher laughed.
> 'Miss Vane's intuition, as they call it, is against it,' said he.
> 'It's not intuition,' retorted Harriet. 'There's no such thing. It's common sense. It's artistic sense, if you like. All those theories – they're all wrong. They're artificial. [. . .] You men [. . .] have let yourselves be carried away by all these figures and time-tables and you've lost sight of what you're really dealing with. But it's all machine-made. It creaks at every joint. It's like – like a bad plot, built up round an idea that won't work. [. . .] Whatever the explanation is, it must be simpler than that – bigger – not so ramped. Can't you see what I mean?' (296–7)

Significantly, only Wimsey can see what Harriet means.

It takes a while for Harriet to realize that what Lord Peter most desires is not gratitude, or even love, at first, but cooperation and mutual respect. Unable to recognize her own deep attraction to him, she trips over her misunderstanding of Wimsey's intentions on the dance floor of the Resplendent lounge, the scene of her previous reflections on female dependency.

Upon their first encountering each other in the hotel lobby a few days before, Wimsey had discussed the Alexis case with Harriet and asked if she would do some interviewing among the victim's professional colleagues at the hotel. Harriet replied that she'd have to get

'a decent frock', since she had arrived in town with only her hiking
clothes. 'Well,' replied Wimsey, 'get a wine-coloured one, then. I've
always wanted to see you in wine-colour' (52). Three days later,
Harriet is wearing the requested wine-coloured frock when Lord
Peter approaches to ask her to dance. He has just come from a conversation with Henry Weldon, a brusque East Anglian gentleman-
farmer who will soon become the prime suspect in Paul Alexis's
murder. 'Now that for a brief moment I have you all to myself,' says
Wimsey, pausing as the music begins.

> 'Well?' said Harriet. She was aware that the wine-coloured frock became
> her.
>   'What,' said Wimsey, 'do you make of Mr Henry Weldon?'
>   'Oh!'
>   This was not quite the question Harriet had expected. She hastily col-
> lected her ideas. It was very necessary that she should be the perfect unemo-
> tional sleuth. (136)

The 'expected' question from Lord Peter would be his facetious,
tireless request that Harriet marry him! And having chosen to wear
the wine-coloured frock that she knows Wimsey prefers, Harriet
almost looks as though she is prepared to consider the idea, or at
least engage in a little 'imitation' coyness on the subject. What
Wimsey offers instead is an opportunity for Harriet to contribute to
a relationship of equals, to help forge the mutual respect and inter-
dependency from which true love may eventuate. Detection, in short,
is his way of courting Harriet.

It is an activity, moreover, that provides, in Sayers's view, a real
benefit to society. The problem facing Harriet as a so-called 'superfluous woman' in a post-Great War world is essentially the same as
that facing Wimsey as a superfluous aristocrat: finding a use for
oneself that will justify one's existence. His class is to Wimsey what
her gender is to Harriet, an incitement to disrespect because neither
aristocrats nor women are seen by post-war society as having anything valuable to contribute to the public good.

This link between the nullifying effects of gender and class bias
becomes most evident when Wimsey's masculinity is called into question by Weldon, who considers his deliberate playboy affectations
'La-di-dah' and 'unmanly' (211). Significantly, Weldon makes these
remarks to Harriet Vane at the precise moment that she, in 'slinky
garment', 'high-heeled beige shoes and sheer silk stockings', and
'black ringlets, skilfully curled' (209), is working hard to 'produce[]
a latent strain of sweet womanliness' in order to seduce Weldon into

revealing what he may know about Alexis's death. Being good detectives, both Wimsey and Vane understand how to exploit the demeaning roles that society assigns them so as to disarm the wariness of a prime suspect.

Blood Won't Tell

In *Have His Carcase*, as elsewhere in the Wimsey corpus, what counts for Sayers regardless of class background is one's adherence to the duties that go with one's profession or occupation, whatever that may be, and one's commitment to placing the skills appropriate to that profession or occupation at the service of society at large. This goes as much for a professional dancer like M. Antoine, who believes that the rich women who dance with him and complain about their unfaithful husbands could use some hard, useful work (166–7), as it does for the Wilvercombe blacksmith who can proudly identify his own workmanship in a mare's cast-off shoe (194–5), a vital piece of evidence.

That there is a moral difference between the casual and the dedicated professional, regardless of class, is made clearest when Wimsey begins to trace the ownership of the murder weapon, a custom-made straight razor. Colonel Belfridge, a former owner of the razor, is a potted example of all that was arrogant and ignorant among the military classes that directed the fighting in the Great War. Between denunciations of 'these damned foreigners' and 'Flapper votes', Belfridge vociferates over the dangers posed to the domestic iron and steel industry without a strong Conservative, that is, anti-Labour, government to keep the workers in their place.

In contrast to Belfridge's preoccupation with steel and his insensitivity to the men who make it, the barber Mr Endicott, who originally sold the Colonel the fatal razor, is more concerned with the men who used the steel razors he sold them. They are nearly all military men, and many of them died in the War. Endicott remembers what happened to each of the fifteen razors he sold because each of them is tied to the fate of the man who bought it. As he recites their stories, Endicott tells a larger tale of how Sayers sees England living now, in the wake of the conflict that shook her generation to its foundations: ships sunk with all hands, the retreat over the Marne, air crashes and insanity, colonial assignments to East Africa, and, later, stock scandals sending investors abroad and callous abuse by Bright Young

Things cutting up canvas with Endicott's blades to make scenery for amateur theatricals (64–6).

The barber particularly remembers Colonel Belfridge: 'oh dear! oh dear! He was a terribly hard man on his razors. [. . .] He was always the same. I think he took the edge off with the strop, instead of putting it on; I do indeed. He didn't keep a man [a valet], you know' (67–8). Endicott's last statement implies that Belfridge was just as hard on any 'man' under him, whether in military or in private life, as on his razors. 'One of the old school, eh?' says Wimsey (68). Endicott's razors are prosaic versions of military swords, and he knows that the metal England produces is no better than the mettle of the men who wield it. Colonel Belfridge has much to say about steel and spaniels, but nothing to say about the soldiers he commanded. Endicott remembers every one of his customers, and those who are alive still remember him. 'They know I value their kind remembrance,' he tells Wimsey (68). Endicott understands the more-than-commercial value of a professional reputation.

In the end, the Russian émigré Paul Alexis makes himself vulnerable to murder because he cannot accept the duties and obligations of his place in life as an ordinary citizen and a professional dancer, like M. Antoine and his ballroom counterparts. The proximate cause of his murder is the threat he poses, as the young fiancé of an ageing widow staying at the Resplendent (Vane's 'predatory hag', in fact), to the expectations of her legitimate heir. What gives Alexis's killer the opportunity to do away with him, however, is his infatuation with the idea that he is a distant but direct descendant of the Romanovs, the Tsarist rulers of Imperial Russia, whose last Emperor, Nicholas II, was executed by the Bolsheviks along with the entire royal family in the Russian Revolution of 1917.

Based on his conviction that he is the fifth-generation descendant of former Tsar Nicholas I and the daughter of a French diplomat, Alexis is easily fooled by his murderer into believing that he has been enlisted by Russian counter-revolutionaries to resume the throne of his mother country and lead his oppressed people to overthrow the Bolshevik plunderers. On the basis of that belief, he is ultimately lured to the desolate Flat-Iron, where, in expectation of a boat that will take him to St Petersburg, his throat is slit from ear to ear.

Alexis's belief in his Romanov blood-line is vital to Sayers's plot, not only with respect to motivation, but also with respect to physical evidence. One of the things that Alexis takes as a sure sign of his Tsarist consanguinity is his haemophilia, a blood condition inherited by all the male Romanovs that impedes clotting and can lead to serious consequences from even minor cuts, bruises, and abrasions. On the level of metonymic connections essential to the plot of detection, Alexis's unknown haemophilia plays havoc with the estimated time of his death on the Flat-Iron, for his unclotted blood gives the impression that he died just moments before Harriet discovered him, rather than several hours earlier. As a result, Wimsey's and Vane's attempted reconstructions of the movements and activities of the young man's unknown murderer are doomed to failure. Appropriately, it is Wimsey, familiar with all the royal houses of Europe, including the pre-Revolutionary Romanovs, who finally guesses Alexis's blood condition, based on his Romanov fantasies, his refusal to shave, and his reported physical timidity.

Symbolically, Paul Alexis's death seems to convey a deeper message relevant to all of the Wimsey novels, but especially to this one, where Alexis's royalist longings have been stimulated by the additional, fabricated prospect of marriage to his royal cousin, 'the fair Feodora' (263), whose photo is actually that of a professional model. Not only does Alexis believe he is the fifth-generation offspring of a liaison between a monarch and a commoner, but his anticipated marriage to 'Feodora' would recapitulate that liaison, with the genders reversed. Both of Alexis's fantasies, past and future, are thus grotesque reflections of a possible marriage between Wimsey and Vane, who find such daydreams, weighed down as they are with the 'burden of gratitude', as repugnant, and about as realistic, as the fairy tale of King Cophetua stooping to marry the beggar maid (153).

The message conveyed by these analogous relationships, in light of the outcome of Alexis's fantasy, is clear: the age of class distinction, deference, and privilege based on blood is a dead dream, as dead as 'the good old days of submissive womanhood' (35), never again to be revived in the aftermath of modern machine warfare and world revolution.

If the ideals that sustained that dream and once gave it meaning are to be revived at all – and they must be, Sayers suggests, or civilization will become little more than a polite veneer for greed, violence, and sexual predation – they will have to prove their usefulness for the betterment of society as a whole. That is an endeavour in which all citizens can and should take part, whether lords or commoners, colonels or barbers, men or women. From now on, blood will not 'tell'.

Part III
American Century

6

Hard-Boiled Detection

History is more or less bunk.
Henry Ford

Henry Ford spoke for many of his fellow Americans when, in a May 1916 interview with the *Chicago Tribune*, he dismissed the importance of history in shaping current affairs. 'It means nothing to me,' added Ford. 'It's tradition. We don't want tradition. We want to live in the present and the only history that is worth a tinker's dam is the history we make today' (Castel).

The Maltese Falcon (1930), by Dashiell Hammett (1894–1961), reverberates with echoes of Ford's verdict on history. Having heard the exciting tale of the golden bird's antiquity, tough-guy detective Sam Spade wonders out loud, 'Is it probable? Is it possible – even barely possible? Or is it the bunk?' (134). Spade's question conveys scepticism toward narrative reconstructions of the past, including alibis and testimonies. Among readers and critics of crime fiction, that attitude is known as 'hard-boiled'.

The Roots of Hard-Boiled Detection

American hard-boiled or 'tough-guy' crime fiction was conceived in part as a direct challenge to the Anglo-American classical tradition inspired by Holmes. Spurning the drawing-room diction of polite society that filled the pages of Wright, Sayers, Christie, and Carr, the tough-guy writers cultivated a brusque, clipped, vernacular style. They also made a point of denigrating the formal puzzle element,

along with the shallow characterizations and implausible conjunc-
tions of events that it seemed to demand. Nonetheless, hard-boiled
authors like Hammett and Raymond Chandler (1888–1959),
Hammett's most important protégé, retained the inductive challenge
of classical detection under a garish surface of fast-paced events,
colourful personalities, and wise-cracking rejoinders. As Julian
Symons notes, 'The problems are composed just as skillfully as those
in an orthodox detective story, but [. . .] they are the beginning and
not the end of the book's interest' (*Bloody*, 147).

That interest, suggests Symons, lies mainly in the enigmas of character, mood, and motive, a strong sense of place, and lots of action.
Heta Pyrhönin argues that, in contrast to the classical detective's
reliance on physical clues to reconstruct the crime, hard-boiled detectives 'often spend the major part of the investigation simply trying
to understand what is going on'. They 'acquire data' by eliciting
responses from their opponents that will reveal hidden interests,
activities, and relationships (114). Often, more than one person has
something to hide. For this reason George Grella distinguishes hard-
boiled from classical detection by appealing to larger generic categories that shape our conceptions of character.

Classical detection, says Grella, belongs to the comedy of manners.
Its characters tend to conform to recognizable comedic types, and
their personalities are little more than temperaments. Each character
has an assigned place in a social cosmos where decorum and con-
viviality are often more urgent matters than morality. Only the criminal has broken ranks in a way that threatens the stability of that
cosmos. The classical detective's job conforms to the requirements of
traditional comedy: to restore order and decorum to a society threatened by the disorder of individual wilfulness. This society is worth
redeeming, and its redemption is often crowned, as in many of
Christie's stories, by an engagement or a marriage.

In contrast to social comedy, the traditional romance unfolds in a
world on the verge of disintegration, as in the Arthurian legends and
medieval tales of knight-errantry. This is a world polluted by self-
interest and full of challenges and snares, in which no one is to be
trusted and all must be tested. The hero, a lone knight, seeks not to
redeem this fallen society, but to maintain his personal integrity in
the face of repeated temptations and deceptions. The 'tough stance'
of hard-boiled detection is accordingly both cynical and sentimental,
according to Grella (105), and quintessentially American in its
idealization of personal autonomy in the face of shadowy coercive
forces, such as organized crime, ruthless corporations, wealthy

families, and corrupt government agencies, including, typically, the regular metropolitan police.

Several cultural, economic, and political developments preceding America's brief participation in the Great War (1917–18) helped to nurture the rise of a detective genre that eventually conformed to this cultural archetype.

From its pre-revolutionary colonization, America had conceived of itself as the land of new beginnings, a place where history, with its traditional political and social arrangements based on class hierarchies and monarchical power, was irrelevant. The Puritans had looked upon the wilderness of New England as a gift from God that they had been chosen to make fruitful. The settlement of the West in the century following the American Revolution had inflated that conviction of divine entitlement into a sense of what journalist John L. O'Sullivan (1813–95) called, in 1839, the nation's 'Manifest Destiny'. America was future-oriented and westward bound, offering apparently limitless freedom and opportunities for self-reinvention. The rags-to-riches tales of Horatio Alger, Jr (1834–99), popular in the last two decades of the 1800s, appealed directly to this faith in individual initiative and achievement, while the cheap dime novels and weeklies of that era, featuring cowboys, detectives, and similar adventure heroes, exploited that faith more obliquely.

These popular, working-class publications came to be known as 'pulps', a term denoting the quickly deteriorating wood-pulp paper on which they were printed. By contrast, so-called 'slicks' like *Collier's* and *McClure's*, whose stories and advertising appealed to middle-class American consumers, used heavier, more expensive rag paper suitable for lithography. Wood-pulp magazine printing was the innovation of New York publisher Frank Munsey, who switched to the cheaper, lighter paper for his general-audience weeklies early in the 1890s in order to save money on paper and postage. Over the next decade his circulation figures skyrocketed (Pronzini and Adrian, 'Introduction', 2).

While Munsey's success posed little immediate threat to the 'slicks', it did cut sharply into sales of the dime novels and rival popular weeklies. These had been the major outlet for action-hero detectives cast in the mould of Vidocq and Bucket, men like Old King Brady and the gymnastic boy-wonder Nick Carter, the best-selling and longest-lived fictional detective of all time. It wasn't long before popular publishers like Beadle and Adams, who had invented the dime novel to sell to barely literate Civil War soldiers, and Street and Smith, creators of *The Nick Carter Library*, took their seats at the pulp-wood table (Goulart, 10). By the end of the First World War, the pulp magazines were driving the dimes off the newsstands and beginning to specialize (Goulart, 13).

As Cynthia Hamilton points out, the master formula for both Westerns and detective fiction in America combined the lessons of social Darwinism with the promise of individual achievement, all set against a general backdrop of lawlessness and its positive mirror-image, unfettered opportunity. It is no accident that these tales of heroic self-determination should have become popular during an era of industrial and corporate triumphalism, when the ordinary citizen, especially the small farmer and immigrant factory worker, was being victimized by America's most successful exemplars of self-empowerment, the industrial 'robber barons' and their financial backers.

Like Alger's fairy tales of entrepreneurial match-boys, the dime detective story and the Western horse-opera began life as compensatory fictions, offering fantasies of individual opportunity and achievement in an America buffed to a patriotic glow for common readers facing a cruel opposing reality. Until that reality could announce itself in the writings of Hammett, Chandler, and their fellow hard-boiled writers, the America of the dime detective tradition, notes Gary Hoppenstand, was 'equated with goodness. Bankers are *good* people. Big business is *good* business. If left to its own device, the city could evolve into a Utopian society' (6), just like the frontier town of the typical Western, which was likewise built on mythical foundations. *The Virginian* (1902), by Owen Wister (1860–1938), whose popular success paved the way for more than half a century of modern cowboy melodramas, appeared four years after historian Frederick Jackson Turner formally announced the closing of the American frontier, while noting its profound impact on the American character.

The growing disparity between American dream and American reality made its first overt appearance in the writings of 'muckraking' journalists and novelists like Upton Sinclair (1878–1968) and Frank Norris (1870–1902). Their exposés of corporate and government corruption helped to encourage American populist reaction against Big Business, Big Banks, and the Big City, where both flourished, playing an important part in the founding of the Progressive Party in 1904. Backed by an agrarian and small-town constituency, the Progressives sought to regulate monopolistic business practices and predatory banking, and to guarantee a minimum wage.

The muckrakers also helped give rise to a Progressive school of American historians. Led by Charles Beard (1874–1948), whose *An Economic Interpretation of the Constitution of the United States*

(1913) scandalized academic and lay readers alike by attributing coarse economic motives to the Founding Fathers, Progressive historians portrayed contemporary America as the result of an ongoing struggle among competing class interests. At the turn of the century, the corporate interests were winning that struggle at the expense of the little guy.

Progressive historians were not revolutionary, like Marxists, just pragmatic, like their muckraking allies in politics and the press. Anticipating the investigative methods and the suspicion of wealth that would characterize tough-guy detectives in the decades to come, they used their knowledge of the past to 'stir[] things up' (79) in the present, as Hammett's nameless detective narrator would later put it in *Red Harvest* (1929), so as to reveal hidden connections and conspiracies among those ultimately responsible for injustice.

Although they shared with Marxist historians a belief that the past was scientifically recoverable, the Progressives did not see history as shaped by laws of inevitable development, or moving in the direction of a 'dictatorship of the proletariat'. History, while knowable, had no 'lessons' to offer about the future. In this conviction they reflected the scepticism shared by Americans in general, from Henry Ford on down to the dye-press operator in his assembly plant, toward any notion that developments in the past necessarily foreclosed possibilities for action in the present. All would have agreed with Ford that 'the only history that is worth a tinker's dam is the history we make today'.

Or Is It?

If America, like Henry Ford, saw attempts to reconstruct the past as 'bunk' by 1916, it is remarkable that the hard-boiled stories appearing in pulp magazines during the ensuing years should have bothered to incorporate as much of the reconstructive puzzle element as they did. It is not unreasonable to speculate that, as in England, widespread social disruption following the Great War bred a compensatory appetite for retrospective invention in middle-class American readers of detective fiction, the very readers who were to become the target audience for authors like Hammett and Chandler.

There was already, of course, a vigorous tradition of classical detection in the United States going back to Anna Katherine Green, and that tradition would remain strong throughout the interwar years. By 1939, however, when Chandler's first Philip Marlowe novel hit the bookstores, hard-boiled detection was seriously challenging its Golden Age competition on the best-seller lists. It did so by incorporating a broader social canvas of credible suspects (including professional criminals) and a world-view more consonant with the deeper cultural anxieties and pragmatism of the Jazz Age. Without the inductive challenge of the puzzle element, however, it is unlikely that this new sub-genre would have prevailed as it did. To this day, although overtaken and surpassed by its crime-suspense rivals, hard-boiled detection remains a vigorous competitor for space on middle-class bookshelves. Like its classical counterpart, it has learned to satisfy the educated reader's need to 'make' history in the act of reading, at a time when the accelerating pace of public events largely defies similar attempts at coherent reconstruction in the real world.

America's hard-boiled adaptation of the classical puzzle element began not long after the end of the war, between the covers of a modest, working-class, action-adventure pulp magazine called *Black Mask*.

Black Mask started life as something of an orphan among pulps. It was founded in 1920 by journalist H. L. Mencken (1880–1956) and his friend, George Jean Nathan (1882–1958), as a money-making scheme to support their upscale publication, *The Smart Set*. Mencken despised the action-packed, proletarian fiction peddled by *Black Mask* and unloaded the magazine after six months at a tidy profit. He backed the wrong horse, however. Under the leadership of retired army Captain Joseph T. Shaw, who took over as editor in 1926, *Black Mask* became a magnet for talented young writers, who soon began to take pride in being 'pointed out as a *Black Mask* man' by their peers (Durham, 54). With the help of contributors like Hammett, the magazine went on, as Ian Ousby says, to 'change the face of crime and mystery fiction in America' (*Guilty*, 95) – and, it is no exaggeration to say, in the world.

In large part the 'tough-guy' contributors to *Black Mask* – including Carroll John Daly (1889–1958), Raoul Whitfield (1898–1945), Erle Stanley Gardner (1889–1970), Cornell Woolrich (1903–68), and Horace McCoy (1897–1955) – were simply responding to the changing face of America itself. Not all of them wrote detective fiction. Woolrich and McCoy, for example, along with novelist James M. Cain (1892–1977), helped to popularize the seedy, low-life thriller that would later dominate crime fiction. Erle Stanley Gardner made the cunning criminal lawyer, Perry Mason, a household name among mystery fans. All of them, however, wrote stories reflecting the changes taking place in cities and towns across the land.

The so-called 'Roaring Twenties' saw spectacular economic growth, but it was based on tottering foundations, as was soon demonstrated by the Crash of 1929, which ushered in the Great Depression. Progressive corporate regulation and labour legislation had not advanced far enough to prevent widespread stock fraud and price manipulation. Corruption at the highest levels of government flourished and violent strike-breaking activities were tolerated, if not sanctioned, by law-enforcement officials alarmed at the world-revolutionary ambitions of the Russian Bolsheviks.

As in England, the 'New Woman' of the late nineteenth century was still posing a challenge to patriarchal stereotypes of her 'place' in society well into the twentieth, a challenge reinforced by the brief incursion of working women into America's wartime economy and the passage of the nineteenth amendment in 1920 granting them the right to vote. Accordingly, female detectives continued to appear in the pages of American crime fiction, just as they did before the war, and not just in Golden Age stories but in the new, hard-boiled tales as well. There, big gals with bad fashion sense like Violet McDade, the creation of Clive F. Adams (1895–1949), performed as independent protagonists, like their dime novel foremothers Calamity Jane and Annie Oakley, while female 'operatives' or 'secretaries' sometimes participated as 'full-fledged members of the [male] hero's band' (Drew, xv). Female criminals also appeared, sometimes as gun molls or outright crooks, but more often in the role of the *femme fatale*, a siren figure animated in American as in British psyches by post-war male insecurity in the face of changing sex-roles and attitudes toward gender.

Far more important than the nineteenth amendment in terms of its contribution to public disorder and cynicism was the passage of the eighteenth amendment prohibiting the sale of alcoholic beverages in 1919. Enacted in response to agitation by temperance societies, Prohibition encouraged a sharp rise in organized crime and public mayhem as rival gangs competed for market-share in the booming bootleg industry. Massive, untaxed profits made it easy to bribe mayors and police to ignore a 'crime' that no one but the most rabid teetotaller considered wrong. The result was public cynicism toward the law and suspicion of those sworn to uphold it, while the spread of an illegal, underground economy nourished other forms of criminal activity, such as loan-sharking, prostitution, gambling, and protection rackets.

Despite America's post-war economic gains, then, new insecurities were undermining public confidence in the promise of the American

Dream. Writers for pulp magazines like *Black Mask* responded by portraying an America in which no one could be trusted, least of all wealthy society types and official law enforcers, and where society itself, especially in the big bad city, seemed to be so thoroughly steeped in graft and self-interest that it was hardly worth rescuing. The most one could expect was that a few innocent lives might be saved from the wreckage, and that the detective, in completing the job he had been hired to do, would save them, or at least avenge their loss. Lacking the respect for 'tradition' and 'history' that helped motivate his Golden Age English counterpart to defend an idealized pre-war way of life, the American tough-guy detective knew he could count on only one thing: himself.

Action vs Plot: Hard-Boiled Detection's Bad Rap

Many critics have taken Spade's question about the Maltese Falcon's history – 'Is it the bunk?' – to indicate Hammett's rejection of narrative truth in general and the carefully plotted, reconstructive narratives of classical detection in particular. Steven Marcus, for instance, has argued that Hammett's tough-guy detective figure not only 'actively undertakes to deconstruct, decompose, and thus demystify the fictional [. . .] reality created by the characters [. . .] with whom he is involved', but also 'tries to substitute his own fictional-hypothetical representation for theirs' (xxi).

Marcus's comments have set the stage for subsequent attempts to make Hammett a forerunner of the more recent avant-garde detective stories of Alain Robbe-Grillet (1922–) or Vladimir Nabokov (1899–1977), where the only reality is an endless succession of narrative fabrications, each achieving, at best, a momentary and fragile plausibility. At the end of *The Maltese Falcon* in particular, according to Sinda Gregory, we are left 'with an indecipherable mystery that has grown larger, more pervasive, and more impenetrable as the book has developed' (89), 'a declaration of the omnipotence of mystery and the failure of human effort to ever dispel it' (88).

This is a bit of an exaggeration, to say the least. At the end of *The Maltese Falcon* we get a complete analeptic account of events, just as we do at the end of a story by Christie or Sayers. Recited at length by Spade to Brigid O'Shaughnessy, this recapitulation sets out the complete array of the novel, including both what has transpired in the course of the narrative and what has led up to the opening scene. Meanwhile, the black bird itself, object of universal desire and the driving force of the plot, has been shown, unmistakably, to be bogus. As Peter Rabinowitz observes, attempts to align *The Maltese Falcon* with recent avant-garde challenges to narrative reliability are doomed to defeat by 'the paradoxically tight-knit ending' ('How', 164).

In fact, no Hammett story ends with uncertainty regarding the material facts of the case. 'From any crime to its author there is a trail,' writes Hammett in 'House Dick' (1923). 'It may be [...] obscure, since matter cannot move without disturbing other matter along its path, [but] there always is – there must be – a trail of some sort. And finding and following such a trail is what a detective is paid to do' (quoted in Wolfe, *Beams* 24). What becomes increasingly indeterminate or undecidable in Hammett's work is not what has happened in the material world it describes, but, as we shall see, what has happened in the mental one.

In short, while Henry Ford may have thought the 'bunk' of history was a foregone conclusion, Spade, who put the matter in an interrogatory form, saw it as an open question.

He was not unique in this respect among tough-guy investigators of the American school, although there is certainly material in the writings of both Hammett and Chandler to give the impression that the success of hard-boiled writing depended on a complete rejection of the classical British model. 'So that's the way you scientific detectives work,' says Dinah Brand when the anonymous narrator of *Red Harvest* admits that his methods have been largely haphazard. 'Plans are all right sometimes,' replies the detective. 'And sometimes just stirring things up is all right – if you're tough enough to survive, and keep your eyes open so you'll see what you want when it comes to the top' (75). As for Chandler, he once wrote that in his stories 'the scene outranked the plot, in the sense that a good plot was one which made good scenes', and added, 'When in doubt have a man come through a door with a gun in his hand' ('Introduction', 1017). Such remarks have led Stephen Knight to argue that Chandler steadfastly rejected 'the mechanistic rational plotting of the organic novel', which classical detection epitomized (*Form*, 152).

It is important, however, to balance such statements against other pronouncements, and against practice as well. *Red Harvest*, for example, capped a series of short stories featuring its anonymous private-eye narrator, an 'operative' employed by the Continental Detective Agency. Contrary to long-standing critical opinion (e.g., Ruehlmann, 70–1), the Continental Op begins literary life as anything but a generic dime-novel action detective. In fact, he is meant to contrast specifically with the unthinking, trigger-happy vigilante figure popularized by Carroll John Daly in the character of Race Williams, whose debut preceded the Op's in *Black Mask* by just four months in 1923.

Often cited as the world's first hard-boiled fictional detective, Williams was exactly the sort of PI a writer could depend on to come bursting through the door with a gun in his hand when imagination took the day off. By contrast, the Op is short, overweight, middle-aged, and easily winded. He is also a cool, wise-cracking, and self-deprecating professional, much like Hammett himself, who had worked for Pinkerton's and knew private investigation inside-out. (The head of Pinkerton's Baltimore office, James Wright, was the model for Hammett's laconic hero.) The Op knows how to use his fists and his gun, but, unlike Williams, he is slow to anger. 'The proper place for guns is after talk has failed,' he says in 'Corkscrew' (1925, 292). Besides restricting his violence largely to self-defence, the Op is also perceptive and inductively shrewd, and nearly all of the Op stories, including the two complete novels in which he figures, make a point of displaying, even telegraphing, his mystery-solving abilities.

Red Harvest is a parodic exception to the previous Op tales not because it rejects induction or the idea of reliable historical reconstruction, but because Hammett's usually self-contained protagonist here finds himself going 'blood simple' (138) and reverting to type in his violent attempts to clean up the town of Personville (pronounced 'Poisonville'). By chapter 20, his 'stirring things up' has made him responsible, directly or indirectly, for sixteen deaths, to the point where even his fellow operative, Dick Foley, refuses to have anything more to do with him.

The Op's inductive abilities remain intact throughout, however, from his first eliminating the gangster Max Thaler as a suspect in the murder of a crusading newspaper editor (35), to his finally exonerating himself for the murder of Dinah Brand, which occurred while he was so doped up on laudanum that he couldn't be sure he hadn't done her in (184–5). In general, when the Op 'stir[s] things up', he does so in order to test hypotheses about the past based on his current state of knowledge. The hard-boiled detective may simply be 'trying to understand what is going on' in the present, as Pyrhönin claims (114), but in order to succeed he must first piece together the events that shaped that present, just like his British counterparts.

Chandler's pronouncements are similarly belied by his practice, and by other statements on the writing of detective fiction. In a letter to Mrs Robert Hogan of 6 March 1947, he says his lack of interest in plot creates difficulties when he tries to force in new material he can't bear to discard. 'I'd write something I liked and then I would have a hell of a time making it fit in to the structure.' But disliking plot and ignoring plot are two different things. 'I have lost months of time because of this stubbornness,' writes Chandler, demonstrating a pig-headed devotion to tight, consistent plotting despite the 'oddities of construction' that may result (MacShane, *Letters*, 87; see also MacShane, *Life*, 67–8).

In fact, Chandler's first book, *The Big Sleep* (1939), makes sophisticated use of what the author himself considered the height of 'literary legerdemain', concealing 'a simple mystery [. . .] behind another mystery' and 'making [the reader] solve the wrong problem' ('Twelve', 1007). Although Chandler later told Howard Hawks, director of the movie version, that he couldn't remember who killed the chauffeur, Owen Taylor (MacShane, *Life*, 126), the fact is that two possibilities are laid out in the book (suicide or murder), each one consistent with the rest of the events in the novel and neither germane to the solution of the initial case or the deeper mystery behind it. Despite immaterial loose ends like these *The Big Sleep* hangs together well, as do most of the books that followed.

Chandler's statement on 'literary legerdemain' appears in an unpublished essay called 'Twelve Notes on the Mystery Story', each numbered entry beginning, 'It must'. For a hard-boiled writer notoriously critical of Golden Age fussiness, Chandler's 'notes' are sometimes hard to distinguish from the 'rules' of Willard Huntington Wright.

Thus, writes Chandler, the mystery story 'must be technically sound', that is, factually correct, 'as to the methods of murder and detection'. 'It must be honest with the reader', which means that '[i]mportant facts not only must not be concealed, they must not be distorted by false emphasis', and 'inferences arising from special knowledge (e.g., Dr Thorndyke)' must be avoided. 'It must have enough essential simplicity to be explained easily when the time comes', but 'baffle a reasonably intelligent reader' (1006–7). Along the way, Chandler tells mystery writers to avoid 'unfairness' to their readers and to make sure that, when the 'inevitable' solution is revealed, 'the fooling was honorable' (1006–7), language that would not be out of place at a meeting of The Detection Club.

But then Chandler himself, though born in Chicago, was raised in England and learned the meaning of 'honour' and 'fairness' at an English preparatory school. The far-reaching consequences of Chandler's expatriate education will become clearer in our next Casebook.

Hammett and History

Samuel Dashiell Hammett was born on 27 May 1894, the second of three children. His father, Richard, was full of plans, but could never hold down a job for very long. Despite young Samuel's native intelligence (he had read, out of curiosity, Kant's *Critique of Pure Reason* at the age of 13, and even understood some of it), the boy had to leave high school after his first year to help support the family. He joined Pinkerton's in 1915, first as a clerk, then as an 'operative' at $20 a week. From the moment Hammett began writing professionally in 1922, this experience as a private investigator gave him an authority no other writer of detective fiction could match.

During the war Hammett enlisted in the army ambulance corps. Before he could be sent overseas, he caught the flu, then tuberculosis, and was medically discharged. He rejoined Pinkerton's and moved to San Francisco in 1921, but deteriorating health soon forced him to abandon detecting and begin, like Sayers in similar circumstances, to write advertising copy. He also started spending a lot of time at the public library.

Almost from the beginning Hammett's aim, as he said, was to make 'literature' out of the 'detective form' (quoted in Johnson, 72). He liked the American vernacular style of Ring Lardner, Jr (1915–2000), but also enjoyed the works of Anatole France (1844–1924) and Henry James (1843–1916), whose *Wings of the Dove* (1902), he claimed, had inspired the plot of *The Maltese Falcon* (Johnson, 36). Hammett had been contributing to *Black Mask* for four years by the time Joseph Shaw began his editorship. The former army captain soon began to 'Hammettize' the magazine's house style, according to Erle Stanley Gardner. As a national champion fencer, Shaw must have appreciated the importance of avoiding wasted motion (Ruehlmann, 58–9).

A stubborn individualist, the young Hammett soon adopted the 'art-for-art's-sake' amoralism of the Victorian decadents and Anglo-American modernists. But his left-leaning populism also led him to connect good writing with the Marxist concept of unalienated labour, that is, work one did for pleasure and personal satisfaction, not just in exchange for money (Johnson, 53). This notion crept into his literary version of professional detection as well. 'I happen to like the work,' says the Op. 'And liking work makes you want to do it as well as you can. Otherwise there'd be no sense to it' ('Gutting', 36). Like the traditional ratiocinative detective, the Op gets his 'fun' not just from 'chasing crooks' but from 'tackling puzzles' and 'solving riddles': 'It's the only kind of sport I know anything about,' he says, 'and I can't imagine a pleasanter future' (34).

While he expressed scorn for 'scientific detection' based on 'photographs, fingerprints, [and] forensics' (Johnson, 18), Hammett was in many respects a throw-back to Enlightenment positivism. 'He saw the modern world of 1924 as characterized by exciting forms of progress,' writes his biographer, Diane Johnson, 'based on science and on reason' (52). His long-term lover and companion, playwright Lillian Hellman (1905–84), noted his 'remarkable mind, neat, accurate, respectful of fact' and his passion for mathematics (xix).

Like any Enlightenment positivist, Hammett trusted his senses. What he mistrusted was what lay beyond them, especially, as Johnson points out, 'human personality', which he doubted 'could be analyzed and quantified' (52). As one of the characters in 'Tulip' (1966), Hammett's fictionalized autobiographical fragment, says about the eponymous Hammett protagonist, it would be naïve 'to expect people [like him] to have any conception of what occupies other people or even to possess any awareness that other people have any interior occupations' (351). Hammett ridiculed deep psychological explanations, especially of the academic variety, with their 'tables and "dawta" and an inventory of human desires and measurements' (quoted in Johnson, 55). This may be one reason why, adept as they are at noting metonymic evidence, Hammett's detectives face their biggest inferential challenges in trying to disentangle the knotted fabric of mutually interdependent, but ultimately superficial, motives that have been woven among a closed circle of suspects.

The Dain Curse (1929), Hammett's second novel and last Op story, is exemplary in this regard. Here the Op rakes over in maddening detail the apparent inconsistencies of motive attributable to each of the major players in the three-part case. The novelist Owen Fitzstephan believes these inconsistencies ultimately defy rational explanation and rest on a deeper 'psychological basis'. The Op disagrees, citing one character in particular as an example: 'You won't find the key to her in any complicated derangements. She was simple as an animal' (246).

Even the simplest motives, however, can defy understanding when the history of events and human actions behind them is not fully known. The Op's stubborn attempts to trace these historical connections in the chapter entitled 'But and If' resemble the speculative analeptic reconstructions of an obsessive-compulsive reader of classical detective fiction. After several minutes, an exasperated

Fitzstephan bursts out, 'Aw, shut up! You're never satisfied until you've got two buts and an if attached to everything' (248). At the end of *The Dain Curse*, we are left in no doubt as to how events have transpired. What remains in doubt is the sanity of the criminal mind behind them.

Narratives of Desire: Getting in Step with Death

The five books Hammett wrote span barely more than a decade, from 1922 to 1934. Many consider his fourth, *The Glass Key* (1931), the finest (see, e.g., Symons, *Bloody*, 148), but the third-person, exteriorized point of view that Hammett adopts with such stunning results here is deployed much more purposefully, and with more forceful thematic and symbolic impact, in the book where he first introduced it, *The Maltese Falcon*.

The Falcon of the title is a legendary statuette of gold inlaid with precious gems and covered with black enamel. It was originally presented in the sixteenth century to Charles V of Spain, so the story goes, by the Knights of St John of Crete in grateful acknowledgement of the king's granting them title to the island of Malta. Recently stolen from its owner, a Russian colonel living in Istanbul, the precious bird is on its way from Hong Kong to San Francisco, where it is eagerly awaited by the three conspirators – Brigid O'Shaughnessy, Joel Cairo, and Caspar Gutman – who stole it. Each is trying to cut the other two out of the deal. Other shady characters linger on the periphery, such as Captain Jacobi of the freighter *La Paloma*, courier of the Falcon; Floyd Thursby, an English gangster; and Gutman's young, trigger-happy gunman, Wilmer Cook.

The tale of the Falcon and its pursuit emerges gradually in the course of the story, which begins with Brigid, a.k.a. Miss Wonderly, appearing one morning at Sam Spade's San Francisco office. Wanting to neutralize Thursby, she pays Spade's partner, Miles Archer, to tail him, telling Spade and Archer that Thursby is preying on a runaway 'sister' of hers. Miles is shot and killed on assignment, and Spade is drawn into the riddle of the Maltese Falcon as he investigates his partner's death. Soon after Miles's murder, Miss Wonderly confesses that her original story was made up. 'Oh, that,' Spade replies. 'We didn't exactly believe your story. [. . .] We believed your two hundred dollars' (33).

Spade's comment points to a theme that runs throughout Hammett's book: the truth of a story is immaterial as long as you can persuade others to believe it, or to behave as if they do. Often, making it worth their while to believe it can help.

Broadly speaking, any story believed to be fact rather than fiction is history. In *The Maltese Falcon* the value of a thing or a person or a course of action depends on the degree to which the story attached to it, him, or her succeeds in gaining credit as history, or in getting others to behave as though it were history. The Falcon itself perfectly demonstrates this point.

According to Gutman, whose tale of the Falcon's origins – 'facts, historical facts', he assures Spade (124) – consumes more than half a chapter of the book, the present value of the bird far exceeds its 'intrinsic value' in gold and jewels. Any one of the wealthy 'modern descendents of the old Order' of the Knights of St John who originally owned the Falcon would, he says, pay a 'far higher, a terrific, price' for it 'once its authenticity was established beyond doubt' (126). That authenticity depends on its provenance, of course, and thus on the factual accuracy of the story that is attached to it. As long as that story is not discredited, it remains history. When the Falcon is revealed to be a fake, however, its history becomes mere story, 'bunk', making it valueless. Ironically, had Gutman himself not decided to test its authenticity by cutting off a 'tiny curl' of the black enamel covering it and revealing lead underneath (201), the Maltese Falcon would have retained its 'immeasurable' (124) value – not for what it was, but for the 'history' that made it a desirable possession for a particular class of customer.

Only the evidence of the senses, empirical evidence, can make history 'bunk' in Hammett's universe. And when history turns out to be 'bunk', value disappears, because value in *The Maltese Falcon* is a direct function of the ability to incite desire in others. This also held true for the feverish speculative economy of 1920s America, where the 'others' included not only consumers, but borrowers and investors. Whether desire is incited by an advertisement, a stock prospectus, a medieval legend, or a sob-story like Brigid O'Shaughnessy's, attributing value to an object of desire always depends on the creation of a plausible narrative. Having written advertising copy for a living, Hammett knew whereof he spoke.

In Hammett's fictive as in his factual world, the value created by narrative always arises from someplace other than the person, act, or thing that seems to have it, and it is realized only in exchange (for other objects, or for money that can be exchanged for other objects), rather than in personal enjoyment. As a Marxist, Hammett would have recognized in this dislocation of the source of value – from the object of one's desire to another's desire for the object – a process that Marx called 'commodity fetishism'. This is the false attribution of an inherent value to material objects that possess it only by virtue of what can be obtained in exchange for them.

Marx felt that ownership of all things in common (namely, 'Communism') could destroy this illusory value-in-exchange and the abuses of capitalist credit, speculation, and exploitation to which it had given rise. Hammett offers no such utopian alternative to commodity fetishism in *The Maltese Falcon*. The detective's only way out of the futile, empty cycle of desire, story, and value-in-exchange lies in his professional commitment to the work at hand, the labour of detecting pursued for its own sake, not for what it can get you, and least of all for pleasure. In this last respect, Spade evinces a much bleaker, more existential vision of detection than his predecessor, the Continental Op, for whom the only 'sense' to doing his job well lay in the 'fun' he got out of it. In fact, Spade carries out his professional duty precisely *because* 'all of [him] wants' to do the opposite (215).

When no meaning or value attaches to persons, things, or actions except as objects of exchange, and where both disappear once the history attached to an object of desire is reduced to story, nothing matters except adherence to a code of behaviour that rejects any basis in desire by resisting the temptation to make behaviour fit into a narrative of desire. Ordinarily, we would expect such a code to base itself on a source of authority that transcends desire, such as religious faith or the will of the people, as expressed in the laws of the democratic state. But the code to which Spade adheres refuses any such prop. Gutman's tale of the Knights of St John, going back to the Crusades, reveals religious faith to be nothing more than a excuse for plunder. Police detectives Polhaus and Dundy show the law to be brutal and incompetent if not corrupt, while Spade himself cuts legal corners with impunity. We are stuck with desire or with meaninglessness, and desire is fatal. The death of Miles Archer, an incurable womanizer, at the hands of Brigid O'Shaughnessy shows that desire can only put you in the path of harm.

To live without desires, however, is more difficult than it may at first appear, and takes constant vigilance. This seems to be the point of Hammett's curious digression in chapter 7, where he has Spade tell Brigid the story of Flitcraft.

Flitcraft is a successful real-estate salesman living in Tacoma, Washington, with a wife, two children, 'and the rest of the appurtenances of successful American living' (62). One day he just disappears. After a few years, Spade is put on the case. He finds Flitcraft in Spokane, living almost exactly the same life he left behind: a successful business, a wife, a baby son, a house in the suburbs, and afternoon golf. Spade asks him why he fled.

Walking to lunch one day in Tacoma, says Flitcraft, he was nearly crushed by an iron beam falling from a construction site.

> The life he knew was a clean orderly sane responsible affair. Now a falling beam had shown him that life was fundamentally none of these things. He, the good citizen-husband-father, could be wiped out between office and restaurant by the accident of a falling beam. He knew then that men died at haphazard like that, and lived only while blind chance spared them. [. . .] What disturbed him was the discovery that in sensibly ordering his affairs he had got out of step and not into step, with life. [. . .] Life could be ended at random by a falling beam: he would change his life at random by going away. (64)

'I don't think he even knew he had settled back naturally into the same groove he had jumped out of in Tacoma,' adds Spade. 'But that's the part of it I always liked' (64).

The Flitcraft story encapsulates the meaning of Hammett's book as an allegory of the American Dream: the desire for financial independence, for a home in the suburbs, afternoon golf, a wife and two kids, 'and the rest of the appurtenances of successful American living' that are made desirable by persuasive narratives. But to live that dream is to walk in one's sleep toward a falling beam. If you're lucky, the beam will miss and wake you up for a moment. But try as you might to stay awake, you'll soon find yourself sleep-walking in 'the same groove' toward another beam. If death comes 'at haphazard', there is no getting 'out of step' with it, except by leaving the 'groove' of desire altogether. Getting 'into step, with life', falling into the routine of the dream, is inevitably getting into step with death.

Outside, Looking At: Being as Doing

Hammett pursues his bleak examination of the nexus of story, desire, and death through an utterly detached, third-person narrative which renders all his characters, but especially Spade, opaque to the reader with respect to their personal histories and motivations, and thus impenetrable with respect to present desire. The rigidity of Hammett's practice extends even to conveying Spade's gradual loss of consciousness, when he has been drugged, through physical descriptions of his slurred speech, the look of his eyes, and his

uncertain steps (129–30). In general, thoughts and feelings throughout the book are signalled by means of gestures, glances, and into-
nations. A single elbow to Joel Cairo's cheek is reduced to a
paragraph-length tally of body parts in motion (48).

In a world where the desires motivating the detective himself
remain as securely hidden from the reader as from everyone under
investigation, not to mention fellow investigators, Spade's ongoing
involvement in the Maltese Falcon case is a constant source of
doubtful speculation. It places the reader in the same unenlightened
position as each of the detective's prospective 'clients' in turn:
O'Shaughnessy, Cairo, and Caspar Gutman, mastermind of the
operation.

Jasmine Yong Hall, tracing the 'inverted' romance elements of
Hammett's reductionistic universe, where every apparent reference to
some transcendental realm of meaning and value collapses into brute
materiality, notes the disturbing effects of Spade's opacity on our traditional assumptions as readers of detective fiction. Perhaps the most
surprising development is Sam's telling Brigid, in the final chapter,
that he knew she was Miles Archer's murderer as soon as he learned
about the burn marks around the bullet-hole in his partner's coat.
They showed that whoever killed him was someone he knew and
trusted. Spade's early awareness of Brigid's guilt, writes Hall, makes
'the whole plot [. . .] a meaningless delay between Archer's murder
and Spade's exposure of Brigid as his killer' (117).

There is something to this, but it doesn't change the fact that the
plot Hammett has constructed is designed to achieve the same goals,
in our reading of it, as those of classical detection: to give the reader's
analeptic imagination a good work-out at nearly every turn of the
page. 'Meaningful' classical detection, however, pursues this task by
letting the reader test material clues against verbal testimonies in
order to arrive at the correct analeptic array of events before the
detective does. The puzzle that Hammett offers readers of *The
Maltese Falcon* is quite different: to reconstruct, from the material
evidence of what he says and does, the motives of Sam Spade.

Hammett uses the mystery of Archer's murder to engage the reader
in an ulterior mystery: What does the detective want? Brought
into the case by Brigid, Sam doesn't hesitate to offer his services to
higher bidders like Cairo, and finally Gutman, who opens negoti-
ations by asking him which of the first two he currently represents.
To Spade's non-committal response Gutman asks, 'Who else is
there?' 'Spade pointed his cigar at his own chest. "There's me," he
said' (108).

But before we jump to the conclusion that Spade is in it only for himself, we should pay attention to his response to Brigid's question in that regard. Told by Spade that he is turning her in for murdering his partner, Brigid asks, 'Would you have done this to me if the falcon had been real and you had been paid your money?' 'Don't be too sure I'm as crooked as I'm supposed to be,' says Spade. 'That kind of reputation might be good business – bringing in high-priced jobs and making it easier to deal with the enemy' (215). If this rationale still sounds mercenary, we should keep in mind that Spade clearly stood to gain much more money from his single deal with Gutman – ten thousand dollars – than he could have earned in half a decade of sleuthing. But Hammett won't even give us that much direct light to see by: Spade doesn't actually deny that he's as crooked as he's supposed to be, only that Brigid can be sure he is.

Hammett does provide other reasons to doubt Spade's crooked-ness, but we must arrive at these by means of circumstantial infer-ence. For instance, almost from the moment Miles is killed, Spade is under suspicion and surveillance by the police because he has been carrying on an affair with Miles's wife, Iva. Once we fully realize the implications of this fact, we can see that Brigid was not the only person Miles would have allowed to get close to him. Putting a bel-ligerent, resentful cop like Lieutenant Dundy onto Brigid's trail might be difficult, to say the least, for a suspect like Spade, who in a pro-fessional capacity has run afoul of Dundy several times. He would only seem to be trying to direct suspicion away from himself. And who could look less likely as a suspect than sweet, helpless Miss Wonderly? Spade has to get more evidence on Brigid, and he has to connect enough of the dots in the case to make that evidence persuasive.

There is also the distinct possibility that Spade is falling in love with Brigid, and is stalling, against his better judgement, for evidence that would exonerate her. Although he clearly suspects her early on, to the point of sneaking out of his flat after their first night together in order to search her apartment, Spade seems genuinely distressed whenever he senses that Brigid is not telling him the truth about her past or about the case. When she finds out that Cairo has offered to hire him for five thousand dollars, she plays her 'trust' card: 'But Mr Spade, you promised to help me. [. . .] I trusted you.' 'Don't let's try to figure out how much you've trusted me,' he said. 'I promised to help you – sure – but you didn't say anything about any black birds' (57).

   In fact, it is impossible to quantify 'trust', to 'figure out how much'
of it Brigid has given Spade, since trust, unlike professional services
or the money one pays for them, is an absolute. Like virginity, it is
given entirely or not at all. Rather than give it, Brigid tries to shame
Spade, implying that she should not have to 'bid for [his] loyalty'.
'What have you given me besides money?' he asks. 'Have you given
me any of your confidence? any of the truth? any help in helping you?
Haven't you tried to buy my loyalty with money and nothing else?'
Brigid, however, doesn't get it: 'I've given you all the money I have.
[. . .] Can I buy you with my body?' Spade kisses her 'roughly and
contemptuously', his face 'hard and furious': 'I'll think it over,' he
replies (57).
   Spade clearly desires Brigid, but his contemptuous kiss shows that
he wants more than her body, the sexual commodity she offers in
exchange for his services – he wants her to open up to him personally as well as physically. It may well be that he is only manipulating
her in an attempt to get information, but his emotional state later on,
when he is about to turn her in, suggests otherwise. As elsewhere in
The Maltese Falcon, feeling here is registered only in physical clues
– Spade's 'pale', 'yellow-white' face and 'croak[ing]' voice (211), his
'bloodshot' eyes (212), the hand that 'shook and jerked' (213) on
Brigid's shoulder, might all be expressions of rage. But if so it is rage
saturated, like his earlier, contemptuous kiss, with desire, and with
something more, sorrow and regret. Spade's 'glittering eyes' (211) and
'wet yellow face' (213) indicate tears. '[M]aybe you love me and
maybe I love you,' he concedes at last, but he doesn't know. 'Does
anybody ever?' (214).
   What Spade does know is that if he's wrong about his feelings for
Brigid he will end up 'play[ing] the sap' (215) for her, and he refuses
to take that risk. He refuses not just because she has done nothing
to make him think he should trust her, but because desire, persist-
ently mistaking story for history, always creates value where there is
none, and acting on it can bring not only disappointment, but death.
   In the end, Spade offers Brigid eight reasons for not letting her go,
but the first and the last, the alpha and omega, as it were, summar-
ize everything that Hammett has to tell us about what makes Spade
tick. First, says Spade, '[w]hen a man's partner is killed he's supposed
to do something about it. It doesn't make any difference what you
thought of him. He was your partner and you're supposed to do
something about it' (213–14). And last, in a statement that Christopher Metress calls 'the sum of these calculations' ('Dashiell', 255),
Spade says, 'I won't because all of me wants to – wants to say to hell

with the consequences and do it – and because – God damn you – you've counted on that with me the same as you counted on that with the others' (215), including Miles Archer.

The question facing Spade throughout *The Maltese Falcon* is precisely the question facing the low-life, crime fiction anti-heroes from whom Metress elsewhere wishes to differentiate him as a force for good, specifically, 'whether or not he can desire at all without initiating a swift process of self-destruction' ('Living', 157). In Spade's world, desire leads to death, and desire is created through stories. We should keep in mind that it was only by accident that the lascivious Archer, and not Spade, should have accompanied Brigid on her evening encounter with Floyd Thursby, and thereby, like Flitcraft but less happily, put himself in the proximity of beams falling. 'I should trust you?' Spade asks her. 'You who knocked off Miles, a man you had nothing against, in cold blood, just like swatting a fly, for the sake of double-crossing Thursby?' (212).

If 'all' of Spade desires Brigid, it's probably wise not to act on that desire. Spade thus chooses to define himself negatively, by what he does *not* want. Feeling nothing but contempt for his dead partner – 'a son of a bitch. [. . .] I meant to kick him out as soon as the year was up' – Spade apparently thinks it safe to pursue Archer's killer, just as he says he's supposed to. It's something for which he has no appetite.

Several critics, including Hall (111–12), have suggested that Brigid's multiple aliases and duplicitous story-telling align her with the Falcon as a spurious object of desire. But no character in *The Maltese Falcon* more clearly matches the tantalizing opacity of the creature of its title than Spade himself. Of course, we should have known what we were up against from the first moment we were invited to picture Hammett's detective anti-hero, whose 'jaw was long and bony', like a beak, 'his chin a jutting v under the flexible v of his mouth'; whose 'nostrils curved back to make another, smaller, v'; whose 'thickish brows' above 'yellow-grey eyes' picked up the 'v *motif*', 'rising outward from twin creases above a hooked nose'; whose 'pale brown hair grew down [. . .] in a point on his forehead' (1); and whose 'steep rounded' sloping shoulders 'made his body seem almost conical – no broader than it was thick' (2), like the deep-chested torso of a bird of prey.

Spade's story-telling skill, as Hall points out, vies with Brigid's in its 'power over the other characters' (112). But as Hammett's opening and final scenes imply, actions speak louder than words. Past or present, they are the only empirical evidence we have of what lies under the skin. When this story andw all the stories in it have ended, one indisputable fact will remain: Brigid O'Shaughnessy is the pigeon 'taking the fall' (211), caught in the talons of a hard-boiled bird named Sam Spade.

Casebook Entry No. 4
No Game for Knights

A Use for 'Bunk'

Published early in 1930, *The Maltese Falcon* offered a timely commentary on the general collapse of value and credit that had begun with the Crash of the stock market the previous October. In short order America began to slide into a long and bitter economic Depression, dragging most of the developed world down with it. Factories closed, unemployment soared, bread lines queued, and shantytowns filled with the homeless.

Despite public works projects, economic reforms, and the repeal of Prohibition that began with the Roosevelt administration in 1933, economic hardship lingered throughout the decade. As Fascism spread through Europe the American worker and his leftist leanings received more sympathetic media treatment, and the sufferings of the unemployed and the working poor were featured more prominently in books, plays, and movies. A 'proletarian' literature of social criticism began to spill over into the crime genre, as exemplified by Horace McCoy's *They Shoot Horses Don't They?* (1935), the story of a desperate mercy killing among the down-and-outs.

In the midst of this economic and political chaos, sales of *Black Mask* and its pulp rivals remained brisk. Not only did their jaundiced view of the world appeal to a disillusioned working-class audience, but the Depression had swelled the pool of cheap, penny-a-word writers from which the pulps could choose their material, keeping costs low (MacShane, *Life*, 44). In 1933 a 44-year-old unemployed accountant living in Los Angeles decided to join their ranks. By

December Raymond Chandler's first story, 'Blackmailers Don't Shoot', was published in *Black Mask*. The following month Dashiell Hammett's fifth novel, *The Thin Man*, appeared. It was the last he ever wrote.

While Hammett took a keen interest in history (it was one of his best subjects in his one year of high school), books like *The Maltese Falcon* suggest that he never saw it as a reliable guide to future action or a source of value. What counted with Hammett was the material fact, and the fewer the narratives attached to that fact the lower the risk of 'playing the sap' by mistaking a lie or a legend for history. For all their sinister behaviour, O'Shaughnessy, Cairo, Wilmer, and Gutman strike Spade, in the end, as saps. 'Jesus God!' he exclaims as the plotters fall to squabbling, 'is this the first thing you guys ever stole? You're a fine lot of lollipops!' (188). The pseudo-historical basis of the conspirators' delusions appears in their consistently calling the capital of modern Turkey 'Constantinople', the name of Istanbul before the Crusades, when the Order of St John supposedly acquired the Falcon. Taken in by the spurious story of what Spade calls 'the dingus', they seek to return to a legendary past that is dead to modern history.

Raymond Chandler, too, wanted to return to a legendary past, not to retrieve an object of great value, but to rescue a personal code of honour made pointless by the Great War's impersonal violence and the vulgar self-interest of the succeeding years. The legendary 'bunk' that, in Hammett's mind, stood in the way of seeing things as they are and the past as it was, Chandler had a use for. If Spade does his duty because none of him wants to, Chandler's Philip Marlowe does his duty because tradition demands it. In this respect, he resembles the detective hero of the Golden Age novelist his creator most despised. Unlike Sayers's Wimsey, however, Marlowe embraces his knightly role in a hopeless gesture of defiance toward a post-war world that cannot countenance it and refuses to be made meaningful by it.

'He didn't seem to be really trying'

Raymond Chandler was born in Chicago on 23 July 1888, to Maurice Chandler and Pearl Eugenie Chandler, who divorced when he was 7. Young Raymond went to live in London with his mother and her relatives, and five years later was enrolled in Dulwich College, a preparatory school for boys. Upon graduation in 1905, he travelled to France and Germany to study the languages, intending to join the British civil service. Two years later, he returned to England, became a naturalized citizen, passed his civil service exam, and secured a position in the Admiralty.

Government work did not suit Chandler, however. He had been bitten by the writing bug. In 1909 he left the Admiralty and began contributing poems, sketches, reviews, and essays to literary journals. His life as a man of letters lasted for some three years before he had to face reality. In 1912 he moved back to the United States, earned a degree in bookkeeping, and found work in Los Angeles.

When war broke out, Chandler enlisted as a British national in the Canadian Army and saw four months of combat at the Western Front. After one particularly devastating barrage he found himself the last surviving member of his unit. Honourably discharged in 1919, he returned to Los Angeles and, in three years, was hired by the Dabney Oil Syndicate. Civilian white-collar work suited Chandler no better than had the government variety. After ten years of increasing absenteeism and erratic behaviour due to alcoholism, Chandler was fired in 1932. Not long afterwards he returned to his old dream, lowering his sights from the literary journals to pulps like *Black Mask*.

Chandler's chivalric themes appear in earnest in his first novel, *The Big Sleep* (1939), whose medieval sources have been traced by Stephen Knight ('Hidden') and Andrew Mathis. The code of knightly fealty, or *comitatus*, that came to play such an important part in his work was a prominent feature of the late Victorian cult of Gothic medievalism, appearing in many of the poems and stories that Chandler would have read as a student at Dulwich. It is easy to accuse him of air-brushing that code, as when, in 'The Simple Art of Murder', he describes its powers of 'redemption' and portrays the hard-boiled private eye as our knightly redeemer: 'But down these mean streets a man must go who is not himself mean,' he writes. This man 'is everything [. . .] a man of honor [. . .] a lonely man [. . .] a proud man' (992), and so on. If Philip Marlowe doesn't quite live up to this portrait, it's because his creator was forced by social and cultural circumstances to question many of the assumptions traditionally informing it, including the gender roles assigned its usual cast: the knightly protagonist, the helpless damsel awaiting rescue, and the deceiving temptress standing in the way.

Leslie Fiedler has argued that American hard-boiled detection in general goes back to the medievalism of Gothic novelists like

Radcliffe, Godwin, and Brown (473). In line with the more prurient Gothic tradition of the Marquis de Sade (1740–1814) and Matthew Lewis (1775–1818), however, the modern private eye, says Fiedler, insists 'on undressing [his] bitches, surveying them with a surly and concupiscent eye before punching, shooting, or consigning them to the gas-chamber. Not only in the cruder and more successful books of Mickey Spillane, but in the more pretentious ones of Raymond Chandler, the detective story has reverted to a kind of populist semi-pornography' (477).

Few critics besides Fiedler would place the formulaic sadism of Mickey Spillane (b. Frank Morrison, 1918) in the same category as Chandler's 'Los Angeles Gothic' (Margolies, 44). Nonetheless, the largely negative reaction to Chandler's treatment of women has continued unabated since Fiedler's book was published in 1960. According to this reading, 'Chandler saw women as sluts or saints' (Wolfe, *Something*, 21), 'gold-diggers, social climbers, nymphomaniacs, psychopaths, monstrous matriarchs, slatternly degenerates' (Thorpe, 68); he is 'pathologically harsh on women' (Mason, 95); his misogyny 'goes without saying' (Christianson, 141); and his 'women (if they are beautiful) are rotten to the core' (Oates, 34). And this includes not only the women Marlowe dislikes. Faced with women who attract him, says Dennis Porter, Marlowe 'demonstrat[es] his mastery over sexual temptation by rejecting, arresting, or in some cases killing' them, in 'a fantasy-fulfilling display of male invulnerability' (185).

Sharon Devaney-Lovinguth has challenged this critical consensus by arguing that Marlowe is a 'modern knight who in order to be a knight rejects, inverts, then remakes chivalric "knightliness"' altogether. One liberating effect of Marlowe's quest in the seven books that Chandler has him narrate is the 'freeing of men and women from the concepts of "knightliness" and "ladyness", from the inadequate and invalid stereotypes assigned by gender' (8).

This critique of 'knightliness' begins on the first page of *The Big Sleep*, with a description of a huge stained-glass window dominating the entrance hall of the Sternwood mansion where Marlowe has just reported for duty. In the window a knight is rescuing

a lady who was tied to a tree and didn't have any clothes on but some very long and convenient hair. The knight had pushed the vizor of his helmet back to be sociable, and he was fiddling with the knots on the ropes that tied the lady to the tree and not getting anywhere. I stood there and thought that if I lived in the house, I would sooner or later have to climb up there and help him. He didn't seem to be really trying. (1–2)

The stained-glass window, as Devaney-Lovinguth observes, announces in typical late-Victorian Gothic style 'the mission that Marlowe will pursue throughout the novels: he will be a "knight" who participates in the freeing of "ladies"' (8). He meets the first lady he will attempt to 'free' in the halls of the Sternwood mansion. She is General Sternwood's voluptuous but mentally impaired younger daughter, Carmen, who introduces herself by turning around and pretending to faint into the arms of the startled detective, like a stereotypical damsel in distress. In fact, Carmen is a nymphomaniac and a psychopathic man-killer. The next time Marlowe sees her it will be in the living room of a high-class pornographer, where, delirious on ether and laudanum, she is posing naked for photos.

Carmen fills the role of the fatally deceiving temptress – the Loathly Lady or reptilian Lamia – of ancient legend. The murderous, epileptic-like fits that overcome her when her sexual advances are rejected by her brother-in-law Rusty Regan, by con man Joe Brody, and by Marlowe himself, have all the hallmarks of demonic possession: 'Her teeth parted and a faint hissing noise came out of her mouth,' says Marlowe when he discovers her waiting for him at one point, naked in his bed. When he turns away, the hissing becomes louder:

> She sat there naked, [...] her face like scraped bone. The hissing noise came tearing out of her mouth as if she had nothing to do with it. There was something behind her eyes, blank as they were, that I had never seen in a woman's eyes. Then her lips moved very slowly and carefully, as if they were artificial lips and had to be manipulated with springs. (157)

Carmen's 'scraped bone' face suggests the scaly snake-head of a Lamia or the skull of a death's-head, and her eyes are 'blank' except for the presence within her of something that can manipulate her like a puppet or automaton.

Critics make a grave error, however, when they assign Carmen exclusively to the role of deadly temptress, for two things have combined to make her what she is, besides her mental disability: her father's neglect and the predatory smut business into which that neglect has driven her. In the end, recognizing Carmen's complete possession by the demons she cannot control and from which no one can protect her, Marlowe chooses to subject her to a modern form of exorcism rather than send her, so to speak, to the stake. Instead of calling the police, he makes Carmen's sister, Vivian, promise to commit her to an asylum (228). *Pace* Fiedler, Spillane's detective hero, Mike Hammer, would be much more likely to have plugged Carmen in the belly.

Psychologically, Carmen is bound by what the English poet William Blake (1757–1827) called 'mind-forged manacles', definitions of her identity that have been fitted to her by a commercialized, patriarchal culture using tools from the workshop of her own brain. Her loss of self-determination makes Carmen, after all, the damsel in distress she pretends to be when she first meets Marlowe. 'He didn't seem to be really trying,' says the hard-boiled detective of the stained-glass knight, revealing, according to Devaney-Lovinguth, 'the sham of the chivalric code which clearly enslaved women – kept them tied up to be gazed upon – even as its knight claimed to be protecting and freeing them' (25).

More precisely, it is what the code became in twentieth-century America, not the code in its most essential form, that demeans and binds women in Chandler's *The Big Sleep*. The naked stained-glass damsel with the 'convenient hair', for example, recalls the pseudo-chivalric legend of Lady Godiva and the original Peeping Tom who gazed at her from behind his shuttered window. This prurient emblem of knighthood is prominently displayed in the home of a retired cavalry officer, the decrepit patriarch of a now-vanished chivalric order, even sharing wall-space with his regimental flags and a portrait of his grandfather, an officer in the Mexican war. The Godiva-like image is matched, says Marlowe, by another nearby (4).

From the first page of *The Big Sleep*, Chandler links sexual depersonalization and coercion to a kitschy – that is to say, mass cultural and commodified – emblem of chivalry. In this respect, he does not so much target Gothic convention, as Devaney-Lovinguth suggests, as use it to take aim at the culture of consumption that the American 'pursuit of happiness' has become. Chandler's critique of the modern debasement of chivalric ideals forms part of a larger critique of the way desire is packaged to be bought and sold in a consumer society, where human relationships themselves are reduced to acts of substitution, utility, and exchange, rather than of faith, fealty, and obligation.

What such a society produces economically, argues Fredric Jameson, are not objects of need, but images of desire, 'fantasms [. . .] the solicitations of various kinds of dream-like mirages and cravings' ('On', 78). In an economy designed to satisfy manufactured cravings rather than real needs, both knights and damsels can easily become proxies, depersonalized instruments for satisfying the desires of customers who will pay for violence and information, or for sexual satisfaction, as long as they can remain personally uninvolved in obtaining them. As we shall see, Chandler even extends this critique to the relationship between the readers of popular crime fiction and what we consume, reminding us that the 'private eye' through which we gaze at gangsters and Godivas in *The Big Sleep* is a proxy 'I' that we have bought and paid for ourselves.

'The client comes first'

Chandler's novel is divided into two halves, which were 'cannibalized' (as Chandler himself put it) from two previous stories, 'Killer in the Rain' (1935) and 'The Curtain' (1936). In the first half, retired General Guy de Brisay Sternwood, whose first and middle names confirm his chivalric typology, has hired Philip Marlowe, private eye, to look into some IOUs sent him by Arthur Geiger, owner of a rare editions bookshop that turns out to be a front for a pornography lending library. The IOUs were written by Sternwood's younger daughter, Carmen, ostensibly for gambling debts. The General has already been victimized by another grifter, Joe Brody, whom he paid $5000 to break off an affair with Carmen. Sternwood hires Marlowe to take Geiger 'off [his] back' (14). In doing so, however, Marlowe must take care to 'make [the] operation as little of a shock to the patient as possible' (15): Sternwood would just as soon not know the dirty details. 'The matter is now in your hands,' he tells Marlowe (15), implying that the detective is free to act as the General's proxy in any way he sees fit, as long as the old man is granted complete deniability.

Marlowe stakes out Geiger's store and home, and hears shots from inside his house. Breaking in the front door, he finds Geiger dead on the floor and Carmen, naked, drugged, and chuckling madly, sitting upright in front of him on an Egyptian-looking throne. After Marlowe takes Carmen home, the rest of the first half of the book is taken up with the discovery of the body of Geiger's murderer, a lovesick Sternwood chauffeur named Owen Taylor, who shot the pornographer when he discovered him photographing Carmen; the tracking down of Carmen's former boyfriend, Joe Brody, who takes over Geiger's pornography racket the day after his murder; and the arrest of Brody's murderer, Geiger's homosexual lover Carol Lundgren, who has killed Brody because he thinks Brody killed Geiger to take over the business.

As this convoluted pornography/blackmail plot unfolds, however, Marlowe finds himself repeatedly being asked – starting with Carmen's older sister, Vivian Regan – if the General had hired him to locate Vivian's missing third husband, Rusty Regan, an ex-bootlegger and ex-officer in the Irish Republican Army.

General Sternwood first mentions Rusty's name when he interviews Marlowe in the stifling heat and humidity of his conservatory. The old man was very attached to his bodyguard, and felt hurt when Regan left without saying goodbye. 'He was the breath of life to me,' he tells Marlowe, 'while he lasted' (11). Sternwood also has practical reasons for wanting his ex-gangster back, feeling certain Rusty would have protected him from blackmailers like Brody (11). In short, former IRA commander Rusty Regan had become the ailing General's trusted knight, and Marlowe, who even resembles Regan (215), is being recruited – and tested – as a possible replacement. The General does not, at this point, ask Marlowe to look for Regan, however, apparently because he suspects that the IRA 'adventurer' may have betrayed him by masterminding Geiger's blackmailing scheme. If so, like every other 'nasty' thing in his life, that is something he would rather not know about.

Since people keep asking him if he's looking for Regan, Marlowe begins to suspect they may have a reason to worry that he might be. 'Test[ing] very high on insubordination' (10), Marlowe takes it upon himself to discover that reason, despite the General's not having asked him. He discovers that Rusty Regan was murdered by Carmen Sternwood when he rejected her sexual advances, and that Vivian has hired a local gangster, Eddie Mars, to help cover up the murder by making it look as though Rusty has run away with Eddie's wife, Mona. Meanwhile, Eddie has begun blackmailing Vivian while keeping Mona in hiding.

Vivian pays off Eddie Mars to protect her sister from the law and her father from the truth. But it is her father's reaction that she seems to fear most. Even the murder of her husband means less to her than 'keeping it from dad' (229). It is important to remember that the General is neither innocent nor naïve. As he tells Marlowe, 'Neither of my daughters has any more moral sense than a cat. Neither have I. No Sternwood ever had' (13). Knowing what his daughters are, however, makes his refusal to see, hear, or speak anything shocking about them appear reckless and irresponsible. Instead of paying attention, he pays money to their thuggish boyfriends. 'My sleep is so close to waking that it is hardly worth the name,' he tells Marlowe from amidst the stifling rugs of his wheelchair, which is parked at the centre of his suffocating greenhouse. Insulating himself from the reality of what his daughters may be up to, the General is already, as it were, 'sleeping the big sleep' (231) that will soon arrive literally with his death.

Everyone around the General conspires to maintain his wilful ignorance concerning the true extent of his family's 'nastiness' (230), including the household staff and, eventually, Marlowe himself. As he feared when he first took this case, it is as though he has agreed to take up residence and become a part of the family, like Rusty before him. If the obligation to 'every detective everywhere' is what finally drives Spade, it's the obligation to his client that finally drives Marlowe, who sees the General as 'a sick man, very frail, very helpless' (156). The rule of *comitatus*, the duty to protect his liege lord's interests at all times, is the first rule of Marlowe's knightly profession, as he explains in his own words to the General: 'I do my best to protect you [. . .]. The client comes first, unless he's crooked' (212–13).

Marlowe's adherence to the rule of *comitatus* is closely linked to his maintaining chastity (not virginity, with which it is often confused, but sexual continence) throughout the book. Specifically, it requires him to resist the sexual temptations of Carmen, who takes a pathological fancy to him, and of Vivian, who tries to seduce him in order to throw him off Rusty's trail (151). Deflecting their advances, Marlowe cites his professional commitment, which is, again, summarized by fidelity to his client: 'Your father didn't hire me to sleep with you,' he tells Vivian (151), and when he finds Carmen naked in his bed he says, 'I'm working for your father. [. . .] He sort of trusts me not to pull any stunts' (156).

Marlowe's predicament is as old as the Arthurian tales of *Le Morte d'Arthur* (1485), by Sir Thomas Malory (d. 1471), in which, as Beverly Kennedy points out, the 'true' knight tries to maintain fealty to his liege lord, satisfy the demands of justice, and remain 'chaste' while overcoming the temptation to pursue his own benefit, to use violence unjustly, or to give in to sexual desire (95–6). In his attempts to negotiate the conflicts between his duty to Sternwood, the temptations of the Sternwood sisters, and the demands of justice in the abstract, Marlowe clearly resembles this 'true' knight. In *The High Window* (1942) he is even called a 'shop-soiled Galahad' (1136). His ultimate quest, however, is not, like Galahad's, to find the Holy Grail, but to find a liege lord worthy of his fealty in a world of ignoble and self-indulgent schemers.

'The orchids are for the sake of the heat'

Sternwood's treatment of his daughters does not make him a good candidate for fealty, however, and calls into question Marlowe's professional acumen. Carmen, for instance, has clearly been abandoned by her father to her own homicidal impulses, and Chandler implies that she is as much their victim as the men she has killed. Ernest Fontana sees General Sternwood as 'a sick, dying lord, who cannot provide Marlowe relevant mastership, but only illusion' (163). Fontana believes that the General's illusions are holdovers from a 'world in which [he] acted with mastery and effect', the world of the 'courageous entrepreneur who develops socially beneficial, primary raw materials' (163), like the oil that made the Sternwoods rich.

There is only one thing wrong with this picture: the idea that Chandler ever believed in a 'heroic' era of capitalistic production. Within one year of being hired by the Dabney Oil Syndicate, he took over the position of chief accountant from a man who had become embroiled in one of the major business scandals of the California oil boom (MacShane, *Life*, 34–7; Marling, 188–200). Eventually fired for what he liked to think was 'insubordination' but was actually drunkenness and philandering on the job (Marling, 200), Chandler was no admirer of capitalist production, having observed its ruthlessly opportunistic workings first-hand among the gushers of Signal Hill, where anyone owning a bungalow in the right spot could become a millionaire overnight. General Sternwood, former cavalry officer turned decrepit oil entrepreneur, is proof of what he learned.

If oil signifies anything in *The Big Sleep*, it is the danger of acquiring too much money, too fast. Fontana is at least half-right: Chandler's 'post-industrial Los Angeles is a world of enervated consumption' (163), not production. The General's 'heroic' period dates from his military years, and his retirement from the rigours of life as a cavalry officer seems to have marked the start of his decline, beginning with the injury he suffered in a steeplechase. As Vivian informs Marlowe to explain why her father is in a wheelchair, the Sternwoods like 'losing games' (59).

Incurred in 'games', not war, in the pursuit of pleasure, not honour, the General's disability represents a life-lesson in the consequences of that constitutionally guaranteed American 'pursuit of happiness' which has reduced even the skills of battle to frivolous, and expensive, 'fun' – a word Chandler rarely uses without cynicism. In *The Big Sleep*, he links it directly to the debasement of chivalric convention. It appears, for instance, when Marlowe describes traffic cops on a rainy day in terms reminiscent of Sir Walter Raleigh spreading his cloak in the puddle for Queen Elizabeth: '[They] had a lot of fun carrying giggling girls across the bad places' (30). Later, the giggles become sinister, even repulsive, when Carmen is reminded of Geiger's murder: 'She just giggled. It was suddenly a lot of fun [. . .] a lot

of nice clean fun. So she giggled. Very cute. The giggles got louder
and ran around the corners of the room like rats behind the wain-
scoting' (66).

Like his taste for soft porn in home décor, the General's 'fun' tends
to take a vicarious form. Unable to smoke, he encourages Marlowe
to light up because he likes the smell. Sniffing the smoke 'like a terrier
at a rathole', Sternwood smiles: ' "A nice state of affairs when a man
has to indulge his vices by proxy," he said dryly. "You are looking
at a very dull survival of a rather gaudy life, a cripple paralyzed
in both legs and with only half of his lower belly" ' (9). For this
superannuated relic of a life lived to its fullest, Marlowe is, like
Rusty Regan before him, 'the breath of life', but good only 'while
he last[s]'.

Even drinking has become a vicarious pleasure for the General.
Unable to partake himself, the old man watches Marlowe sip brandy
while licking his lips 'over and over again, drawing one lip over the
other with a funeral absorption, like an undertaker dry-washing his
hands' (9). Being the 'old buzzard' that he is (206), Sternwood draws
sustenance not only from other men's pleasures, but also from other
men's suffering. Regan 'spent hours with me', he tells Marlowe,
'drinking brandy by the quart and telling me stories of the Irish revolution' (11). Of Rusty's contributions to these bull sessions, Vivian
says, 'He was a lot of fun for Dad' (18).

At one point, General Sternwood tells Marlowe, 'I seem to exist
largely on heat, like a newborn spider' (9). Venomous and predatory,
'sleeping the big sleep' of his crepuscular second childhood, the
General lives 'on' – and in – a life-giving 'heat' that is artificial,
second-hand, not his own. Even the orchids he grows in the conservatory are just 'an excuse for the heat', he tells Marlowe, who could
not help noticing their 'cloying smell' upon entering: 'The plants filled
the place, a forest of them, with nasty meaty leaves and stalks like
the newly washed fingers of dead men' (7). Unprompted by
Marlowe's reflections, General Sternwood calls his specimens 'nasty
things', with flesh 'like the flesh of men' and a 'perfume' like 'the
rotten sweetness of a prostitute' (9).

Fontana takes the General's nightmarish orchids to be 'metaphors
for his daughters' (162). Enclosed in this insulated environment,
however, they seem more specifically to represent the over-protected
Carmen, whose single-minded obsession blends her only object of
desire – the 'flesh of men' – with the principal weapon she uses to
subdue that object – 'the rotten sweetness of a prostitute'. Alterna-
tively, as Marlowe's related image of 'dead men's fingers' suggests,

Carmen's desire is invariably redirected toward murder when her first object is denied her.

The implications of the orchid metaphor seem to extend to the General's marriage to the woman with whom he fathered Carmen and her sister: 'the orchids are *an excuse* for the heat'. He has no love for them. In fact, they disgust him. 'Vivian is spoiled, exacting, smart and quite ruthless,' he tells Marlowe. 'Carmen is a child who likes to pull wings off flies' (13). It was for the sake of the 'heat', his sexual passion, that he fathered 'nasty things' like Carmen and Vivian. They were just 'an excuse' for satisfying his lust. These perverse implications of the General's hot-house atmosphere are later reprised just as Marlowe is about to examine a volume of smut that one of Geiger's skittish clients had abandoned in an outdoor planter: 'The air was as still as the air in General Sternwood's orchid house' (26).

'Silver Wig'

By the time Marlowe finds Carmen waiting naked in his bed, he is forced to admit, 'Knights had no meaning in this game. It wasn't a game for knights' (156). But whether or not the game they are forced to play respects the law of *comitatus*, whether or not they can remain gentlemen 'of the old school' (202) or must themselves become 'a part of the nastiness' (230) by covering it up so that others can sleep 'the big sleep', Chandler's 'true' knights still play the game as best they can, and to them, he suggests, some credit at least is due. In *The Big Sleep*, one such true knight is a woman, Eddie Mars's wife, Mona.

When Marlowe discovers Mona's hideout, he is ambushed by Eddie's gunman, Lash Canino, who knocks him unconscious and ties him up before going out to look for a place to bury his corpse in the nearby hills. As Marlowe comes to, he sees a woman 'sitting near a lamp [. . .] in a good light', and 'so platinumed that her hair shone like a silver fruit bowl' (190). When she speaks, Mona's 'smooth silvery voice' matches her hair colour: 'What did you expect, Mr Marlowe,' she asks, 'orchids?' (191).

Mona is no hot-house plant. This scene inverts the roles of rescuing knight and helpless maiden depicted on General Sternwood's stained-glass window, which also needs to be seen in a good light to achieve its full effect. In a few moments, Mona will release Marlowe from his 'knots' and enable him to escape, endangering her own life as a result when Canino returns. As Mona's silvery attributes and first name (from the Old English for 'moon') suggest, she is a daughter of

Diana, the huntress, who has also served as patroness to several of Mona's literary antecedents, such as the warrior-princess Camilla, leader of the Volscians in Virgil's *Aeneid*, and Britomart in *The Faerie Queene* (1589–96), by Edmund Spenser (1552?-99).

Mona's platinum-coloured hair, which reminds Marlowe of an upended silver bowl, is in fact a wig, which she removes to be sociable, like the knight raising his vizor in the General's window: 'She reached up and yanked it off. Her own hair was clipped short, like a boy's' (194). Gleaming metallically on Mona's cropped head, the removable wig also resembles a helmet, representing her knightly status and chaste devotion to her husband, Eddie Mars. She has disfigured herself, she says, not because she had to, but to show her husband that she is 'willing to do what he wanted me to – hide out. That he didn't need to have me guarded. I wouldn't let him down. I love him' (194). When Marlowe conveys the dangerous information that he knows who she is, Mona's eyes 'flash [. . .] sharply', and the 'sweep of their glance' is 'like the sweep of a sword' (192).

Of course, Mars is no more worthy of Mona's fealty than is Marlowe's client of his, but every attempt to persuade her of this fact is met, initially, with anger and denial: '[H]e's not a killer,' she says repeatedly. 'Not personally,' Marlowe replies. 'He has Canino', making Eddie 'a killer by remote control' (194). Though shaken by Marlowe's arguments to the point of releasing him, and thus compromising her devotion to her husband, Mona will not abandon Eddie Mars, despite her obvious attraction to Marlowe, upon whom she bestows a kiss as cold 'as ice' and, presumably, as chaste. Mona remains behind, professing the belief that her spousal loyalty to Mars will protect her from Canino (197).

Even after Canino ends up using Mona as a human shield in his final confrontation with Marlowe, she goes back to her husband, though their reunion at District Attorney Wilde's house suggests that her eyes have been opened. When Eddie enters the room and greets her, she refuses to look at him or speak to him (208). The book ends with Marlowe stopping at a bar for a couple of double Scotches. 'They didn't do any good,' he says. 'All they did was make me think of Silver-Wig, and I never saw her again' (231). If Mona in her 'silver fruit bowl' is, as Devaney-Lovinguth suggests, Marlowe's Holy Grail (51), then she represents that perfect dream of knightly *comitatus*, of fealty and chastity combined in one object, which in this fallen world must always remain out of reach.

Mona's predicament represents the tragedy of the modern-day 'true' knight who, like Marlowe himself, cannot find a liege lord

worthy of her, one who shares her sense of fairness and right conduct.
At the same time, she cannot abandon the ideals of fealty, chastity,
and justice that define her chivalric identity – that is, her identity not
as a woman or a man, but as something more than a mere instrument of others' needs and desires, like Carmen. Mona's release of
Marlowe brings her close to 'testing high on insubordination', like
the man she rescues, but in the end, also like Marlowe, she cannot
bring herself to betray the man to whom she has committed herself,
even though that makes her 'part of the nastiness' she abhors.

Marlowe's Complicity and Ours: 'The Soldier's Eye'

Clearly, Mona Mars's role in *The Big Sleep* makes it hard to gener-
alize about Chandler's attitude toward women. They are admirable
when they behave in a knightly fashion. And so are grifters. Harry
Jones, a two-bit numbers runner, is Mona's male equivalent. '[A]
small man in a big man's world', Jones tries to sell Marlowe information about Mona's whereabouts so that he and his girlfriend,
Agnes, can skip town. 'There was something I liked about him' (168),
says Marlowe. Unlike any other hoodlum in the book, proud Harry
Jones sticks by his 'frail', even when Canino, who has learned
that Agnes knows where Mona is hiding, threatens him with death
unless he reveals Agnes's whereabouts. Jones gives Canino a false
address, but he never lives to find out if his ploy worked because
Canino kills him immediately afterwards with a shot of cyanide-laced
whiskey.

Harry Jones's murder is one of the most disturbing scenes in *The
Big Sleep*. As it unfolds, Marlowe crouches in an adjoining room,
peering through a crack in the door frame. He can see nothing except
the door-jamb, but he overhears everything, including Harry's 'sharp
cough' and 'violent wretching' (175). Marlowe does not, however,
intervene, because he has no gun and thinks Canino is bluffing. His
misjudgement contributes to Jones's death, and makes him, yet again,
'part of the nastiness' that confronts him at every turn. Peering
through the door-jamb, Marlowe also overhears himself referred to,
for the first time in the book, with an appropriately nasty epithet,
'peeper', which is used three times by Canino (172, 174) and once
by Jones himself (173).

Eddie Mars uses a different term for Marlowe. Named for the god
of war, Mars is used to hiring mercenaries like Canino to do his dirty
business. He calls Marlowe 'soldier', not 'peeper', repeating the term

six times when they first meet (69–75). Together, 'peeper' and 'soldier' exhaust the roles available to 'knights' like Marlowe in a world where knights have no place. Upon completing his job as a 'peeper' for General Sternwood outside the room where Jones was killed, Marlowe will soon have an opportunity to fulfil his duties as the General's new 'soldier' as well, behaving just as ruthlessly as the former IRA Commander he has been hired to replace when he kills Lash Canino while remaining hidden in the dark, something, as he himself remarks, that 'a gentleman of the old school' would never do (202).

Sternwood's butler, Norris, thinks Marlowe has 'the soldier's eye' (215), like Regan. It can hardly be an accident that Chandler, who had seen vicious combat during the Great War, dresses his lords and their knights in uniform colours. Marlowe, an ex-lawman fired for insubordination, reports to Sternwood's front door all in blue, the colour of law enforcement, and 'neat, clean, shaved, and sober', army-talk for 'ready for inspection'. Eddie Mars and his two henchmen, Geiger and Canino, are dressed all in grey (36), black (68), and brown (186–7), respectively, the colours of German and Italian Fascism, whose armies were already marching across the face of Europe. Twenty years before, the Great War had reduced the 'old school' glory of face-to-face combat to the horror of mechanized slaughter. Appearing just months before the outbreak of another Great War, Chandler's militaristic imagery in *The Big Sleep* is unmistakable in its implications: the 'soldier's eye' of the private eye has become the 'Private's' eye. Knights who played the honour game from now on would become its pawns, the unquestioning instruments of proxy violence.

The eye of the soldier, like that of the 'peeper', is ever alert for danger but emotionally detached, and because it is 'private', it is also discreet with its intelligence. In this game of discretion and detachment, Chandler implies, his readers are complicit. Marlowe's private 'eye' is also, after all, the proxy 'I' through which, in Marlowe's first-person narration, we get to 'peep' at 'the nastiness' while remaining, like General Sternwood and Eddie Mars, apart from it. Because Marlowe, our store-bought 'private eye', stays awake, we are allowed to 'sleep[] the big sleep', to dream the waking dream of sex and violence that is twentieth-century America's hard-boiled version of Gothic. Chandler indicates Marlowe's enabling role in our voyeuristic complicity at fleeting moments throughout the book. The evening after Geiger's murder, for instance, Marlowe has nightmares in which he chases Geiger and a nude Carmen while trying to take their photograph (42). Later, he pretends to be a pornographer himself, reassuring Geiger's salesgirl, Agnes, 'I'm in the business too' (52).

'Hollywood's made to order for it' (81), Marlowe tells Brody. And so is Carmen Sternwood. Hollywood, the American dream-factory and master cylinder of its consumer culture, is the home of the stars, and the first syllable of 'Sternwood' is German for 'star', making 'Sternwood', macaronically, 'Star-wood'. Marlowe, however, seems impervious to Carmen's allure. From the moment he beheld her sitting naked in Geiger's living room, he says, he felt neither embarrassment nor lust: 'As a naked girl she was not there in that room at all. She was just a dope. To me she was always just a dope' (36).

What Sam Spade's opacity is to the central themes of *The Maltese Falcon*, Carmen Sternwood's objectification is to the cultural commentary of *The Big Sleep*. Whether posing nude or murdering the men who reject her nakedness, Carmen is never 'there'. In both cases, she is literally de-personalized, as emptied of soul as her 'blank' eyes suggest. Thoroughly habituated to being nothing more than an object in the male's detached, pornographic gaze, Carmen cannot relate to any male except as such an object. When her need to be the focus of erotic attention is denied, her only recourse is violence. She must eliminate the undesiring gaze that reveals to her her own emptiness. She must make the man to whom that gaze belongs stop not-noticing her, stop not-desiring her. Otherwise, she will cease to exist in the only way that has any meaning for her.

Chandler's foregrounding of Carmen's pathology helps us understand what it is about her that Marlowe finds so disturbing, even infuriating. When Carmen leaves his room after her failed attempt at seduction, he reacts with violence. Looking down at his bed, he sees '[t]he imprint of her head [. . .] still in the pillow, of her small corrupt body still on the sheets. I put the empty glass down and tore the bed to pieces savagely' (159).

Marlowe's reaction has been cited as evidence of misogyny and sexual frustration. But it is fundamentally different in kind from both. Chandler's studied use of the word 'imprint' recalls the photographic 'prints' in which Carmen's body has been commodified by pornographers like Geiger and used as a means of blackmail by punks like Brody. Carmen herself is already little more than a walking, talking *Playboy* centrefold, an endlessly replicable object of desire who is never really 'there'.

Marlowe's fury is literally directed, then, not at Carmen, but at her erotic simulacrum, the phantasm to which she has been reduced in the circulation of desire through commodity exchange. Marlowe's own bed has become the photographic plate, as it were, of this ghostly, ectoplasmic 'imprint', and there is no way to make sense of his savage reaction without assuming that, at some level, he feels sexually aroused by what the 'head' and 'body' of Carmen have left there. His rage, however, reflects not frustration, but dread. For Chandler, this is the ultimate horror of vicarious sex: its objects are ghoulish, un-dead.

To his credit, the chaste Marlowe never acts on these impulses, but rather seeks to re-humanize the female body that Carmen's own father and the faceless power of modern consumerism have robbed of its very soul. To the end Marlowe remains, as he tells Carmen, 'your friend – in spite of yourself. You and I have to keep on being friends, and this isn't the way to do it' (155). If indeed knights have 'no meaning in this game', it may be because no knight can save a damsel who is 'not there'.

7

Cold War, Cops, and Counterculture

The last six decades in the history of fictional detection have witnessed developments abroad as well as in the United States and Britain, but none have had an impact on the genre comparable to those that took place in the eras of Poe, Doyle, Sayers, and Chandler.

With few exceptions, the most important transformations have taken place in America, which soon after World War II found itself defending its dominant global position against the Communist regimes of the Soviet Union and China. With the deployment of intercontinental nuclear weaponry in the 1950s, this ongoing 'Cold War' threatened to become 'hot', taking on apocalyptic implications as fears arose that history might soon end altogether with the annihilation of the human race. Despite, or perhaps because of, these anxieties, faith in the traditional positivist and historicist methods of historical reconstruction remained largely unshaken among readers in the popular literary mainstream, who, after a slight hiatus of enthusiasm in the 1960s/1970s, restored the novel of detection to market respectability. Among intellectuals, academicians, and other high-brow readers and writers, however, a more sceptical view of historical evidence and narrative reliability began to find expression in the so-called 'post-modern' detective story, which deliberately upended many of the formulaic assumptions of popular detection.

Hammer and Archer

After *The Big Sleep*, Raymond Chandler wrote six more Philip Marlowe mysteries. At the end of the last, *Playback* (1958), Marlowe decides to abandon his 'blank' and 'meaningless' (870) existence as a private detective and marry Linda Loring, the rich man's daughter who had proposed to him in his previous adventure, *The Long Goodbye* (1953). To judge from the clichéd tough talk and contrived sentimentality of *Playback*, Chandler had grown as weary of detection as his famous PI. The shallow materialism of American post-war life, as reflected in the commercial and residential sprawl of southern California, seems to have had something to do with that weariness. Beginning with *The Little Sister* (1949), Marlowe's digressions on vacuous Golden State life-styles became longer and more frequent: 'California, the department-store state', he quips at the end of one such jeremiad. 'The most of everything and the best of nothing' (80).

By 1959, the year of Chandler's death, two new avatars of the hard-boiled dick that he had raised to middle-brow respectability had appeared on the scene. In personality and world-view no two private detectives could have been more complete opposites, but each in his own way reflected the new political and cultural realities of the Cold War era.

Mike Hammer, the creation of former comic-book writer Mickey Spillane (b. Frank Morrison Spillane, 1918–), was a reincarnation of the avenging vigilantes of the early pulps, re-tooled to focus and reflect back to Spillane's largely male, high-school-educated readership the anti-intellectual fury of a triumphant America facing down the apocalyptic threat posed by godless Communism and its effete 'fellow-travellers': college-educated professionals, homosexuals, and sexy, demanding females. The title of Hammer's first adventure, *I, the Jury* (1947), conveys the self-righteous tenor of the whole series. As William Ruehlmann points out, Hammer never demands a fee to hunt down scum and Commies, but undertakes such assignments willingly and with enthusiasm, like the instrument of an angry God (98). After discovering the corpse of his disabled war buddy Jack Williams, shot dead while crawling toward his wheelchair, Hammer announces to the cops, 'The law is fine. But this time I'm the law, and I'm not going to be cold and impartial' (11). And he isn't.

The sadism and voyeurism, the puritanical hypocrisy and misogyny, and the holier-than-thou disrespect for legal 'niceties' that fill the Mike Hammer books are repugnant. And yet they remain among the best-selling detective stories of all time. This popularity, extending well beyond Spillane's natural audience demographic – *Kiss Me Deadly* (1952) appeared on the *New York Times* best-seller list, for example – is not simply a matter of the author's conservative Cold War ideology, nor the disingenuous prurience of Hammer's first-person point of view. For one thing, Spillane knows how to build suspense, even using characters as shallow as a soup dish. Also, like the hard-boiled mentors on which he draws, Spillane rarely abandons the puzzle element, challenging his readers' powers of imaginative, analeptic invention up to the very end.

Although the House Un-American Activities Committee (HUAC) began hearings on suspected Communist infiltration among American citizens in 1947, Spillane's anti-Communist vendetta did not begin in earnest until 1951, with *One Lonely Night*. The year before, war had broken out with Communist North Korea, Senator Joseph McCarthy of Wisconsin had publicly announced that Soviet spies were infiltrating the State Department, and the HUAC had resumed its hearings, focusing on the Hollywood film industry. Dashiell Hammett, among others who refused to testify against fellow left-wing authors and screenwriters, was sentenced to six months in prison for contempt of Congress. In this pervasive atmosphere of anti-Communist hysteria, writes Woody Haut, 'the basic themes of proletariat writing' in the 1930s, such as 'the corrosive power of money, class antagonism, [and] capitalism's ability to corrode the community', were co-opted by anti-Communist paranoia and suspicion, losing their politically critical edge (5).

Sean McCann has shown how the centralizing tendencies of the Federal bureaucracy that were nurtured by the social welfare programmes of the Depression became intensified by the war effort, leading to the rise within the government and its service bureaus of an educated, intellectual class of administrative professionals. These white-collar 'mandarins', like their artistic and academic colleagues, were generally resented and distrusted by small-town, anti-Communist conservatives like Joe McCarthy, and by many of the working-class veterans to whom Spillane's books appealed. At the same time, industrial acceptance of unionization, post-war prosperity, and legislation making housing and education affordable for returning soldiers and their families had created an ambitious, upwardly mobile, and status-conscious class of industrial and trade union workers capable of earning 'middle-class' incomes.

Many among this post-war adult generation, moving into the three-bedroom housing projects and strip malls flourishing just outside the major cities, possessed at least a smattering of college experience thanks to the GI Bill. Like their white-collar suburban counterparts, they also had high educational and professional expectations for their children, the so-called 'Baby Boomers', who swelled the elementary schools of post-war America and, as adolescents and college students, rebelled in life-style, musical taste, and political outlook against nearly everything their parents stood for. This was the generation raised according to the principles of Dr Benjamin Spock (1903–98), who in his best-selling *Baby and Child Care* (1946) counselled reason and patience in raising kids and cautioned parents against using violence to keep them in line.

Ross Macdonald (b. Kenneth Millar, 1915–83) rode the rising wave of these intergenerational anxieties to both middle-class and academic literary respectability. Unlike Spillane, who saw the world in Manichaean black and white, Macdonald adopted a politically liberal and tolerant outlook, depicting the new alienation between parents and children as the result of mutual misunderstanding, and as amenable to reconciliation. Like his predecessor Raymond Chandler, he addressed his work to a readership that believed in making the cultural and literary values traditionally associated with an upper-class education democratically accessible to all.

Macdonald was born Kenneth Millar in 1915 in Los Gatos, California, the only son of Canadian parents who returned to their homeland two years later. Millar's father abandoned the family soon afterwards, and when he was 6 the boy's mother sent him to live with relatives. She never took him back. After a dozen years of being shunted among his Canadian kin, Millar came to look upon California as the golden land of his birthright, and himself as a young prince in exile. Thence, he says, arose the underlying theme of many of his novels, 'to repossess my American birthplace by imaginative means' ('Archer', 16). His first detective story, 'Find the Woman' (1945), introduced the subject that would later come to dominate his work: the missing or abandoned child. Stylistically, Millar's debt to Chandler was unmistakable.

Not long after he took up writing, Millar and his wife settled in Santa Barbara, California, the 'Santa Teresa' of his fictional world. His long-running series detective Lew Archer debuted in *The Moving Target* (1949), but it was not until ten years later, with *The Galton Case* (1959), that Ross Macdonald, as he was then known, began to introduce into the Archer novels material more directly related to the trauma of his own abandonment as a child.

In 1956 Macdonald had undergone psychotherapy after a nervous breakdown triggered by his daughter's arrest for vehicular homicide. His 'talking cure' had brought to the surface repressed memories and feelings from his earliest years, all related to his abandonment by parents he had never really known. *The Galton Case* was his way of coming to terms with that devastating rejection. In a move that would become typical of his later work, Macdonald traced the origin of such traumas back to the generation of grandparents who had begun the cycle by alienating their own children. In this way, the question of blame was suspended along an implicitly endless chain of victimized generations, into the distant past.

Unlike Spillane's Hammer, Macdonald's Lew Archer (whose last name is derived from that of Sam Spade's doomed partner, Miles) does not pursue vengeance, but like a good psychotherapist serves as a catalyst for understanding and forgiveness, and, above all, for self-forgiveness, among the people he encounters while solving a case. This includes not only young adult children and their conscience-stricken parents and grandparents, but grifters, thugs, and their disreputable female companions as well. 'I don't know why I'm telling you all this,' the respectable Mrs Marion Matheson says to Archer in *The Galton Case*, momentarily interrupting the story of her sordid past relationship with the hoodlum Peter Culligan. 'Why don't you stop me?' (53). Fran Lemberg, slatternly wife of con man Roy Lemberg, feels a similar urge to unburden herself: 'I'm talking too much,' she says, just before echoing Mrs Matheson: 'I don't know why I'm telling you all this. In my experience, the guys do most of the talking. I guess you have a talkable-attable face.' 'You're welcome to the use of it,' Archer replies (94).

In his essay 'Writing *The Galton Case*', Macdonald noted how 'the literary detective has provided writers since Poe with a disguise, a kind of welder's mask enabling us to handle dangerous, hot material' (47). In 'The Writer as Detective Hero', he notes that for writers like Chandler, that mask embodied an ego ideal: Chandler *was* Marlowe, the detective as writer (the private 'I' telling the story) and as redeemer. Archer, however, is not Macdonald, but rather 'a consciousness in which the meanings of other lives emerge', as in the quiet, attentive presence of a psychiatrist (121). 'These other people are for me the main thing,' writes Macdonald. '[T]hey are often more intimately related to me and my life than Lew Archer is' (121).

In *The Galton Case* Macdonald's most obvious self-projection is young John Galton, son of Tony Galton and heir to the Galton fortune, who discovers his true identity by undertaking to play-act, as part of an intended scam that goes haywire, the very person he turns out to be. Archer questions John's claims of gradual self-enlightenment until nearly the end of the book, beginning with the young man's fortuitous appearance in southern California at just the moment when Archer's client, the aged and ill Mrs Galton, has hired the detective to find her missing heir.

Like Macdonald, John had never known his father. He was born in California and taken to Canada in infancy, where he grew up imagining himself an exiled prince, and later took acting classes at the University of Michigan, where Macdonald earned his Ph.D. in English. When Archer questions John's apparently 'sudden interest' in tracing his roots back to California, implying that the young man's motives are pecuniary, John replies, 'It wasn't a sudden interest. Ask any orphan how important it is to him' (128). Later, just moments before his true identity is sealed with the metonymic evidence of a long-lost ruby ring, Archer asks again, 'Money had nothing to do with it?' 'There's more than money to a man's inheritance,' John says. 'Above everything else, I wanted to be sure of my identity' (235).

Macdonald's growing attention to what came to be known as 'the Generation Gap' came on the heels of America's new preoccupation with juvenile delinquency, as reflected in movies like *The Wild One* (1953) and *Rebel without a Cause* (1955). 'What are you rebelling against?' a local girl asks a young Marlon Brando, who plays a motorcycle gang leader in *The Wild One*. 'Whatta ya got?' Brando replies. The rock'n'roll revolution was just getting underway, led by Elvis Presley and Bill Haley and the Comets. Its anti-establishment mood soon found political ballast in the Civil Rights movement's demand for equal opportunity for African Americans, beginning with universal enforcement of the Supreme Court's *Brown* vs *Board of Education* decision of 1954 ending racial segregation in the nation's schools.

White college students, including some of the earliest born of the Baby Boomers, participated in this struggle. The political base they fashioned was further energized by the Free Speech campus movement of the early 1960s and, ultimately, the anti-Vietnam War demonstrations and ghetto riots of the late 1960s and early 1970s. Meanwhile, marijuana, hallucinogens, and harder drugs provided disaffected young people with surer means than the music of The Beatles and The Doors by which to 'turn on, tune in, and drop out' of a mainstream American society they perceived as irredeemably materialistic, racist, violent, and corrupt.

What Macdonald offered his adult readers was not a fantasy of defeating the youth revolution by beating it into submission with night-sticks or showing it the error of its ways with movies like *Reefer Madness* (1947), but rather the promise of reconciliation with their children through confession, reciprocal understanding, and mutual forgiveness. His plots generally make good on that promise while affirming many of the basic values that shaped the Boomers' condemnation of America's 'plastic' way of life, which Macdonald pillories in the shape of ugly impersonal suburbs (where fathers are absent during the day), commercial sprawl, the impunity of wealth, and, increasingly, environmental degradation.

Also contributing to Macdonald's middle-brow popularity was his command of the plain idiom of the great hard-boiled writers, a style he borrowed from Chandler, who had first made it attractive to a mainstream audience. Macdonald made it even more respectable by soft-pedalling its traditional in-your-face, chip-on-the-shoulder insouciance. While there are still scenes of violence and wise-cracking between Archer and the bad guys, Macdonald gets in most of his licks at nouveau-riche vulgarity and class snobbery by subtler means. For instance, on the first page of *The Galton Case* Archer ascends to the waiting room of attorney Gordon Sable's office in a 'private elevator' that 'lifted you from a bare little lobby into an atmosphere of elegant simplicity. It created the impression that after years of struggle you were rising effortlessly to your natural level, one of the chosen' (3). Archer continues the charade of having so risen by sitting down in a 'Harvard chair' and reading the *Wall Street Journal*. It doesn't take long, however, for Sable's secretary to catch on and 'relax[] her formal manner': 'I wasn't one of the chosen after all,' Archer concedes (3).

Macdonald's opening scene not only establishes Archer as a regular guy (despite his familiarity with Paul Klee paintings and Jacob Epstein bronze sculptures), but anticipates the fortunes of young John Galton as he suddenly finds himself 'after years of struggle' 'rising effortlessly' to a level he hopes is 'natural', but from which he may, like the mythical Icarus nearing the sun, plunge seaward as a result of flying too high. The Icarus myth is only one of several alluded to in *The Galton Case*, and bird and flight imagery also plays an important thematic role.

In all of his books, Ross Macdonald took care to fabricate a tightly woven thematic structure by means of reiterated symbols, resonant allusions, and compelling scenes of what the ancient Greek tragedians called *peripety* – plot reversal – and *anagnorisis* – unexpected revelation or discovery. Indeed, in the history of fictional detection, whether classical or hard-boiled, there is probably no more natural-seeming (at least on first reading) and at the same time more densely implicatory stylist than Macdonald. His craftsmanship has helped make him, in the eyes of epigones like Robert B. Parker (1932–) and many critics, the third great name in the twentieth-century history of American tough-guy detection.

The complex layering of his novels was something Macdonald set out quite deliberately to achieve, and he carried through those intentions most emphatically with respect to plot, which he saw 'as a vehicle of meaning': 'The surprise with which a detective novel concludes should set up tragic vibrations which run backward through the entire structure. Which means that the structure must be single, and *intended*' ('Writer', 120). Using dozens of subtly symbolic pieces of evidence and dove-tailing testimonies in each novel, Macdonald evolved one of the most efficient narrative engines in modern detection, and certainly the most efficient among works of the hard-boiled school, for inciting readers to invent analeptic arrays.

Macdonald's reputation continued to grow throughout the turbulent 1960s and well into the 1970s. His sales were bolstered, like Spillane's, by the paperback revolution that began in 1939 with the founding of Pocket Books. By the time Lew Archer appeared on the scene, writers for middle-brow as well as low-brow audiences could publish first edition paperbacks directly for a mass market, rather than awaiting sales figures for initial hardback editions. Closely paralleling this paperback trend were sales of crime-related fiction in general, and especially police procedurals.

Call the Cops

Like its nineteenth-century predecessor, the *roman policier*, the modern police procedural features an official investigator or team of investigators filling the role of detective protagonist and includes a great deal of the technical and administrative detail that supposedly characterizes everyday police work. In its modern form, the genre usually adds off-duty vignettes and story-lines concerning the detective's family life or personal relationships, friendly or otherwise, with his or her colleagues.

While public demand for it emerged just after the war, helped along by the ground-breaking radio (1949) and then television (1952) series, *Dragnet*, the police procedural first achieved widespread popularity in the 1960s as a result of public concern over the rapid rise in urban crime rates. Although violent crime has somewhat abated in recent years, at least in the United States, with the ageing of the Baby-Boom generation of young male criminals, this sub-type of official detection has continued to hold market share, partly through its ability to spin off into related sub-genres, such as crime-scene forensics and medical pathology.

In the United States, the police procedural was inaugurated by Lawrence V. Treat (1903–98) in *V as in Victim* (1945), which introduced many of the now standard features of the genre, including family difficulties, career anxieties, and personal conflicts with peers. Hillary Waugh (1920–) carried on the tradition with *Last Seen Wearing* (1952) and a later series featuring investigator Fred Fellows. Meanwhile, the American grandmaster of police procedurals, Ed McBain (b. Salvatore Lombino, 1926–2005), inaugurated his long-running 87th Precinct series with *Cop-Hater* (1956), eventually perfecting the multiple-plot form that was to become the staple of television police dramas following the debut of *Hill Street Blues* (1981–7), written and directed by Steven Bochco (1943–).

More recently, the dark, gritty, monumental LA police procedurals of James Ellroy (1948–), beginning with *Black Dahlia* (1987) and extending through the rest of his so-called 'LA Quartet' of *The Big Nowhere* (1988), *L. A. Confidential* (1990), and *White Jazz* (1992), have infused the southern California of late Chandler and early Macdonald with the cultural neuroses and conspiratorial paranoia of the American 1980s and 1990s. In some ways, Ellroy's cynical revision of 1950s Los Angeles can be said to have been anticipated, as early as 1957, by the nightmarish vision of New York City found in the Harlem police procedurals of Chester Himes (1909–84), which featured black police detectives Coffin Ed Johnson and Grave Digger Jones.

Himes, a one-time petty crook and jailbird, did not achieve widespread recognition as a writer until after he emigrated to France in 1953, where the tradition of the *roman policier* had originated. Enlisted to contribute to Éditions Galliard's *Série noir* ('Dark Series') of translated American crime writing, Himes wrote his first police novel, *For Love of Immabelle* (1957), in English, translating it into French the following year. It won the distinguished *Grand prix de la littérature policière*, a first for a non-French book. All of Himes's subsequent Harlem police procedurals were published initially in French, and then translated into English.

While Himes himself had never lived in Harlem, the black ghetto depicted in his pages spoke directly, despite its aura of surrealism, to issues being raised by a new generation of angry black protest writers and activists. Unlike many in his African American cohort, however, Himes reserved his most biting sarcasm for the charlatans, drug-dealers, and religious con men of his own race who infest the community that Johnson and Jones, working-class cops at heart, attempt to keep within the bounds of law and order. 'This is Harlem,' Grave

Digger tells white Detective Sergeant Brody in *The Crazy Kill* (1959). '[F]olks in Harlem do things for reasons nobody else would think of' (56). As Sean McCann observes, 'Himes maintained a distinctly unenthusiastic attitude toward the idea of racial identity for most of his life', 'cast[ing] race as a potent, but empty, fiction' (262). As the white backlash against civil rights became more violent, however, Himes's liberal attachment to 'larger notions of solidarity', such as 'the brotherhood of man' (260–1), began to give way to more overt criticism of systemic white racism.

While the paperback book revolution helped drive older pulp magazines like *Black Mask* out of business, the percentage of crime paperbacks, including police procedurals, devoted specifically to mysteries fell drastically at first, from 50 per cent in 1945 to only 13 per cent ten years later (Haut, 6). These figures make Spillane's and Macdonald's durability all the more remarkable. The appearance of television detectives in shows like *Dragnet*, *Perry Mason*, *Naked City*, and *77 Sunset Strip* played some part in reducing the American market for written detection, but in addition the popular literary appetite was beginning to shift away from detective mysteries and toward 'caper' crime fiction, Cold War spy stories, and psychological thrillers.

Nonetheless, traditional tough-guy police detectives and private eyes have never fallen entirely out of favour, as is clearly demonstrated by the success of more recent hard-boiled writers like Andrew Vachss (1942–), whose 'Burke' is rooted in the vigilante avenger-figure popularized by Daly and Spillane. Robert B. Parker seems most deliberately to have seized the mantle of his predecessors with the creation of the long-running series of mysteries featuring Boston PI Spenser and his tough, black sidekick Hawk, a civilian descendant of Jones and Johnson by way of early 1970s 'Blaxploitation' films like *Shaft* (1971). In recent years, the hard-boiled tradition has found some of its most vigorous exponents, ironically enough, among those writers – feminist, ethnic, and African American – who have set out to challenge some of its oldest conventions. These we shall turn to in a moment.

In Britain, it took a long time for the hard-boiled revolution to challenge mainstream classical detection in any serious way. Christie began to include observations on the deteriorating conditions of postwar English life in books like *A Murder is Announced* (1950) and *Mrs McGinty's Dead* (1953). Others, as Julian Symons notes, became caught in a 'desperate struggle [. . .] to adapt to new conditions and ways of feeling' (*Bloody*, 161). The war, the Holocaust, the atomic devastation of Hiroshima and Nagasaki, all had demonstrated the limited impact of reason when pitted against the powers of darkness, and Golden Age authors now had to acknowledge the transformation of their tidy world of country villages and manor houses, of eccentric sleuths and convenient fingerprints, into 'a world much more like that of *Red Harvest*' (Symons, *Bloody*, 161).

Official law enforcement had meanwhile become more sophisticated and forensically advanced, and government agencies were more respected. (The police were part of the same organization, after all, that had won the war.) As a result, British amateur and even private professional detectives lost much of their authority, and their methods became hopelessly anachronistic. Those that survived did so by becoming more fallible and emotionally complex, and the puzzle plots in which they were featured came to depend less on bizarre weapons and exotic clues than previously. Humour often helped overcome any lingering implausibility.

By the next generation, classical detection had largely shifted its focus from amateur to official police investigation. Beginning with two separate series by John Creasey (1908–73), one in the 1940s (featuring Detective inspector Roger West) and the other in the 1950s (featuring Detective George Gideon), the British police procedural was further invigorated by the work of Alan Hunter and Maurice Proctor in the second half of that decade and reached widespread respectability in the 1960s with books like *From Doon to Death* (1964), by Ruth Rendell (1930–). Through the continuing efforts of Chief Inspector Reginald Wexford and his sidekick Inspector Burden, Rendell went on to become one of the most successful of the post-war British detective writers at incorporating a grittier, even vulgar, realism in her portraits of lower-class life.

Among writers who featured police investigators, Rendell's contemporary, P. D. James (1920–) achieved instant celebrity with *Cover Her Face* (1962) and a reputation for unflinching realism with *Shroud for a Nightingale* (1962), which was set in a remote country hospital. James's harrowing description of the carbolic acid poisoning by feeding-tube of a young nurse-volunteer remains a narrative *tour de force* of grim, clear-eyed horror. Like Sayers, James eventually became dissatisfied with the generic constraints of detection and began to venture into the more traditional terrain of the realistic novel, taking her quiet, intense, and highly intellectual poet-police investigator, Adam Dalgleish, along with her.

Three other living writers of British police detection deserve mention here. The first is Colin Dexter (1930–), whose Inspector

Morse of the Thames Valley CID, a hybrid of proletarian, intellectual, and bohemian tendencies, was introduced to the world in *Last Bus to Woodstock* (1975), along with his stolid middle-class protégé, Sergeant Lewis. A bit too fond of his mid-day pint of ale, Oxford-educated Morse is a bachelor and a loner, a lover of opera, and a highly unorthodox investigator who often runs afoul of his superiors by ignoring official police procedure.

Detective Inspector John Rebus, who shares his contemporary Edinburgh beat with creator Ian Rankin (1960–), often comes across as a Caledonian version of Morse: an irascible, inspired loner; survivor of several failed relationships, including one marriage; lover of good wine, good books, and music. He has even acquired his own version of a Sergeant-Lewis-like sidekick in the person of young Detective Constable Brian Holmes. Much more so than Morse, however, Rebus seems a direct descendant of hard-boiled PIs like Chandler's Philip Marlowe. In *Hide and Seek* (1990), Rankin's homage is revealed both explicitly (97) and implicitly, as Rebus finds himself facing a sordid conspiracy that reaches to the highest levels of Edinburgh's legal establishment and decides, in the end, to comply with his superiors' cover-up, becoming thereby, like Marlowe in *The Big Sleep*, a part of the nastiness he had set out to eradicate. Rankin's Edinburgh is the present-day equivalent of Chandler's LA – beautiful but corrupt, money-mad, and beyond redemption.

The third contemporary writer of police procedurals worth mentioning here is Elizabeth George (1949–), American creator of the English aristocratic Inspector Thomas Lynley and working class Detective Sergeant Barbara Havers. Their adventures, now spanning a decade and a half since the publication of *A Great Deliverance* (1988), reveal not only the friction and *frisson* of gender difference, but also the deleterious effects of an embattled sense of class entitlement and class resentment that seems an ineradicable part of British culture.

Despite this post-war shift to official police detection, the puzzle-focused or 'cosy' detective story featuring an amateur investigator has survived on both sides of the Atlantic, if with a smaller readership, relatively speaking, than in its heyday.

Such stories still adhere to the norms of Golden Age detection, including restricting the story to a relatively small, well-defined community of suspects. Among writers of recent and contemporary classical detection are Harry Kemelman (1908–96), whose amateur detective Rabbi David Small began his investigative career helping the members of his synagogue in *Friday the Rabbi Slept Late* (1964);

Martha Grimes (1931–), whose Inspector Richard Jury novels unfold in the English village of Long Piddleton; Amanda Cross (b. Carolyn G. Heilbrun, 1926–2003), a confessed admirer of Dorothy Sayers who set her Professor Kate Fansler novels at a New York college suspiciously resembling Columbia University; Jane Langton (1922–), whose Homer Kelley, a Harvard academic, does his sleuthing largely in Boston's insular suburbs; and John Mortimer (1923–), creator of the 'Rumpole of the Bailey' series of English courtroom mysteries.

Other New Developments

One of the most widespread post-war developments in popular mystery literature has been detection's loss of predominance in the crime hierarchy and its displacement by the 'caper' crime story, the psychological thriller, and gangster fiction. Much of what is now published in these categories comes under the heading of *noir*, a term that French film-makers and critics coined to describe the 'dark' and 'shadowy' look of 1930s American underworld films such as *Little Caesar* (1930) and *Scarface* (1932), both written by W. R. Burnett (1899–1982). The term came to embrace the world of criminal duplicity and deceit not only endemic to the genre of professionalized crime, but also assumed to lie just beneath the innocent surface of everyday American life. During the 1930s and 1940s this world was compellingly realized in the work of writers such as James M. Cain and Cornell Woolrich, most famously in Cain's *The Postman Always Rings Twice* (1934) and *Double Indemnity* (1936), and in Woolrich's *I Married a Dead Man* (1948), written under the name 'William Irish'.

Noir rose sharply in popularity after the war, riding the success of books by Jim Thompson (1906–77) and Patricia Highsmith (1921–95). Thompson's *The Killer Inside Me* (1952) conveys by its title alone the outlook its author adopted throughout his work. Highsmith, whose most famous series features the pleasant, polite, and morally vacuous young murderer and confidence man Tom Ripley, eschewed the puzzle element and moral viewpoint of detection in favour of an empathetic, if dispassionate, evocation of the criminal mind.

In recent years, serial killers have begun to hog the *noir* half-light, two of the most notorious being Patrick Bateman, the young, trendy Wall Street broker and sexual psychopath who narrates *American Psycho* (1991), by Bret Easton Ellis (1964–), and Hannibal 'the

Cannibal' Lecter, mind-game master of *Silence of the Lambs* (1989), by Thomas Harris (1940–). American gangsters have also flourished since the publication by Mario Puzo (1920–99) of *The Godfather* (1969), which film director Francis Ford Coppola (1939–) brought to the screen in 1972. In the 2004 Emmy competition the HBO TV series *The Sopranos*, which had followed the fortunes of a New Jersey organized crime family for four seasons, won more nominations than any other show in television history.

Aside from authors of psychological thrillers and organized crime fiction, many writers over the last several decades have pursued successful careers adhering to the 'caper' format. Two have stood out: former Federal prosecutor George V. Higgins (1939–99), whose impeccable ear for sleazy dialogue helped make his first crime novel, *The Friends of Eddie Coyle* (1972), an immediate best-seller, and one of Higgins's most prolific protégés, Elmore Leonard (1925–), who began his literary career writing Westerns and turned to crime fiction when the market for cowboy soap operas dried up at the end of the 1960s.

Leonard took Higgins's trademark tone and turned it into a superbly malleable instrument for revealing the inner thoughts and vividly idiosyncratic personalities of his buffoonish but deadly protagonists. Although he began to incorporate Old West allusions as early as *City Primeval: High Noon in Detroit* (1980), it was not until *Killshot* (1989) that Leonard undertook a deeper critical examination of the myths and stereotypes of the American frontier. By refocusing these through the lens of contemporary life and exploiting the mastery he had achieved in the use of voice and persona, Leonard showed how deeply embedded in their nation's frontier ethos was the way Americans lived, and killed, today.

Another new development in post-war detection has been the growth of an international market for detective fiction, and the increasing popularity of detective and crime fiction written in languages other than English.

Detective writing outside the United States and Great Britain had, up to World War II, taken place mainly in France, where the *roman policier* remained an important crime sub-genre. Drawing on this tradition, the Belgian writer Georges Simenon (1903–89) achieved international fame with the creation of Inspector Jules Maigret of the Paris Sûreté in *M. Gallet, décédé* (*The Death of Monsieur Gallet*, 1931). In more than seventy subsequent books translated into dozens of languages, Maigret went on to probe the psyches of his suspects, largely at the expense of detection in the classical sense, making the

Maigret corpus an important impetus in the growth of the psychological crime novel in both America and Britain.

With this major exception, however, the general direction of international influence in the writing of crime fiction of all sorts has been
one-way. Mystery stories, police procedurals, and private detection
have all flourished in locales ranging from Hong Kong to Amsterdam
to Botswana, but aside from a handful of European writers,
American crime and detective fiction has enjoyed a major imbalance
of trade in influence, exporting much more than it has imported. In
part, this was simply a result of the overwhelming demand for crime
fiction in the American popular literary marketplace, relative to the
rest of the world. In part, it was due to the parochial monolinguism
of American readers generally, writers and critics included, despite,
or rather because of, the dominant position of the United States in
world culture.

One of the most important exceptions to this rule was the English
and American publication, in translation, of *The Name of the Rose*
(1983) by the Italian scholar Umberto Eco (1932–). A work full of
erudite allusions to Catholic theology, Aristotelian poetics, medieval
philosophy, and contemporary semiotics (the study of signs), *The
Name of the Rose* achieved popular as well as international success
through Eco's ingenious appropriation of the personalities and
methods of detection made world-famous by the Sherlock Holmes
canon. This appropriation begins with the name of Eco's monkish
chief investigator, William of Baskerville, whose anachronistically
empirical, inductive procedures scandalize the inhabitants of a
fourteenth-century monastery where a series of gruesome and
baffling murders has begun to unfold.

Along with the Judge Dee novels of Robert van Gulik (1910–67),
set in seventh-century China and published in the late 1950s, and the
medieval Brother Cadfael adventures of Ellis Peters (1913–95), which
had begun to appear in 1977, Eco's book helped to launch a new
wave of 'historical' detective novels set in various eras of the near
and distant past, ranging from ancient Rome to nineteenth-century
New York City. As Robin Winks notes, this may be 'the most rapidly
growing branch of the genre' at present (*Detective as Historian*, x).

Winks suggests that one reason for historical detection's sudden
popularity is traditional history's recent turn away from narrative as
a reliable means of representing the past. 'Historians moved too far
away from their origins, as storytellers: now storytellers may bring
historians back to those roots,' writes Winks (x). In fact, however,
the shelves of most bookstores and libraries today are groaning under

the weight of historical story-telling, in the form of biographies, military histories, and sports sagas, as well as accessible lay explanations of important past events like the signing of the American Constitution or the invention of computers. It is academic history, not popular history, that has struggled in recent years with the challenge of what has come to be called 'postmodernism', wherein narratives of the past claiming to be factual are analysed and interpreted as though they were fictional texts.

The Challenge of Postmodernism

Postmodern sociologists like Jean-François Lyotard, along with like-minded philosophers of history like Hayden White and Patrick Joyce, have questioned the ability of any narrative to resist the inherent biases and limited point of view of its author, not to mention the distortions of its own rhetorical devices, in attempting to convey historical truth. The stories through which material documents and artefacts of the past have traditionally been made meaningful in relation to one another and to present-day experience are seen by such critics as devices for arbitrarily imposing meaning, causal or otherwise, on those relationships. Such distortions, it is alleged, often arise from a desire for professional advancement, personal enrichment, or class, gender, or racial dominance.

In part, these developments in the practice and writing of history have grown out of the sense of relativism in historical interpretation signalled by the work of historicists like Collingwood and Croce in the interwar years. They were also anticipated, culturally, by a new and generically subversive challenge to popular detection that began to emerge at the end of the interwar period. This challenge was mounted by a high-brow, intellectual variant of detection with which Eco's much later book was immediately identified by many of its academic readers: postmodern or, as Julian Symons calls it, 'parodic' detection (*Bloody*, 220).

Postmodern detection, according to Michael Holquist, 'exploits detective stories by expanding and changing certain possibilities in them' (165). Among these are the typically unrealized possibilities of an open-ended plot, undecidable conflicts in testimony, indecipherable clues, and impenetrable motives – in short, all the wayward possibilities of real life that the traditional detective story deliberately excludes from its highly rational, causally coherent universe. Postmodern detection can be said formally to have begun with the

publication of 'The Garden of Forking Paths', by Argentinian writer
Jorge Luis Borges (1899–1986). A self-conscious homage to Poe's
'Murders in the Rue Morgue', the story was published in 1941, the
centenary of Poe's tale.

The 'Garden' of Borges's title is an imaginary one, wherein a
labyrinthine path corresponding to every possible future development
of every passing moment of time 'forks' into an infinite number of
parallel and intersecting future universes. This 'Garden' is also the
cryptic subject of a book being written by a reclusive sinologist
whose murder, when announced in the newspapers, will serve as a
coded message indicating the location of a hidden gun emplacement
during an engagement of World War I, the period in which the story
is set.

The specific connections between Poe's story and Borges's, which
is as much a spy as a detective tale, need not concern us here, but in
this and subsequent variations on Poe's other two Dupin cases Borges
made evident one of postmodern detection's most important themes:
the way in which material objects, events, and actions in the world,
which we take to have an existence preceding and apart from the
words we use to describe them, are assigned their meanings by the
very narratives within which they are made to appear as 'facts'. From
the viewpoint of postmodernism, there is no final array awaiting us
at the end of the narrative of detection; ideally, all imaginable arrays,
all of the 'forking paths' in the 'garden' of the text, have an equal
claim to finality.

To assign this degree of power to narrative in general, however, is
ultimately to deny it to any narrative in particular. Succeeding writers
of postmodern detection like Alain Robbe-Grillet (1922–) have
accordingly multiplied or suspended narratives of causality, calling
into question the reliability of memory and the attribution of motive
in novels like *Les Gommes* (*The Erasers*, 1953) and *Le Voyeur*
(1955). Robbe-Grillet's is a world of objects that resist appropriation
by narrative, and of narratives that appropriate their own narrators.

Robbe-Grillet's contemporary, Russian émigré Vladimir Nabokov
(1899–1977), similarly parodied the American crime novel in *Lolita*
(1955) and plots of detection in *Pale Fire* (1962), a tale of envy,
murder, and unreliable narration set in a small college town. Others
have queried the contrived successes of fictional detection. In *Das
Versprechen* (*The Pledge*, 1958), Swiss writer Friedrich Dürrenmatt
(1921–90) portrayed the self-defeating obsession of a detective who
sacrifices his job and his happiness to make good on his 'pledge' to
the mother of a murdered little girl that he will catch her killer. His

failure after many years makes his entire life pointless. The killer meanwhile dies in an auto accident.

With few exceptions, postmodern detection has not found a broad market among ordinary fans of detective fiction, perhaps because it frustrates the middle-class urge for imaginative reconstruction and closure that traditional detection is designed to satisfy. As *The Name of the Rose* has demonstrated, however, there are exceptions. The popular works of Paul Auster (1947–) include his *New York Trilogy* (1985–6), which pays homage, implicitly and explicitly, to the mind-bending, self-reflexive narratives of Poe's Gothic tales, incorporating plot elements and names not just from the Dupin stories, but from elsewhere in the Poe canon as well, including 'The Man of the Crowd', 'William Wilson' (1839), and *The Narrative of Arthur Gordon Pym* (1850).

Another interesting, but comic, pair of exceptions are two adventures written by the late British sci-fi parodist Douglas Adams (1952–2001) featuring Dirk Gently, the 'holistic' detective: *Dirk Gently's Holistic Detective Agency* (1987) and *The Long Dark Tea-Time of the Soul* (1988). Adams's eponymous PI goes about solving crimes using methods based on contemporary catastrophe theory, which posits the interconnected nature of all physical events in a random universe. Accordingly, Gently will often begin his investigations by following a lead wholly unrelated to the obvious clues of traditional detection, with absurd and hilarious, but serendipitously effective, results.

Alternative Detection

A more mainstream challenge to traditional detection has arisen on several related fronts in the last two decades, especially among American writers. Fuelled by the movements against racism and the Vietnam War in the 1960s and against sexism in the 1970s, these 'alternative' sub-genres began to question the traditional reliance of fictional detection, particularly in the hard-boiled tradition, on Western, white, male protagonists. 'Alternative' detection may, accordingly, be divided into three groups: ethnic/post-colonial, African American, and feminist/gay/lesbian. Among these groups are writers who belong to more than one category.

Alternative detective writers seek to challenge traditional assumptions about the nationality, race, and gender of investigative authority by placing a culturally non-conforming protagonist in the position of primary investigator. Typically, this person will bring to the task of investigation skills and abilities not ordinarily attributed to Western, white, male detectives, and face obstacles that his or her traditional counterparts need never face. These obstacles arise mainly from the prejudices of the dominant culture. Sometimes the point is to reveal the hidden biases that readers themselves may bring to the genre of detection, but more often it is to reflect back to a self-selected class of 'alternative'-minded readers their personal understanding of the ways in which white patriarchal discrimination against the ethnic, racial, or female Other has become endemic to modern Western society.

What distinguishes the position of the alternative detective figure within the tradition of detection is how his or her cultural difference or 'alterity' finds expression within the constraints of what the post-colonial theorist Homi Bhabha calls the 'liminal space' between cultures (4). We have already encountered the concept of the liminal in examining the rise of the traditional white male detective, who since the days of the thief-taker has straddled the *limen* or threshold between law-abiding society and the criminal element. In alternative sub-genres the *limen* is drawn along the boundary between genders, races, or ethnic groups, with the detective occupying the 'liminal space' between the group he or she has been born into (black, female, Hispanic, and so on) and the group he or she has chosen to join, but from which he or she has traditionally been excluded, namely, the group of white male detectives.

Often, writers of alternative detection will take over this liminal space in the name of the excluded birth group and mount a direct offensive on the cultural prerogatives of the oppressor. Some critics applaud this kind of explicit ideological critique as a form of resistance that 'teach[es] [. . .] readers to read' from a politically committed point of view (Reddy, 176). Few readers who are not already in favour of resistance wish to be 'taught' it in this manner, however, and few resistance-minded authors of detective fiction could stay in business solely by trying to teach them. The result is often a simplistic reversal of the principal characters' traditional roles, with all virtue accruing to the non-traditional detective figure and all vice assigned to the white, Western, male antagonist, whether colleague or criminal.

More interesting work, and no less compelling as an interrogation of 'Things as They Are', has appeared among writers who try to maintain the ambiguity of the non-traditional detective's liminal position by exploring the legitimate, but finally irreconcilable, demands on his or her allegiance made from both sides of the line. This kind of 'interstitial passage between fixed identifications', as Bhabha calls it, 'opens up the possibility of [. . .] entertain[ing] difference without assumed or imposed hierarchy' (4).

Post-colonial detection of this 'interstitial' type, according to Ed Christian, explores how the alternative detective's own 'cultural attitudes' influence his or her 'approach to criminal investigation' (2). Christian identifies the 'practical anthropology' that emerges from this process as crucial to helping readers of all cultural backgrounds understand the 'way people are as they are and why there are benefits to being that way', leading not necessarily to resistance, but to 'tolerance of diversity and hybridity' (2). The latter term, also coined by Bhabha (4), indicates a process whereby former colonizer and colonized begin to take on each other's perspectives and values, transforming 'liminality' from a 'neither/nor' to a 'both/and' region of cultural overlap. As Gina and Andrew Macdonald put it, the most interesting post-colonial detectives stand at a cultural 'crossroads' (63) from which a universally human perspective can begin to emerge and prevail among readers.

John Cawelti has noted that post-colonial detective fiction has precursors dating from the Golden Age, when the search for eccentricity began to embrace exotic nations and races 'as a means of exploring rather than condemning other cultures' ('Canonization', 10). Earl Derr Biggers's Charlie Chan, whose first adventure dates to 1925; the Japanese sleuth 'Mr Moto', whom John P. Marquand (1893–1960) created in 1935; and the half-Aborigine police detective Napoleon Bonaparte conceived by Arthur Upfield (1890–1964) in 1928, all date from this period. Since the 1960s two of the most popular post-colonial detectives have been the Indian police investigator Inspector Ghote, created in 1964 by British writer H. R. F. Keating (b. 1926), and the black police detective Mickey Zondi, partnered since 1971 with white Afrikaner Tromp Kramer in the South African novels of James McClure (1939–). In 2002, private professional detective Precious Ramotswe, founder of 'The No. 1 Ladies Detective Agency' in Gaborone, Botswana, began to attract an enthusiastic readership for Alexander McCall Smith (1948–), who has prolonged her adventures in subsequent books.

Some alternative detection writers identify the basic inductive methods of the genre itself with Western patriarchal oppression, based as these methods are on modes of historical reconstruction originating with the male-dominated sciences of the European Enlightenment. However, there is a limit to how much of the genre's traditional methodology alternative writers can discard without falling outside the generic boundaries altogether.

As a case in point, the Macdonalds cite the novels of C. Q. Yarbro (1942–), featuring Ojibway investigator Charlie Spotted Moon (70–1). Here, native American sweat-lodge visions and magic sticks take the place of material clues and fingerprint kits at the expense of detection's most culturally universal feature: the power to activate, in the reader's mind, an ongoing process of imaginative reconstruction independent of but parallel to that of the detective. This inferential process is as culturally widespread as ritualizations of birth, marriage, and death, and as old as the tracking of game. In contrast to Yarbro's native American window-dressing, argue the Macdonalds, the Navajo police detectives of Tony Hillerman (1925–), Joe Leaphorn and Jim Chee, represent true 'crossroads heroes' who must 'pick and choose among the best of each culture – native American and Euro-American – into which birth and profession, respectively, have thrust them (74–6).

Despite its superficial resemblance to post-colonial detection, African American detection constitutes a special alternative category, in which notions of 'liminality' and 'hybridity' require considerable revision. For one thing, African American detectives, whether male or female, must work through the pervasive and lingering impact of institutionalized antebellum black slavery. Born both black and American, African Americans are not free to choose either category of identification, and the two are interconnected in a way that defeats most attempts to reconcile them.

As a result, Stephen Soitos points out, black investigators labour under what the black sociologist W. E. B. Du Bois called a 'double consciousness' unknown to traditional white detectives. Specifically, they are forced by their upbringing to see themselves as second-class citizens in the eyes of the dominant white American culture before they can see themselves as citizens of the 'America' defined by that culture (Soitos, 35). The 'Blues Detective', as Soitos calls him or her, must struggle against this white-mediated mirror-relationship with respect to his or her own subjectivity in order to achieve the dignity and sense of self-worth that have naturally been accorded white male detectives.

This kind of 'double consciousness' is particularly evident in the Easy Rawlins series of detective novels by Walter Mosley (1952–), beginning with *Devil in a Blue Dress* (1995).

The first of seven books so far (as of 2005) in Mosley's long-running Los Angeles saga, *Devil in a Blue Dress* relates how World

War II veteran Ezekiel 'Easy' Rawlins is transformed from a factory worker in an aircraft plant into an unlicensed detective – or, more accurately, spy – in the black neighbourhoods of South Central Los Angeles. Part of the great migration of blacks from the American South seeking jobs in post-war southern California, Easy is fired from his job by a racist foreman for insubordination. Having house payments to meet, Rawlins starts taking fees to gather information about his neighbours in the African American community. Sometimes he is hired by his neighbours, and sometimes by the largely white Los Angeles police department, which has few contacts in the black community.

Easy begins his underground career by agreeing to find a young white jazz singer named Daphne Monet, the 'Devil in a Blue Dress' of the title, who likes the 'company of Negroes' (18). The man who hires him, a sadistic, cold-blooded killer dressed entirely in white whose name, Dewitt Albright, further conveys his racial symbolism, is himself working for a prominent white citizen named Todd Carter. Carter's love for Daphne has, inexplicably, driven her into hiding.

Easy's investigation leads him to Daphne, but as he, too, falls in love with her he comes face to face with his unexamined feelings about white women, feelings exacerbated by his sexual experiences with Frenchwomen in the liberation of Paris during the war. Like Daphne, whose apparent French ancestry they share, these women also had blue eyes, and one in particular wore a blue dress.

The ambiguities and ironies of Easy's incipient love for Daphne, and what that love says about his own 'uneasy' sense of racial identity in a white-dominated society, are intensified by a secret revealed only at the end of the novel. They are made more complex throughout by Mosley's sophisticated juxtaposition of one 'white man's war' (193), the one against Nazism, with another, the war against crime, in both of which black men like Easy are fooled or forced to participate. As Liam Kennedy points out, Mosley is also very aware of the white American hard-boiled tradition, which he often subjects to 'defamiliarization and inversion as he plots the urban scene around the perspective of a black subject' (227). The opening chapter of *Devil in a Blue Dress*, for instance, reverses the perspective of the opening chapter of Chandler's *Farewell, My Lovely* (1940), which unfolds in a black Los Angeles bar.

Mosley's fiction arrives at the end of a long history of black detection extending back to 1901, when Pauline Hopkins (1859–1930) first began serial publication of *Hagar's Daughter: A Story of Southern Caste Prejudice*, featuring the black female detective Venus

Johnson. Chester Himes's Harlem police procedurals, a watershed in this tradition, had a major impact on Mosley. While there is still disagreement, as Robert Crooks indicates, over whether or not the official police affiliation of Himes's black Harlem detectives Jones and Johnson make them 'tactical' inside strategists against racial discrimination or 'complicitous' advocates of assimilation (189), by the time he finished his career Himes had clearly come to embrace a broader 'strategic' critique of the entire socio-economic system of white racism (189–92). Similarly, while some critics think Easy's precarious balance between white and black identities reflects Mosley's own lack of conviction (Berger, 292), others see this as 'an engaging aspect of [Easy's] evolving self-awareness' (Muller, 295). Some even consider Mosley heir to the 'strategic' view of endemic racism that was Himes's final legacy (Crooks, 183).

The fastest-growing category of alternative detection today is feminist and gay/lesbian, especially of the hard-boiled variety. The recent surge of feminist detection was inspired in part by P. D. James's two Cordeila Gray novels, beginning with *An Unsuitable Job for a Woman* (1972). Five years later *Edwin of the Iron Shoes* (1977), by Marcia Muller (1944–), introduced series private detective Sharon McCone to American readers. Muller's hard-boiled successors include Katherine V. Forrest (1939–), creator of lesbian Los Angeles cop Kate Delafield, and forensic pathologist Patricia Cornwell (b. 1956), who packs plenty of grisly detail into the adventures of State Medical Examiner Kate Scarpetta. Two of the most durable exponents of American feminism over the last two decades, however, have been Sara Paretsky (1947–) and Sue Grafton (1940–). Both made their debut in 1982, Paretsky with *Indemnity Only*, Grafton with *'A' is for Alibi*.

Paretsky's Polish-American private eye V. I. Warshawski is probably the toughest of the feminist hard-boiled detectives. Daughter of a Chicago cop, she is little given to sentiment as she hunts down the masculinist stooges of the patriarchal system and their shadowy bosses. Paretsky focuses on institutionalized forms of oppression and corruption, and her Ph.D. in history has provided her with the necessary tools for solid research into the massive machinery of day-to-day exploitation. Warshawski clearly belongs to what the Macdonalds call the current 'trend of having the detective act out headline issues' (88). Her toughness, however, verges on ideological self-defeat, at least insofar as feminism typically rejects the resort to violence as a trait of patriarchy. Meanwhile, the villainy of Warshawski's male foes can approach the flat monstrosity of melodrama. In *Blood Shot* (1988), the male culprit becomes a veritable Swiss Army knife of hyper-masculinist threats: paedophile, wife abuser, con man, and corrupt politician.

Given her tom-boy appearance and taste for guns and weight-lifting, Sue Grafton's Kinsey Millhone seems to be just a more 'butch' version of Warshawski. But there are important differences between the two. While Grafton appears to be as indebted to generic convention as Paretsky (Rabinowitz, 'Reader', 335), she takes better advantage of the opportunities for ambiguity afforded her by the male hard-boiled tradition. Warshawski's path in life has been modelled for her by her father, but Millhone was orphaned at the age of 5 when both her parents died in a car crash. Raised by her pragmatic spinster aunt, Kinsey has been spared the cultural indoctrination in femininity to which her peers have been subjected, but her overt contempt for the stereotypical female accoutrements of gender often seems like a defensive form of acting out, betraying an existential vulnerability true to the basic spirit of Hammett and Chandler.

As Grafton's alphabetic series of novels continued (as of this writing it has reached *'R' is for Ricochet* [2004]), the mystery of Kinsey's own identity became thematic. This was not a matter of sexual orientation (she is unambiguously drawn to the opposite sex, sometimes to the detriment of her sleuthing abilities) so much as her family history and conflicted relationship to common, enculturated notions of gender.

In *'F' is for Fugitive* (1989), Kinsey finds herself involved in a case requiring her to move in with a dysfunctional family and unwittingly assume the role, within the familial power structure, of the fugitive adult son she has been hired to find. This places her squarely in the path of an older sister's sibling hostility. Meanwhile, Kinsey's relationships with the patriarch and the sickly mother of the clan bring up irrational childhood feelings of anger at being abandoned by her parents, especially her father. Thus, the 'fugitive' in Grafton's title takes on added significance as it applies to Kinsey's own 'fugitive' status from the culturally legitimated American family, to which 'F' might also refer in a covert manner.

Kinsey's relationship with the Fowlers (another 'F'!) becomes so strained that at one point she states that living with them has made orphanhood look good. In *'J' is for Judgment* (1993), she discovers that she has an extended family, whose existence her aunt kept from her as she was growing up. Here and in several succeeding books one of the moral dilemmas facing Kinsey becomes whether or not to preserve and strengthen these new ties, or retreat into the emotional cocoon of her solitary life-style. Thus Grafton takes many of the standard features of the masculine hard-boiled hero – detachment, toughness, cynicism – and gives them a personal history that distinguishes her detective heroine not only from her masculine precursors, but also from many of her alternative feminist contemporaries.

Grafton's own personal history, as well as her allusions to the hard-boiled tradition, offer signposts to the imaginative origins of Kinsey Millhone. Grafton was a child of alcoholic parents, who acquired her love of fictional detection from her father, C. W. Grafton, a Louisville attorney and detective writer. When her mother became a chronic invalid, Grafton's father left his wife's care entirely in the hands of Sue and her older sister, Ann, and checked out of the family emotionally (Kaufman and Kay, 376–9). 'Ann' is the name that Grafton gave the hostile older sister in 'F', and the selfish and emotionally distant Royce Fowler and his sickly wife, Oribelle, seem to be modelled on Grafton's own parents.

While Grafton clearly learned her hard-boiled skills from masters like Hammett and Chandler, Ross Macdonald may have had the most serious impact on her writing. Kinsey Millhone, like Lew Archer, rents office space in Macdonald's fictional equivalent of Santa Barbara, 'Santa Teresa', and Kinsey's initials match those of Kenneth Millar. In a deeper sense, orphaned Kinsey's search for a sound foundation of identity, her sense of abandonment and ambivalent need for connection, her tendencies to act out parent–child scenarios with acquaintances and clients, all linked to the gradual discovery of her unknown relatives, recapitulate Macdonald's most important thematic preoccupations. 'None of us had survived the wounds of our fathers,' says Kinsey at the end of 'F' is for Fugitive (306), perhaps one of the most accurate, and certainly one of the saddest, indictments of patriarchy in the whole corpus of feminist detection.

Epilogue
The End of History?

Three years after the destruction of the Berlin Wall in 1989, Francis Fukuyama declared 'the end of history', by which he meant the end of disputes over the ultimate outcome of the centuries-long struggle to define the purpose and meaning of history. The collapse of the Soviet Union meant the defeat of Marxism, the last widely credited teleological view of historical development, capping a struggle that had begun with the Western Enlightenment's earliest challenges to Judaeo-Christian salvation history in the eighteenth century. There would be no dictatorship of the proletariat waiting at the end of a coherent and inexorable historical process, only the ongoing, haphazard globalization of free trade and individual property rights, with the prospect of increasing democratization.

Although the outcome of the current struggle between Western secularism and Islamic fundamentalism remains in doubt, Fukuyama's vision of a static-state future dominated by liberal democracies and capitalist economies suggests that the international market for detection, which Cawelti calls the quintessential popular genre of 'individualistic, bourgeois democracy' ('Canonization', 13), will continue to grow. The outcome of history may have ended, but demand for the West's premier popular genre aimed at inciting in readers the active, imaginative reconstruction of past events has not.

In any case, there can be little doubt that since 1989 America's hegemony over detective fiction, like that of its British predecessor, has rapidly been going the way of its Cold War political agenda. Hegemony has now become a virtual diaspora, and detective fiction's literary colonies around the world have been declaring their independence. In nearly every developed and developing nation, from

Sweden, where the works of Henning Mankel have been filling the best-seller shelves since 1991, to Japan, where the stories of Edogawa Rampo outsell those of any American writer and provide material for *manga* (comics) and *anime* (cartoons), detective and crime fiction are sending down roots into native soils and bearing indigenous fruits for export.

At the same time, with the so-called 'End of History' as a stable narrative entity, new stresses are cracking the plaster of Enlightenment faith in a factually recoverable history, a faith that underwrote the rise and eventual triumph of detection among the popular genres of the West. These stresses have become evident in part as a result of the continuing infiltration of the popular crime genre by the postmodern critique of detection and its inductive methods, which has characterized the academic and high-brow reaction to popular detection for more than half a century now. The ultimate outcome of this infiltration remains unclear, but Dan Brown's best-selling *The Da Vinci Code* (2002) provides one tentative signpost.

Brown's foray into the putative netherworld of Catholic conservatism, goddess worship, the Knights Templar, and the Holy Grail has raised eyebrows, and hackles, at its factual claims for the existence of a secret hoard of documents proving Jesus' marriage to Mary Magdalene (presumably the true meaning of the Grail legend) and his paternity of a line of descendants down to the present day. The suspense of Brown's tale depends on the assumption that these documents pose so great a threat to patriarchal Christianity that the Catholic Church would stop at nothing, not even murder, to get hold of them.

In a conversation between a French cryptologist and a British expert on the Grail legend, Brown coyly implies that his readers bear the responsibility for taking such claims at face value. Sophie, the cryptologist, points out that even a 'documented genealogy of Christ's bloodline' is 'not proof. Historians could not possibly confirm its authenticity.' 'No more so than they can confirm the authenticity of the Bible,' replies Grail specialist Sir Leigh Teabing. '[H]istory is always written by the winners,' he continues. 'The Sangreal documents simply tell the *other* side of the Christ story. In the end, which side of the story you believe becomes a matter of faith and personal exploration' (256).

In short, the readers of such documents, like the readers of Brown's text, will have to decide the truth for themselves, on no firmer basis than personal 'faith', or lack thereof. Overlooked in Brown's pop version of postmodernism are all the standard methods of contemporary historiography, including chemical analysis and carbon-dating, for establishing, not beyond a shadow of a doubt but with a high degree of inductive probability, the age and provenance of ancient documents such as those supposedly stashed in the Grail. But no matter, implies Brown: just like *The Da Vinci Code* itself, ancient documents must rest their claims to authority on nothing more than their ability to induce a willing suspension of disbelief in their readers.

What is missing from Brown's trendy hybridization of feminism, paganism, and conspiracy theory is what gives its most obvious antecedent in hard-boiled detective fiction philosophical fibre. When challenged to establish the provenance and authenticity of a similar tale concerning a long-hidden treasure of the medieval Knights of St John, Sam Spade doesn't hesitate to ask, 'Is it probable? Is it possible – even barely possible? Or is it the bunk?' In pursuit of answers to his questions, he sends his secretary Effie Perrine to find out what her cousin at Berkeley, who is working on his doctorate in history, can make of the fantastic 'history' of the Maltese Falcon. Before the verdict is in, Spade finds his question answered when Gutman takes his penknife to the Falcon's shiny scalp. As the West learned long before the fall of the Berlin Wall, when material evidence trumps testimony, that's the end of history, or at least one particular version of it.

Despite the popularity of *The Da Vinci Code* and the currently beleaguered status of history as world narrative, there is plenty of evidence to suggest that the puzzle element, with its ancillary faith in the reconstructive powers of inductive reason, continues to thrive in the international community of detective fiction, including its countries of origin, Britain and America. As noted in the previous chapter, the classical, 'cosy' mystery of analytical detection, that durable relic of the Golden Age, remains alive and well, as current sales figures for Christie's Poirot and Marple adventures attest.

Meanwhile, in addition to St Mary Meade, nearly every village, town, moderately sized city, and region of the Anglophone world can now boast its own resident fictional detective, with his or her own distinct history and idiosyncratic personality. The United States alone is now home to a Louisiana swamp-rat (James Lee Burke's Dave Robicheaux), an upper-Midwestern cat-lover (Lilian Jackson Braun's Jim Qwilleran), an Atlanta DA descendant of the Cherokee Nation (Sallie Bissell's Mary Crow), a lesbian Denver patrol officer with a thing for S&M (Kate Allen's Alison Kane), and a rain-soaked Seattle police detective of 'the old school' (Ridley Pearson's Lou Boldt), among many others.

Almost without exception, whether amateur, private professional, or municipal; white, black, brown, or yellow; male, female, or transgender; straight, gay, or bi-sexual; proletarian or propertied or somewhere in between, every one of these sleuths carries the literary genetic markers of his or her detective forebears.

Watch for one coming soon to a dark alley near you.

Works Cited

Primary Works (quoted or discussed at length; see under *Secondary Works* for criticism by detective writers)

Borges, Jorge Luis. 'The Garden of Forking Paths'. In *Collected Fictions*. Trans. Andrew Hurley. New York: Penguin Putnam, 1998, pp. 119–28.

Braddon, Mary E. *Birds of Prey*. London: Ward, Lock, and Tyler, n.d.

Braddon, Mary E. *Lady Audley's Secret*. London: Virago, 1985.

Brown, Dan. *The Da Vinci Code*. New York: Doubleday, 2003.

Chandler, Raymond. *The Big Sleep*. New York: Vintage, 1988.

Chandler, Raymond. *The High Window*. In Raymond Chandler, *Stories and Early Novels*. New York: Library of America, 1995, pp. 985–1177.

Chandler, Raymond. *Later Novels and Other Writings*. New York: Library of America, 1995.

Chandler, Raymond. *The Little Sister*. New York: Vintage, 1988.

Chandler, Raymond. *Playback*. In Chandler, *Later*, pp. 735–871.

Chesterton, G[ilbert] K[eith]. 'The Blue Cross'. In Chesterton, *Penguin*, pp. 9–22.

Chesterton, G[ilbert] K[eith]. 'The Hammer of God'. In Chesterton, *Penguin*, pp. 118–30.

Chesterton, G[ilbert] K[eith]. *The Penguin Complete Father Brown*. London: Penguin, 1981.

Chesterton, G[ilbert] K[eith]. 'The Secret of Father Brown'. In Chesterton, *Penguin*, pp. 461–7.

Chesterton, G[ilbert] K[eith]. 'The Secret Garden'. In Chesterton, *Penguin*, pp. 23–39.

Christie, Agatha. *Murder at the Vicarage*. New York: Dell, 1958.

Christie, Agatha. *The Mysterious Affair at Stys*. New York: Dodd, Mead, 1927.

Collins, Wilkie. *The Moonstone*. Ed. Anthea Trodd. New York: Oxford University Press, 1982.

Collins, Wilkie. *The Woman in White*. London: Sampson, Low, 1860.

Cox, Michael, ed. *Victorian Tales of Mystery and Detection: An Oxford Anthology*. Oxford: Oxford University Press, 1992.

Dickens, Charles. *Bleak House*. Eds George Ford and Sylvere Monod. New York: W. W. Norton, 1977.

Dickens, Charles. *The Mystery of Edwin Drood*. Ed. Arthur J. Cox. London: Penguin, 1974.

Doyle, Arthur Conan. 'The Adventure of the Abbey Grange'. In Doyle, *Sherlock*, 1.881–901.

Doyle, Arthur Conan. 'The Adventure of the Six Napoleons'. In Doyle, *Sherlock*, 1.806–25.

Doyle, Arthur Conan. *Beyond the City*. In Arthur Conan Doyle, *Works*. New York: Black's, 1928, pp. 623–94.

Doyle, Arthur Conan. 'A Case of Identity'. In Doyle, *Sherlock*, 1.251–67.

Doyle, Arthur Conan. *The Hound of the Baskervilles*. In Doyle, *Sherlock*, 2.1–146.

Doyle, Arthur Conan. 'The Musgrave Ritual'. In Doyle, *Sherlock*, 1.527–43.

Doyle, Arthur Conan. 'The Red-Headed League'. In Doyle, *Sherlock*, 1.230–51.

Doyle, Arthur Conan. 'A Scandal in Bohemia'. In Doyle, *Sherlock*, 1.209–29.

Doyle, Arthur Conan. *Sherlock Holmes: The Complete Novels and Stories*. 2 vols. Ed. Loren Estlerman. New York: Bantam Books, 1986.

Doyle, Arthur Conan. *The Sign of Four*. In Doyle, *Sherlock*, 1.105–205.

Doyle, Arthur Conan. *A Study in Scarlet*. In Doyle, *Sherlock*, 1.1–104.

Eco, Umberto. *The Name of the Rose*. Trans. William Weaver. New York: Harcourt Brace Jovanovich, 1983.

Freeman, R. Austin. 'The Case of Oscar Brodski'. In Freeman, *Famous*, pp. 3–52.

Freeman, R. Austin. *The Famous Cases of Dr Thorndyke*. London: Hodder and Stoughton, 1931.

Freeman, R. Austin. 'The Old Lag'. In Freeman, *Famous*, pp. 235–69.

Freeman, R. Austin. *The Singing Bone*. In *Famous*, pp. 3–234.

Gaboriau, Émile. *The Honor of the Name*. New York: Scribner's, 1923.

Gaboriau, Émile. *Monsieur Lecoq*. New York: Scribner's, 1926.

Gaboriau, Émile. *The Widow Lerouge*. New York: Scribner's, 1923.

Godwin, William. *Caleb Williams, or Things as They Are*. Ed. Maurice Hindle. London: Penguin, 1988.

Grafton, Sue. *'F' is for Fugitive*. New York: Bantam, 1990.

Green, Anna Katharine. *The Leavenworth Case: A Lawyer's Story*. Concord, NH: Modern Age Books, 1937.

Hammett, Dashiell, *The Big Knockover*. New York: Vintage, 1972.

Hammett, Dashiell. *'Corkscrew'*. In Hammett, *Big*, pp. 250–304.

Hammett, Dashiell. *Complete Novels*. New York: Library of America, 1999.

Hammett, Dashiell. *The Dain Curse*. In Hammett, *Complete*, pp. 189–386.

Hammett, Dashiell. 'The Gutting of Couffignal'. In Hammett, *Big*, pp. 3–38.

Hammett, Dashiell. *The Maltese Falcon*. New York: Vintage, 1989.

Hammett, Dashiell. *Red Harvest*. In Hammett, Complete, pp. 1–187.

Hammett, Dashiell. 'Tulip'. In Hammett, *Big*, pp. 305–52.

Himes, Chester. *The Crazy Kill*. Chatham, NJ: Chatham Bookseller, 1959.

Knapp, Andrew, and William Baldwin, eds. *The Newgate Calendar*. [. . .] 4 vols. London: J. Robins and Co., Ivy Lane, Paternoster Row, 1824–5.

Macdonald, Ross. *The Galton Case*. New York: Vintage, 1996.

Morrison, Arthur. 'The Ivy Cottage Mystery'. In Cox, pp. 342–64.

Mosley, Walter. *Devil in a Blue Dress*. New York: Norton, 1990.

Poe, Edgar Allan. *Essays and Reviews*. Ed. G. R. Thompson. New York: Library of America, 1984.

Poe, Edgar Allan. 'The Man of the Crowd'. In Poe, *Selected*, pp. 179–88.

Poe, Edgar Allan. 'The Murders in the Rue Morgue'. In Poe, *Selected*, pp. 189–224.

Poe, Edgar Allan. 'The Purloined Letter'. In Poe, *Selected*, pp. 330–49.

Poe, Edgar Allan. *Selected Writings*. Ed. David Galloway. Harmondsworth: Penguin, 1979.

Pronzini, Bill, and Jack Adrian, eds. *Hard-Boiled: An Anthology of American Crime Stories*. New York: Oxford University Press, 1995.

Radcliffe, Ann. *The Mysteries of Udolpho*. Ed. Bonamy Dobree. Oxford: Oxford University Press, 1980.

Rankin, Ian. *Hide and Seek*. London: Orion Books, 1998.

Rohmer, Sax. *The Mystery of Fu Manchu*. In *The Fu Manchu Omnibus*. London: Allison and Busby, 1995, pp. 1–217.

Russell, William ('Thomas Waters'). *Recollections of a Detective Police-Officer*. Boston: Wentworth and Company, 1859.

Sayers, Dorothy L. *Clouds of Witnesses*. New York: Harper and Row, 1987.

Sayers, Dorothy L. *Have His Carcase*. New York: Harper and Row, 1986.

Sayers, Dorothy L. *Unnatural Death*. London: Victor Gollancz, 1972.

Sayers, Dorothy L. *The Unpleasantness at the Bellona Club*. New York: Harper and Row, 1987.

Sayers, Dorothy L. *Whose Body?* New York: Harper and Row, 1987.

Spillane, Mickey. *I, the Jury*. New York: Dutton, 1947.

Surr, Thomas Skinner. *Richmond; or, Scenes in the Life of a Bow Street Officer*. [. . .] 2 vols. New York: J. & J. Harper, 1827.

Taylor, Tom. 'The Ticket-of-Leave Man'. In Montrose J. Moses, *Representative British Dramas, Victorian and Modern*. Boston: Little, Brown, 1931, pp. 225–67.

Twain, Mark. 'A Double-Barreled Detective Story'. In Charles Neider, ed., *The Complete Short Stories of Mark Twain*. New York: Doubleday, 1957, pp. 423–69.

Vidocq, Eugène-François. *Memoirs of Vidocq, Principal Agent of the French Police until 1827, written by himself*. Philadelphia, PA: E. L. Carey & A. Hart, 1834.

Secondary Works (post-1775; quoted, cited, or referred to)

Althusser, Louis. *Lenin and Philosophy and Other Essays*. Trans. Ben Brewster. London: New Left Books, 1971.

Anonymous. 'Women Would Rather Date Darcy than James Bond'. Online at *http://www.orangeprize.co.uk/news/bedtime.shtml*.

Archer, R. L. *Secondary Education in the Nineteenth Century*. Cambridge: Cambridge University Press, 1932.

Auden, W. H. 'The Guilty Vicarage'. In Winks, *Detective Fiction*, pp. 15–24.

Baring-Gould, William S. *The Annotated Sherlock Holmes*. 2 vols. New York: Clarkson N. Potter, 1967.

Barrett, Lindon. 'Presence of Mind: Detection and Racialization in "The Murders in the Rue Morgue" '. In Kennedy and Weissberg, pp. 157–76.

Barthes, Roland. *Mythologies*. Trans. Annette Lavers. New York: Hill and Wang, 1972.

Beer, Gillian. *Darwin's Plots: Evolutionary Narrative in Darwin, George Eliot, and Nineteenth-Century Fiction*. London: Routledge & Kegan Paul, 1983.

Benjamin, Walter. 'On Some Motifs in Baudelaire'. In *Illuminations*. Trans. Harry Zohn. New York: Schocken Books, 1968, pp. 155–94.

Berger, Roger A. ' "The Black Dick": Race, Sexuality, and Discourse in the L. A. Novels of Walter Mosley', *African American Review* 31:2 (1997): 281–94.

Bhabha, Homi K. *The Location of Culture*. New York: Routledge, 1994.

Bloch, Ernest. 'A Philosophical View of the Detective Novel'. In *The Utopian Function of Art and Literature: Selected Essays*. Trans. Jack Zipes and Frank Mecklenberg. Cambridge, MA: MIT Press, 1988, pp. 245–64.

Brooks, Peter. *Reading for the Plot: Design and Intention in Narrative*. New York: Knopf, 1984.

Browne, Janet. *Charles Darwin: Voyaging*. Princeton: Princeton University Press, 1995.

Caillois, Roger. 'The Detective Novel as Game'. In Most and Stowe, pp. 1–12.

Caprettini, Gian Paolo. 'Peirce, Holmes, Popper.' In Eco and Sebeok, pp. 135–53.

Carr, John Dickson. *The Life of Sir Arthur Conan Doyle*. New York: Vintage Books, 1975.

Castel, Albert. 'Henry Ford's Time Machine'. Online at *http://away.com/primedia/transport/henry_ford_1.html*.

Cawelti, John G. *Adventure, Mystery, and Romance: Formula Stories as Art and Popular Culture*. Chicago: University of Chicago Press.

Cawelti, John G. 'Canonization, Modern Literature, and the Detective Story'. In Delameter and Prigozy, pp. 5–16.

Chambers, Robert. *Vestiges of the Natural History of the Creation and Other Evolutionary Writings*. Ed. James A. Secord. Chicago: University of Chicago Press, 1994.

Champigny, Robert. *What Will Have Happened: A Philosophical and Technical Essay on Mystery Stories*. Bloomington: Indiana University Press, 1977.

Chandler, Raymond. 'Introduction to "The Simple Art of Murder"'. In Chandler, *Later*, pp. 1016–19.

Chandler, Raymond. 'The Simple Art of Murder'. In Chandler, *Later*, pp. 977–92.

Chandler, Raymond. 'Twelve Notes on the Mystery Story'. In Chandler, *Later*, pp. 1004–11.

Chesterton, G[ilbert] K[eith]. 'A Defence of Detective Stories'. In Haycraft, pp. 3–6.

Christian, Ed, ed. *The Post-Colonial Detective*. New York: Palgrave, 2001.

Christianson, Scott R. 'A Heap of Broken Images: Hardboiled Detective Fiction and the Discourse(s) of Modernity'. In Walker and Frazer, pp. 135–48.

Christie, Agatha. *An Autobiography*. London: Collins, 1977.

Cohen, Michael. *Murder Most Fair: The Appeal of Mystery Fiction*. Madison, NJ: Fairleigh Dickinson University Press, 2000.

Collingwood, R. G., *The Idea of History*. Oxford: Clarendon Press, 1946,

Craig, Patricia, and Mary Cadogan. *The Lady Investigates: Women Detectives and Spies in Fiction*. London: Victor Gollancz, 1981.

Crooks, Robert. 'From the Far Side of the Urban Frontier: The Detective Fiction of Chester Himes and Walter Mosley'. In Kostas Myrsiades and Linda Myrsiades, eds, *Race-ing Representation: Voice, History, and Sexuality*. Lanham, MD: Rowman & Littlefield, 1998, pp. 175–99.

Cuvier, Georges. *Essay on the Theory of the Earth, with Mineralogical Notes, and an Account of Cuvier's Geological Discoveries, [trans.] by Professor Jameson*. 3rd edition, 1817; rpt New York: Arno Press, 1978.

Darwin, Charles. *The Origin of Species by Means of Natural Selection, or The Preservation of Favored Races in the Struggle for Life*. 2nd edition, 1860; rpt New York: J. A. Hill and Company, 1904.

Dayan, Joan. 'Amorous Bondage: Poe, Ladies, and Slaves'. In Rosenheim and Rachman, pp. 179–209.

Delameter, Jerome H., and Ruth Prigozy, eds. *Theory and Practice of Classic Detective Fiction*. Westport, CT: Greenwood Press, 1997.

De Quincey, Thomas. *The Works of Thomas De Quincey*. 21 vols. Ed. Grevel Lindop. London: Pickering and Chatto, 2000.

Devaney-Lovinguth, Sharon. *Modernism and Gender in the Novels of Raymond Chandler*. Ph.D. dissertation. University of Alabama, 1993.

Dove, George N. 'The Detection Formula and the Act of Reading'. In Walker and Frazer, pp. 25–37.

Doyle, Arthur Conan. *Memories and Adventures*. London: Greenhill Books, 1988.

Drew, Bernard A. *Hard-Boiled Dames: Stories Featuring Women Detectives, Reporters, Adventurers, and Criminals from the Pulp Fiction Magazines of the 1930s*. New York: St Martin's Press, 1986.

Durham, Philip. 'The Black Mask School'. In David Madden, ed., *Tough Guy Writers of the Thirties*. Carbondale, IL: Southern Illinois University Press, 1968, pp. 51–79.

Durkin, Mary Brian. *Dorothy L. Sayers*. Boston: Twayne Publishers, 1980.

Eco, Umberto. 'Horns, Hooves, Insteps: Some Hypotheses on Three Types of Abduction'. In Eco and Sebeok, pp. 198–220.

Eco, Umberto, and Thomas A. Sebeok, eds. *The Sign of Three: Dupin, Holmes, Peirce*. Bloomington, IN: Indiana University Press, 1983.

Eliot, T[homas] S[tearns]. 'Wilkie Collins and Dickens'. In *Selected Essays, 1917–1932*. New York: Harcourt, Brace, and Co., 1932, pp. 373–82.

Evans, Richard. *In Defense of History*. New York: Norton, 1999.

Fiedler, Leslie A. *Love and Death in the American Novel*. New York: Criterion Books, 1960.

Fontana, Ernest. 'Chivalry and Modernity in Raymond Chandler's *The Big Sleep*'. In Van Dover, pp. 159–65.

Foucault, Michel. *Discipline and Punish: The Birth of the Prison*. Trans. Alan Sheridan. New York: Vintage Books, 1979.

Frank, Lawrence. *Victorian Detective Fiction and the Nature of Evidence: The Scientific Investigations of Poe, Dickens, and Doyle*. New York: Palgrave Macmillan, 2003.

Freud, Sigmund. *Introductory Lectures on Psychoanalysis*. Trans. and ed. James Strachey. New York: W. W. Norton, 1966.

Freud, Sigmund. *Standard Edition of the Complete Psychological Works*. Trans. James Strachey. 24 vols. London: Hogarth Press, 1953.

Fukuyama, Francis. *The End of History and the Last Man*. New York: Free Press, 1992.

Fussell, Paul. *The Great War and Modern Memory*. New York: Oxford University Press, 1975.

Geikie, Archibald. *The Founders of Geology*. 2nd edition, 1905; rpt New York: Dover, 1962.

Genette, Gérard. *Narrative Discourse: An Essay in Method*. Trans. Jane E. Levin. Foreword by Jonathan Culler. Ithaca, NY: Cornell University Press, 1980.

Gilbert, Sandra M., and Susan Gubar. *No Man's Land: The Place of the Woman Writer in the Twentieth Century*. Vol. 1. New Haven, CT: Yale University Press, 1988.

Ginzburg, Carlo. *Clues, Myths, and the Historical Method*. Trans. John and Anne C. Tedeschi. Baltimore, MD: Johns Hopkins University Press, 1989.

Goulart, Ron. *Cheap Thrills: An Informal History of the Pulp Magazines*. New Rochelle, NY: Arlington House, 1972.

Gould, Stephen J. *The Mismeasure of Man*. New York: W. W. Norton & Co., 1981.

Gramsci, Antonio. *Letters from Prison*. Ed. Frank Rosengarten. Trans. Raymond Rosenthal. New York: Columbia University Press, 1994.

Gregory, Sinda. *Private Investigations: The Novels of Dashiell Hammett.* Carbondale, IL: Southern Illinois University Press, 1985.

Grella, George. 'Murder and the Mean Streets: The Hard Boiled Detective Novel'. In Winks, *Detective Fiction,* pp. 103–20.

Grossvogel, David I.. *Mystery and Its Fictions: From Oedipus to Agatha Christie.* Baltimore, MD: Johns Hopkins University Press, 1979.

Hall, Jasmine Yong. 'Jameson, Genre, and Gumshoes: The Maltese Falcon as Inverted Romance'. In Walker and Frazer, pp. 109–19.

Hamilton, Cynthia S. *From High Noon to Midnight: Western and Hard-Boiled Detective Fiction in America.* Iowa City, IA: University of Iowa Press, 1987.

Hardwick, Michael. *The Complete Guide to Sherlock Holmes.* New York: St Martin's Press, 1986.

Haut, Woody. *Pulp Culture: Hardboiled Fiction and the Cold War.* London: Serpent's Tail, 1995.

Haycraft, Howard, ed. *The Art of the Mystery Story: A Collection of Critical Essays.* Introd. Robin Winks. 2nd edition. New York: Carroll and Graf, 1992.

Hellman, Lillian. 'Introduction'. In Hammett, *Big,* pp. v–xxv.

Hill, Reginald. 'Holmes: The Hamlet of Crime Fiction'. In Keating, pp. 20–41.

Hollingsworth, Keith. *The Newgate Novel, 1830–1847: Bulwer, Ainsworth, Dickens, & Thackeray.* Detroit, MI: Wayne State University Press, 1963.

Holquist, Michael. 'Whodunit and Other Questions: Metaphysical Detective Stories in Postwar Fiction'. In Most and Stowe, pp. 149–74.

Homer. *The Iliad.* Trans. Richard Lattimore. Chicago: University of Chicago Press, 1951.

Homer. *The Odyssey.* Trans. Richard Lattimore. Chicago: University of Chicago Press, 1956.

Hoppenstand, Gary. *The Dime Novel Detective.* Bowling Green, OH: Bowling Green University Press, 1982.

Horkheimer, Max, and Theodor W. Adorno. *Dialectic of Enlightenment.* Trans. John Cumming. New York: Herder and Herder, 1972.

Huhn, Peter. 'The Detective as Reader: Narrativity and Reading Concepts in Detective Fiction', *Modern Fiction Studies* 33:3 (1987): 451–66.

Hutton, James. *Theory of the Earth; or an Investigation of the Laws observable in the Composition, Dissolution, and Restoration of Land upon the Globe.* 1788. In George W. White, ed., *Contributions to the History of Geology.* Vol. 5. Darien, CT: Hafner Publishing Co., 1970, pp. 31–131.

Irwin, John T. *The Mystery to a Solution: Poe, Borges, and the Analytical Detective Story.* Baltimore, MD: Johns Hopkins University Press, 1994.

Jameson, Fredric. 'On Raymond Chandler'. In Van Dover, pp. 65–87.

Jameson, Fredric. *The Political Unconscious: Narrative as a Socially Symbolic Act.* Ithaca, NY: Cornell University Press, 1981.

Jeffers, H. Paul. *Bloody Business: An Anecdotal History of Scotland Yard.* New York: Pharos Books, 1992.

Johnson, Diane. *Dashiell Hammett: A Life.* New York: Random House, 1983.

Joyce, Patrick. 'History and Postmodernism', *Past and Present* 133 (1991): 204–9.

Kaufman, Natalie Hevener, and Carol McGinnis Kay. *'G' is for Grafton: The World of Kinsey Millhone.* New York: Henry Holt and Co,, 2000.

Kayman, Martin A. *From Bow Street to Baker Street: Mystery, Detection, and Narrative.* London: Macmillan, 1992.

Keating, H. R. F., ed. *Crime Writers.* London: British Broadcasting Corporation, 1978.

Keats, John. *Letters of John Keats.* Ed. Robert Gittings. Oxford: Oxford University Press, 1977.

Kennedy, Beverley. *Knighthood in the Morte Darthur.* 2nd edition. Cambridge: D. S. Brewer, 1992.

Kennedy, J. Gerald, and Lilianne Weissberg, eds. *Romancing the Shadow: Poe and Race.* Oxford: Oxford University Press, 2001.

Kennedy, Liam. 'Black Noir: Race and Urban Space in Walter Mosley's Detective Fiction'. In Klein, *Diversity*, pp. 224–39.

Klein, Kathleen Gregory, ed. *Diversity and Detective Fiction.* Bowling Green, OH: Bowling Green State University Popular Press, 1999.

Klein, Kathleen Gregory. *The Woman Detective: Gender and Genre.* Urbana, IL: University of Illinois Press, 1988.

Knight, Stephen. *Form and Ideology in Crime Fiction.* Bloomington, IN: Indiana University Press, 1980.

Knight, Stephen. 'Hidden Dragon'. 'The Case of the Hidden Dragon: Style, Simile, and Gender in The Big Sleep', *Q/W/E/R/T/Y: arts, littératures & civilisations du monde Anglophone* 5 (1995): 259–66.

Koselleck, Reinhart. *Futures Past: On the Semantics of Historical Time.* Trans. Keith Tribe. Cambridge, MA: MIT Press, 1985.

Kozicki, Henry. *Tennyson and Clio: History in the Major Poems.* Baltimore, MD: Johns Hopkins University Press, 1979.

Lemire, Elise. ' "The Murders in the Rue Morgue": Amalgamation Discourses and the Race Riots of 1838 in Poe's Philadelphia'. In Kennedy and Weissberg, pp. 177–204.

Leverenz, David. 'Poe and Gentry Virginia'. In Rosenheim and Rachman, pp. 210–36.

Lewis, Terrance L. *Dorothy L. Sayers' Wimsey and Interwar British Society.* Lewiston, NY: Edwin Mellen Press, 1994.

Löwith, Karl. *Meaning in History: The Theological Implications of the Philosophy of History.* Chicago: University of Chicago Press, 1949.

Lyotard, Jean-François. *The Postmodern Condition: A Report on Knowledge.* Trans. Geoff Bennington and Brian Massumi. Foreword by Fredric Jameson. Minneapolis, MN: University of Minnesota Press, 1984.

McCann, Sean. *Hard-Boiled Crime Fiction and the Rise and Fall of New Deal Liberalism*. Durham, NC: Duke University Press, 2000.

Macdonald, Gina, and Andrew Macdonald. 'Ethnic Detectives in Popular Fiction: New Directions for an American Genre'. In Klein, *Diversity*, pp. 60–113.

Macdonald, Ross. 'Archer in Jeopardy'. In Macdonald, *Self-Portrait*, pp. 15–16.

Macdonald, Ross. *Self-Portrait: Ceaselessly Into the Past*. Santa Barbara, CA: Capra Press, 1981.

Macdonald, Ross. 'The Writer as Detective Hero'. In Macdonald, *Self-Portrait*, pp. 113–22.

Macdonald, Ross. '*Writing The Galton Case*'. In Macdonald, *Self-Portrait*, pp. 47–60.

MacShane, Frank. *The Life of Raymond Chandler*. New York: E. P. Dutton, 1976.

MacShane, Frank. *Selected Letters of Raymond Chandler*. New York: Dell, 1981.

Marcus, Steven. 'Introduction'. In *The Continental Op*. Ed. Steven Marcus. New York: Vintage Books, 1974, pp. ix–xxxi.

Margolies, Edward. *Which Way Did He Go? The Private Eye in Dashiell Hammett, Raymond Chandler, Chester Himes, and Ross Macdonald*. New York: Holmes and Meier, 1982.

Marling, William. *The American Roman Noir: Hammett, Cain, and Chandler*. Athens, GA: University of Georgia Press, 1995.

Mason, Michael. 'Marlowe, Men and Women'. In Miriam Gross, ed., *The World of Raymond Chandler*. New York: A & W Publishers, 1977, pp. 90–101.

Mathis, Andrew E. '*The Big Sleep*: The Celtic Connection', *Clues* 18:2 (1997): 81–97.

Messac, Régis. *Le 'Detective Novel' et l'influence de la pensée scientifique*. Paris: Librairie Ancienne Honoré Champion, 1929.

Metress, Christopher. 'Dashiell Hammett and the Challenge of the New Individualism: Rereading *Red Harvest* and *The Maltese Falcon*'. *Essays in Literature* 17:4 (1990): 242–60.

Metress, Christopher. 'Living Degree Zero: Masculinity and the Threat of Desire in the *Roman Noir*'. In Peter F. Murphy, ed., *Fictions of Masculinity: Crossing Cultures, Crossing Sexualities*. New York: New York University Press, 1994, pp. 154–84.

Mill, John Stuart. 'The Spirit of the Age'. In *Mill: Texts, Commentaries*. Ed. Alan Ryan. New York: W. W. Norton, 1997, pp. 3–40.

Miller, D. A. *The Novel and the Police*. Berkeley, CA: University of California Press, 1988.

Milligan, Barry. *Pains and Pleasures: Opium and the Orient in Nineteenth-Century British Culture*. Charlottesville, VA: University Press of Virginia, 1995.

Moretti, Franco. 'Clues'. In *Signs Taken for Wonders: Essays in the Sociology of Literary Forms*. Trans. Susan Fischer. London: Verso, 1983, pp. 130–56.

Morrison, Robert. 'Poe's De Quincey, Poe's Dupin', *Essays in Criticism* 51:4 (2001): 424–41.

Most, Glenn W., and William W. Stowe, eds. *The Poetics of Murder: Detective Fiction and Literary Theory*. New York: Harcourt Brace, 1983.

Mowat, Charles Loch. *Britain Between the Wars, 1918–1940*. Chicago: University of Chicago Press, 1955.

Muller, Gilbert H. 'Double Agent: The Los Angeles Crime Cycle of Walter Mosley'. In David Fine, ed., *Los Angeles in Fiction: A Collection of Essays*. Albuquerque, NM: University of New Mexico Press, 1995, pp. 287–301.

Murch, Alma E. *The Development of the Detective Novel*. Rev. edition. London: Peter Owen, 1968.

Nicolson, Marjorie. 'The Professor and the Detective'. In Haycraft, pp. 110–27.

Oates, Joyce Carol. 'The Simple Art of Murder'. *New York Review of Books*, 21 December, 1995, pp. 32–40.

Oliphant, Margaret. 'Sensation Novels'. *Blackwood's Edinburgh Magazine* 54:5 (1862): 564–84.

Ousby, Ian. *Bloodhounds of Heaven: The Detective in English Fiction from Godwin to Doyle*. Cambridge, MA: Harvard University Press, 1976.

Ousby, Ian. *Guilty Parties: A Mystery Lover's Companion*. New York: Thames and Hudson, 1997.

Owen, Kathleen Belin. ' "The Game's Afoot": Predecessors and Pursuits of a Postmodern Detective Novel'. In Delameter and Prigozy, pp. 73–84.

Pavett, Mike. 'Introduction'. In Keating, pp. 8–19.

Perkin, Harold. *The Rise of Professional Society: England Since 1880*. London: Routledge, 1989.

Person, Leland S. 'Poe's Philosophy of Amalgamation: Reading Racism in the Tales'. In Kennedy and Weissberg, pp. 205–24.

Porter, Dennis. *The Pursuit of Crime: Art and Ideology in Detective Fiction*. New Haven, CT: Yale University Press, 1981.

Priestman, Martin. *Detective Fiction and Literature: The Figure in the Carpet*. London: Macmillan, 1990.

Pronzini, Bill, and Jack Adrian. 'Introduction'. In Pronzini and Adrian, *Hard-Boiled*, pp. 3–19 (see Primary Works).

Pyrhönin, Heta. *Mayhem and Murder: Narrative and Moral Problems in the Detective Story*. Toronto: University of Toronto Press, 1999.

Rabinowitz, Peter J. ' "How Did You Know He Licked His Lips?": Second Person Knowledge and First Person Power in *The Maltese Falcon*'. In James Phelan and Peter J. Rabinowitz, eds, *Understanding Narrative*. Columbus, OH: Ohio State University Press, 1994, pp. 157–77.

Rabinowitz, Peter J. ' "Reader, I blew him away": Convention and Transgression in Sue Grafton'. In Alison Booth, ed., *Famous Last Words: Changes in Gender and Narrative Closure*. Charlottesville, VA: University Press of Virginia, 1993, pp. 326–44.

Reddy, Maureen T. 'The Feminist Counter-Tradition in Crime: Cross, Grafton, Paretsky, and Wilson'. In Walker and Frazer, pp. 174–87.

Reed, John R. 'English Imperialism and the Unacknowledged Crime of *The Moonstone*', *Clio* 2:3 (1973): 281–90.

Reynolds, David S. *Beneath the American Renaissance: The Subversive Imagination in the Age of Emerson and Melville*. Cambridge, MA: Harvard University Press, 1988.

Roach, John. *A History of Secondary Education in England, 1800–1870*. New York: Longman, 1986.

Rosenheim, Shawn, and Stephen Rachman, eds. *The American Face of Edgar Allan Poe*. Baltimore, MD: Johns Hopkins University Press, 1995.

Ruehlmann, William. *Saint with a Gun: The Unlawful American Private Eye*. New York: New York University Press, 1974.

Russell, Colin A. *Science and Social Change, 1700–1900*. London: Macmillan, 1983.

Rycroft, Charles. 'A Detective Story: Psychoanalytic Observations', *Psycho-Analytic Quarterly* 26 (1957): 229–45.

Said, Edward. *Orientalism*. New York: Pantheon, 1978.

Sayers, Dorothy. 'The Omnibus of Crime'. In Haycraft, pp. 71–109.

Sebeok, Thomas A. 'One, Two, Three Spells UBERTY'. In Eco and Sebeok, pp. 1–10.

Secord, James A. *Victorian Sensation: The Extraordinary Publication, Reception, and Secret Authorship of Vestiges of the Natural Creation*. Chicago: University of Chicago Press, 2000.

Slung, Michele B. 'Introduction'. In Michele B. Slung, ed., *Crime on Her Mind: Fifteen Stories of Female Sleuths from the Victorian Era to the Forties*. New York: Pantheon, 1975, pp. xv–xxx.

Snow, C. P. *The Two Cultures and the Scientific Revolution*. New York: Cambridge University Press, 1961.

Soitos, Stephen F. *The Blues Detective: A Study of African American Detective Fiction*. Amherst, MA: University of Massachusetts Press, 1996.

Stashower, Daniel. *Teller of Tales: The Life of Arthur Conan Doyle*. New York: Holt, 1999.

Stead, Philip John. *Vidocq: A Biography*. New York: Roy, 1954.

Stowe, William W. 'From Semiotics to Hermeneutics: Modes of Detection in Doyle and Chandler'. In Most and Stowe, pp. 366–86.

Symons, Julian. *Bloody Murder: From the Detective Story to the Crime Novel*. 3rd edition. New York: Mysterious Press, 1992.

Symons, Julian. *Conan Doyle: Portrait of an Artist*. 1979; rpt New York: Mysterious Press, 1987.

Thomas, Ronald R. *Detective Fiction and the Rise of Forensic Science*. Cambridge: Cambridge University Press, 1999.

Thompson, Jon. *Fiction, Crime, and Empire*. Urbana, IL: University of Illinois Press, 1993.

Thorpe, Edward. *Chandlertown: The Los Angeles of Philip Marlowe*. New York: St Martin's Press, 1983.

Todorov, Tzvetan. *The Poetics of Prose*. Trans. Richard Howard. Foreword Jonathan Culler. Ithaca, NY: Cornell University Press, 1977.

Trigger, Bruce G. *A History of Archaeological Thought*. Cambridge: Cambridge University Press, 1989.

Van Dover, J. K., ed. *The Critical Response to Raymond Chandler*. Westport, CT: Greenwood, 1995.

Wald, Gayle F. 'Strong Poison: Love and the Novelistic in Dorothy Sayers'. In Walker and Frazer, pp. 98–108.

Walker, Ronald G., and June M. Frazer, eds. *The Cunning Craft: Original Essays on Detective Fiction and Contemporary Literary Theory*. Macomb, IL: Western Illinois University Press, 1990.

Watson, Colin. *Snobbery with Violence: English Crime Stories and their Audience*. 2nd edition. London: Methuen, 1987.

Whalen, Terrence. 'Average Racism: Poe, Slavery, and the Wages of Literary Nationalism'. In Kennedy and Weissberg, pp. 3–40.

Wheeler, Michael. *English Fiction of the Victorian Period, 1830–1890*. 2nd edition. New York: Longman, 1994.

White, Hayden. *The Content of the Form: Narrative, Discourse, and Historical Representation*. Baltimore, MD: Johns Hopkins University Press, 1987.

Wilbur, Richard. 'The Poe Mystery Case', in *Responses: Prose Pieces, 1953–1976*. New York: Harcourt Brace Jovanovich, 1976, pp. 127–39.

Winks, Robin W. 'Preface'. In Ray B. Browne and Lawrence A. Kreiser, Jr, eds. *The Detective as Historian: History and Art in Historical Crime Fiction*. Bowling Green, OH: Bowling Green State University Popular Press, 2000. pp. ix–xiii.

Winks, Robin W., ed. *Detective Fiction: A Collection of Critical Essays*. Englewood Cliffs, NJ: Prentice-Hall, 1980.

Wolfe, Peter. *Beams Falling: The Art of Dashiell Hammett*. Bowling Green, OH: Bowling Green State University Popular Press, 1980.

Wolfe, Peter. *Something More than Night: The Case of Raymond Chandler*. Bowling Green, OH: Bowling Green State University Popular Press, 1985.

Wordsworth, William. *The Prelude*. In Stephen Gill, ed., *William Wordsworth: Works*. Oxford: Oxford University Press, 1984.

Wright, William Huntington ('S. S. van Dine'). 'Twenty Rules for Writing Detective Stories'. In Haycraft, pp. 189–93.

Wrong, E. M. 'Crime and Detection'. In Haycraft, pp. 18–29.

Yeo, Richard. 'Science and Intellectual Authority in Mid-Nineteenth-Century Britain: Robert Chambers and *Vestiges of the Natural History of Creation*'. In Patrick Brantlinger, ed., *Energy and Entropy: Science and Culture in Victorian Britain*. Bloomington, IN: Indiana University Press, 1989, pp. 1–27.

Index